# When Buy Means Sell

## An Investor's Guide to Investing When It Counts

Eric Shkolnik

**McGraw-Hill**

New York   Chicago   San Francisco   Lisbon   London   Madrid
Mexico City   Milan   New Delhi   San Juan   Seoul
Singapore   Sydney   Toronto

The McGraw·Hill Companies

**Library of Congress Cataloging-in-Publication Data**

Shkolnik, Eric.
   When buy means sell: an investor's guide to investing when it counts / by Eric Shkolnik
        p.     cm.
   ISBN 0-07-138706-4 (acid free)
   1. Stocks. 2. Securities. 3. Speculation. I. Title

   HG4661 .S444 2002
   332.63'22—dc21                                                      2002005906

1 2 3 4 5 6 7 8 9 0 AGM/AGM 0 9 8 7 6 5 4 3 2

ISBN: 0-07-138706-4

This publication is designed to provide accurate and authoritative information in regard to the subject matter covered. It is sold with the understanding that neither the author nor the publisher is engaged in rendering legal, accounting, futures/securities trading, or other professional service. If legal advice or other expert assistance is required, the services of a competent professional person should be sought.

*From a declaration of principles jointly adapted by a committee of the American Bar Association and a committee of publishers.*

 This book is printed on recycled, acid-free paper containing a minimum of 50% recycled, de-inked fiber.

McGraw-Hill books are available at special quantity discounts to use as premiums and sales promotions, or for use in corporate training programs. For more information, please write to the Director of Special Sales, Professional Publishing, McGraw-Hill, Two Penn Plaza, New York, NY 10121-2298. Or contact your local bookstore.

# CONTENTS

*Dedicated to the memory of my cousin*
*Victor Davidovich*

# ACKNOWLEDGMENTS

This book was truly a collaborative effort by people whose encouragement and support are invaluable.

I would like to thank my parents and my brother, who had the wisdom to leave the Soviet Union in the 1970s for a better future in America. I can say with certainty, had we stayed there my life would have turned out entirely differently.

My wife and my two dear sons provide me with a happy home, love, and inner peace. It is their continued support and overwhelming confidence in my undertakings that propel me to the success I enjoy today.

Thank you to the amazing people at MarketPerform.com, who contributed long hours and endless efforts in the development of my vision. Phil Brin and Alex Rabinovich have made MarketPerform a reality.

To Boris Tiomkin, who took the time from his demanding schedule to offer advice and much needed criticism for the benefit of our product.

To my dear friends Katherine Dovlatov and Anthony Direnzo, who spent countless hours editing and revising the manuscript, offering ideas, encouragement, and valuable comments.

To my editor at McGraw-Hill, Kelli Christiansen, who not only had the timely vision for this book and its contents, but who also was involved in the editorial process chapter by chapter.

Thank you all. This book is as much your book as it is mine.

# INTRODUCTION

My personal story of becoming an investor—if I could be called that back in the 1980s—in all probability is very ordinary. The first stock I ever bought was on the advice of a friend who worked as a secretary for a successful financial adviser. The advice was based on a rumor that a company, whose symbol I can no longer remember, was going to be bought out within a week or two by a much larger competitor at a very big premium.

That was the day that I finally decided to take the plunge. I selected my broker, picked up the phone, opened my trading account, and threw my $10,000 into the abyss. Later that same evening, just after sitting down for dinner with my family, I consciously acknowledged my actions. I said to my wife, "Darling, today we bought $10,000 worth of stock, and please don't worry because this is a sure thing."

To this day I remember her less than enthusiastic reaction. "How come you didn't consult with me?" she asked. "Didn't we agree to make major decisions together? What do you know about this company? Have you even bothered to look around for a second opinion? The least you could have done is call me. You will lose all our money!" Her voice was rising and she became visibly upset. Even though I had arrived home famished after a long day and had not yet had a chance to touch my food, my hunger was gone. My wife was right. And I would soon discover exactly how right she was.

During the next 3 weeks, I would call the automated phone system at Citibank every hour on the hour to get the latest delayed

1

quote on my stock. It was exciting during the first few days as the stock price climbed a bit. But when it started to fall, I felt at once both ashamed and dismayed. Not only had we dipped below our original $10,000 investment, but my wife's voice was now ringing in my ears as well. I was now asking myself the same questions, and a few more: Why didn't I consult with her? What does this company make? Did I get a second opinion? Did I look at its financial statements? And then the inevitable: How could I have been so stupid?

My patience finally ran out 3 weeks later, and I sold the stock for about $6,000 and closed the account. My wife was triumphant and she gave me hell—that was well deserved, I must admit. I was determined not to repeat the same mistake again. I had learned my lesson.

I embarked on my next investment journey approximately 6 months later. The seas were even rougher the second time around, but it's not as if I had learned nothing from my first ordeal.

Lesson 1: Investing is a family affair. I opened an account with Merrill Lynch and invested about $30,000. This time I had spoken with my wife in advance, and we had agreed that it was the right move. (Losing money is painful enough by itself, and I surely did not need to heap marital discord on top of it.) Anyway, it all started out well. I even made money on the first stock purchase. I bought a stock, whose symbol again I can no longer remember, for approximately $2,000 and sold it for $3,200 within couple of weeks. I remember the excitement of telling all my friends about this wonderful experience and about my newfound investment prowess. I immediately bought shares in the next few companies that my broker recommended. I had tasted the appetizer, and now I wanted to move on to the main course.

Lesson 2: Don't confuse appetizer with bait. Within the next year, and culminating in the unfortunate purchase of options in Micron Technology and Sybase, I lost the whole account, even exceeding my $30,000 by the interest my account "earned."

After this second investment fiasco, I was out of the market for approximately a year and a half. It is interesting to note that a $4,000 loss the first time around made me take a leave of absence from the market for roughly 6 months; losing $30,000 kept me out of action for more than a year.

These first investment steps (or missteps) reminded me of some of my other, more informed financial experiences such as gambling excursions to Atlantic City, where I've played roughly 10 times in my life. I consider these trips more informed because I knew exactly what I was getting myself into: odds stacked against me, house winnings nearly assured, but always the possibility of getting lucky. On seven of the ten trips I lost money, and on three of them I won a bit. Not a great average, but that is not the parallel I'm drawing. The salient point is that my average wait time for returning to the casinos after a winning trip is about 6 weeks. On the other hand, my average hiatus after a losing visit is usually at least a year. I also noticed that the more money I lost, the longer was the break between that trip and the next one. Although the specific parameters vary, this is a frequently found pattern, albeit somewhat counterintuitive. Perhaps there is a Ph.D. dissertation in the timeouts people take after receiving a financial battering. But the occasional win often results in greater vulnerability. A streak of good luck often makes one become more cavalier, with the false sense of skill and security that comes with convincing oneself that it wasn't luck at all. You drop your guard, are less careful, and make more slips. And sooner or later you get nailed.

These tendencies are not mine alone. Many others share the feelings of immunity and invulnerability to loss after winning as well as the converse, the anxiety and despair after the inevitable loss. Later in the book, we will touch briefly on a paper written by William Sharpe, who shared the 1990 Nobel Prize in economics for his research describing patterns of aversion to risk and how they increase with wins and decrease with losses. Sharpe describes how these tendencies are responsible for extended and exaggerated bull and bear markets.

So where did I go wrong? What were the main reasons for my poor investment decisions, and how could I improve my track record in the future? Further on we will discuss this in detail, but for now suffice it to say that I made many classic mistakes in my drive to time the market. Diversification took a backseat. Planning and strategy went out the window. And informed decision making wasn't even in the travel plans. We'll discuss the more reasoned approaches to investing later, but first let's set the stage with some other "brilliant" strategies.

My neighbor (we'll call him Jack) has a rather peculiar strategy for buying and selling stocks. It involves half of his extended family, specifically the in-laws. His wife, a lovely lady who never discusses her finances with strangers, has a fairly large family with active business interests. Now Jack can't stand a single member of her family, and according to him the feeling is mutual, aside from his wife, whom he loves dearly. The reciprocal distaste and disrespect for one another likely stem from issues surrounding the family-owned business, where they all work, and there is a lot of friction among these very strong personalities.

Since they spend a lot of time together, on average 6 days a week, besides arguing about their daily business routines, they do engage in occasional civil conversations. And what do they talk about most? You guessed it. They always discuss their latest stock picks. Not only do they tell each other which stock they bought and sold, but they also reveal the stock price. This creates a never-ending foolish strategy of buying stocks at a lower price than their extremely disliked relatives.

Quite often when I see Jack, our conversation goes something like this: "My mother-in-law just bought AOL for $49 and I got it for $46. Oh, if you could only know how much I hate this woman, and you should have seen her face when I told her that I bought it for $46. I literally ruined her day." Or "Frankie, my wife's cousin, bought Microsoft at $50 when I paid $110. I hate him." This investment approach continued for many years, and I was consistently updated in the elevator, until so much money was lost that he finally sold all his stocks and bought municipal and corporate bonds, or at least that's what he told me.

Another acquaintance of mine who confused bull market for brains took stock trading a step further. He decided to change his carrier altogether. We're all aware of the stellar rise and then meteoric fall of the day-trading game. In the late 1990s, it was almost hard to lose on Wall Street or at least hard to find people who would admit losing. But those who jumped in at the cusp are especially worth discussing. The following story is reminiscent of people who got caught up in the frenzy at the tail end of the boom.

It happened in early 2000. This acquaintance (let's call him George), a Peoplesoft programmer capable of earning $120 to $140 per hour, decided to quit his job to become a day trader. He found a day-trading school with a 3-month training program on all the ins and outs of day trading. He spent hundreds of dollars on books about day trading, and he energetically began his new career. His thinking was, "Why do I need to work for someone else when there are opportunities to trade while sitting at home or at these day-trading farms?" He invested approximately $100,000 of his hard-earned money and promised his wife $10,000 in income per month from trading. That's 10 percent per month, or 120 percent per year! Does that seem a little optimistic? Perhaps it's even unrealistic.

Well, what surprised me was that he delivered on his promise the first month, and in the second month, he brought home $16,000. They were both thrilled at the foresight that brought them into this new world of success. The third month was April 2000. The NASDAQ tanked, and he lost it all. Fortunately, he did not lose his programming skills. He was away from his programming career for only 3 months. Although it was an expensive endeavor, at least he got his job back.

In the late 1990s, the markets were in an unusual realm, and many investors were convinced of their phenomenal stock-picking ability and cleverness. Many stocks they touched doubled or more in a very short time. A stock that increased in value a mere 25 percent was labeled a loser and left them feeling nauseous and frustrated. What surprises me—but then again it shouldn't—is that many of those same individuals continue to stick with their false impressions of what it takes to make money in the market, even though many of them have lost 50 to 90 percent in their portfolios. And don't think that the professionals such as analysts, venture capitalists, and so forth were immune either.

## Confidence Is the Thing You Had Before You Knew Better

There is no escaping the endless flood of investment advice from all over the Internet, television networks, magazines, and newspapers. We quite often hear and read the pundits confidently proclaiming what stock we should buy or sell. These gurus tell us about all the exceptional opportunities that exist. I remember Jim Cramer, senior partner of the Cramer Berkowitz hedge fund and cofounder of TheStreet.com (TSCM), pushing TheStreet's stock when it was around $5 a share. He boldly explained, while banging the table and waving his finger at the camera, that the company had $5 in cash per share and naturally was one of the finest buying opportunities available. Soon after those remarks TSCM declined to $1.25. Recently it was trading around $2.75.

Cramer recently started to offer his buy and sell signals through an e-mail service for $39 per month. For all intents and purposes, this service will let you execute trades virtually along with Cramer. Minutes after Cramer buys a stock, subscribers will get an e-mail notification to do the same. The same occurs when he turns bearish on a security he owns and decides to unload it. I would love to track this service for a few years before deciding on registering for a subscription.

Then there was a guest on CNBC who claimed that Cisco's (CSCO) trading range was locked between $28 and $32. He went on to recommend buying CSCO at about $28 and selling it at about $32 for a quick turnaround. Proving that no analyst's prognostications could box in CSCO stock, the share price promptly plummeted to $13 within a month after that interview.

Yet another "expert" was recommending Pier 1 Imports (PIR) smack in the middle of the 1998 financial crisis in overseas markets. PIR is a specialty retailer of imported decorative home furnishings, gifts, and related items. Many of the goods that PIR imports are from South Korea. Because Korea was in recession at that time, the goods being purchased by PIR would be cheaper, he claimed, which in turn would make the store chain more profitable. It made perfect sense to me, and I bought a few shares of Pier 1 Imports at $30. I sold it 2 years later for around $9.

It is easy to see that financial advisers will talk interminably about their investment prowess when they happen to make the right investment decisions. They tell stories of how they bought or recommended a particular stock at $10 and sold it 6 months later for $25. They continually remind anyone who cares to take heed— sometimes a paying customer—of their greatest triumphs. We often hear something along the lines of, "I told you so last time and you didn't listen. Now's your chance to jump in." Of course, this is just human nature. And in their defense, the investing public is a finicky bunch. We quickly forget about the triumphs of our advisers, and, unforgiving, we hold them responsible for their latest stock pick, on which we just lost a small fortune. Our lasting motto is: What have you done for us lately?

Nevertheless, why do we rarely hear about the bad advice? Have you ever heard a financial adviser or one of the investor newsletters admit that their last 10 stock picks were disasters? When was the last time one recommended that you stay away from their "recommended" list or perhaps even consider it as a shorting strategy? We don't even hear this from the losers' competitors! Is this some sort of conspiracy or just a bunch of people who realize they all live in glass houses?

It is clear that simply and consistently following the recommendations of these gurus will, more often than not, help you lose your money. But if my neighbor Jack, my acquaintance George, and the most popular market analysts can't be trusted to deliver sound investment advice, who can?

## Peer Pressure: We Are Like Children All Over Again

Among children, one of the most powerful impetuses to action is peer pressure. Properly directed, it can have very positive results. But more often it "falls into the wrong hands." For instance, peer pressure is the way most young smokers are influenced to begin their habit, particularly when their friends have already started. They think they look cool, and they convince themselves that smoking makes them seem more mature and sophisticated. They rationalize that it makes them more appealing to the opposite sex.

As adults, of course we know better. Having lived through those wonder years, and now possibly bringing up kids of our own, we understand the foolishness of our earlier actions and the immaturity and insecurity that caused us to follow the crowd. We now see how ridiculous it is to feel the need to jump in on every fad or habit. And we would be irresponsible parents if we failed to impress this newfound wisdom on our offspring. We remind our children to choose their friends carefully and not to associate with troublemakers or others who might have a negative influence on them. We constantly remind them not to smoke, drink, have sex, and so forth.

Yes, of course. We adults know better . . .

But unfortunately, we do the same stupid things just to be part of the crowd. It's part peer pressure and part herd mentality. We do this in one way or another all our lives, and we never really outgrow it. And when it comes to the financial aspects of our lives, we throw different names at it. "Keeping up with the Joneses" is all part of the same behavior. Or we just rationalize the behavior, claiming that we're trying to make ends meet, build the American Dream, and provide for our families.

One of the greatest challenges we face every day is to provide our families with the wherewithal to enjoy the lifestyles we choose. This requires earning enough money to pay our mortgage or rent, go on vacation, or buy stylish clothes—in short, making a decent and comfortable living. And then there's the fact that we also want to save enough money to put our kids through school and to retire at an early age.

It is this constant pressure to earn more and more money, combined with the appeal of the stock market and its potential to multiply our salaries, that draws us into the game. And yet we're not all prepared or trained to maintain the level head necessary for informed investing. Add the bull market of the 1990s to the mix, with its preponderance of promoters, and our common sense gets short-circuited. CNBC, CNNfn, and other media outlets bombard us with exciting and enticing stories of overnight millionaires. People come out of the woodwork to tell us tales of how they bought stocks at $1 and sold them 6 months later for $70. We all want a piece of the action. We sense the means to the end.

During the creation of the Internet bubble in the late 1990s, people would recount stories of venture capitalists (VCs) pouring millions of dollars into companies that after 2 years in business could barely muster $10,000 in sales—sales, not earnings. The craze went so far that it seemed companies with positive cashflow were not fashionable enough to consider as investments. After all, a company whose valuation was based on what used to be considered sound fundamentals, like future earnings, book value, intrinsic value, P/E, and so on, was now disparaged as "brick and mortar." These companies aimed for mere single- or double-digit percentage growth. But why set your sights so low when the dot coms promised to return several times your original investment, sometimes in a matter of weeks? Warren Buffett was reviled as a has-been.

Prominent analysts allocated a company valuation that was based on the number of people logging on and clicking their way around the Web site—sometimes referred to as *page views*—or some other ridiculous approach. It seemed that the deeper in the red a company was, the better its potential. When I started building MarketPerform.com, one venture capitalist told me, "Just take out a large banner ad saying, 'I have a dot-com idea and all I need is $5 million.' People will trip over themselves to give you money to get in on the ground floor."

And it wasn't only the investors caving in to the peer pressure. Businesses as well were following, sometimes because they saw the opportunity for a sharp rise and immediate cash out, but sometimes because it was the only game in town. Look at the number of companies that went public during this time. The prospectuses accompanying many initial public offerings (IPOs) were loaded with warnings that the company has been losing money and would likely continue to lose for the foreseeable future. Some of these ventures had no real prospect or even a specific target, for that matter, of becoming profitable. The business plan was nothing more than IPO with a bunch of words surrounding it. High burn rate was the measure of success.

Had everyone taken leave of his or her senses?

I offer another personal experience about a company in which I invested a substantial amount, only to lose it all. (Believe me, it took a while to learn.) The management of this business was being shaped by peer pressure, but I didn't realize this in time.

It was back in 1996, when we decided that our consulting business needed a Web presence. We hired a system administrator/ programmer to build our Web site, and we signed a contract a few weeks later with PSINet, our new Internet provider, for a dedicated line. The Web site was up and running in no time. Everything was great. I was so happy with PSINet and their service that I took Peter Lynch's advice to invest in companies you know. I bought a good number of shares in PSINet, and they did quite well. PSINet was growing very quickly, the service was wonderful, and all was excellent.

Then a friend of mine, who had just raised some money for his fledgling dot-com company, told me that he signed a different sort of deal with PSINet. For 6 percent of his firm, which had yet to generate any sales at all, PSINet would give him $400,000 in cash plus $3 million in services. These services included communications lines, computer hardware, computer software, programmers, and system administrators to be available 24 hours a day, 7 days a week in case something went wrong. I should have smelled it then. The corollary to Lynch's suggestion should be to *divest* from companies you understand to be doing stupid things. Why did a company like PSINet, which appeared to have a working business model and was growing quickly, need a deal like this?

It's simple. Everyone else was doing it. Deals like that abounded by both companies and individuals alike. Everywhere you turned companies were dishing out options to their new and excited employees as well as to their service providers. Projects that normally entailed significant expenses were paid for in options. Cash was no longer king. It was a new and very dangerous paradigm. Everyone had dot-com fever. But now even viable businesses were mortgaging their revenues for a piece of a dot com.

The craze overwhelmed even the more conservative segment of investors and molded them into Internet players. People who are more the IBM and GE types bought AtHome for $50 and Rhythms Net Connections for $36. Others felt that CSCO, at around $60 per share, was a steal. Millions of others gave up on any semblance of sound investment strategy, like diversifying and staying clear of overheated, fashion-crazed industries. We all threw in the collective towel and went with the rest of the herd. Some turned before reaching the edge of the cliff, but many were not so lucky.

In June 2001 PSINet filed for bankruptcy protection under Chapter 11; AtHome and many other high fliers didn't have to wait much longer to join PSINet. Those who thought CSCO was a bargain at $60 last year have changed their mind and think it's overpriced at $17 today.

## Analysis Versus Prophesy and MarketPerform.com

I knew, after reading a library of books on investing and after having invested on my own for years, that diversification was the only method that can bring consistent success to an investor. But how does one diversify effectively and intelligently? There are only so many stocks that we as individuals can examine and track. How does one build diversified investment strategies and then execute them?

Surely mutual funds are a great investment intermediary, but they can entail certain tax implications that are beyond your control, and that can be devastating to your pocketbook, as we will discuss in more detail later in the book. And then there are index funds, which can track the market or any number of slices and segments thereof, minus a fee for management. Index funds allow investors to follow the market blindly, which is generally recommended for the casual investor.

Nevertheless, people often get the itch to try their own hand, to become involved, and to take a chance and make a bet. So how does the average investor build a dynamic and diversified investment portfolio? I can serve as an example. Given my own technology background, I understand the hi-tech sector relatively well. This does not afford me the ability to pick consistent winners in that sector, as evidenced from previously described experiences, but at least I am equipped to do some basic investigation. When it comes to something like biotechnology or energy, however, I am a total buffoon. So how am I to diversify among many sectors and industries when my own knowledge is so limited?

When a friend gave me a dartboard for a birthday present (a sad commentary on my investment insights of the past), I considered throwing darts at a newspaper stock table. This was only half in fun. What really stopped me was the fact that I was living in an apartment at the time. With my aim in darts about as good as my aim in investing back then, I took pity on my walls. And if my children saw me doing this, I'd have "a lot o' splainin' to do" when they wanted to do the same. Just in the nick of time, while browsing through the Yahoo! finance section, I came upon a research listing called "upgrades and downgrades." The many stocks on that list implied diversification. The many different financial institutions covering these stocks also gave breadth of coverage, implying more diversification. As I looked further, I found that the Yahoo! finance section was not the only source of this information. There were plenty of upgrades and downgrades on CNBC, CNNfn, and many other financial media sources as well. For one reason or another, this information continued to intrigue my curiosity.

At one point I showed the upgrades section to a friend who had worked as a research assistant following the South American telecommunications industry. When I asked his counsel on whether I should buy some of the companies that were upgraded, his reply was, "Do me a favor. Don't listen to this stuff. It's all bull!" But what about the downgrades? Should I perhaps buy some of them? My friend's reply to that question was the same. Confused for a moment, I made a mental note of it and got busy with my real job.

Usually in the morning when I get ready for work, I turn on my television to watch the latest news about world affairs, the market, and the economy. Every morning around 8 A.M., Maria Bartiromo would start delivering the latest upgrade and downgrade reports she received from financial institutions on the Squawk Box segment of the show. "This morning," she would start, "Morgan Stanley upgraded IBM from Neutral to its Outperform rating. The analyst quoted that mainframe sales were picking up and IBM's professional services division is experiencing 30 percent growth." Then she would continue, "Goldman Sachs just downgraded Campbell Soup from its Recommended List to its Market Perform rating." Maria would continue with a few sentences about why the analyst lowered his or her rating for Campbell Soup and so on.

As I was getting dressed and at the same time trying to make sure that my kids were getting ready for school and brushing their teeth, I started asking myself a few basic questions: What does Morgan Stanley's Outperform rating mean? What is Morgan Stanley's Outperform rating's average annual return? Is it 5 or 10 percent? Perhaps it's more than that. Perhaps it's less. And finally, does Morgan Stanley's Outperform rating produce a better return than Morgan Stanley's Neutral rating? Subsequently, the same question could be applied to Goldman Sachs's Market Perform rating. What kind of return does this rating produce? And furthermore, how much better does Goldman's Recommended List (which is their top recommendation, resembling a Strong Buy at other firms) do than its Market Underperform rating (which is their lowest recommendation, resembling a Sell at other firms)?

Searching for answers to these basic questions yielded little information. But there was nothing to be found. I read material that explained Strong Buy, Top Pick, or Recommended List means that one should buy that stock. A Buy or Outperform recommendation means hold the stock if you have it but don't purchase it if you don't already have some in your portfolio. Moreover, a Hold,

Neutral, Market Perform, or Maintain recommendation means sell that stock if you have it and stay away from it if you don't. And of course, the rarely used Sell recommendation probably means drop dead, finita la comedia, but in truth no one ever said what Sell really means. So I started wondering, with the ways the markets *really* work, could Sell possibly mean a Strong Buy?

Mixed signals from Wall Street have caused many investors to buy when they should have sold and to sell when they should have held onto a stock. After the tech wreck of 2000 and 2001, when both the NASDAQ and the S&P 500 Index fell to levels unseen literally in years, investors who followed the recommendations of analysts, newsletter writers, so-called investment gurus, and even friends started asking questions about what the ratings bandied about in the media actually mean. Neutral? Market Perform? How can today's investor decipher the language of Wall Street? What is an investor to do when Buy means Sell or Sell means Buy?

Our journey for the rest of the book will cover a number of subjects. As a first step, it is imperative to identify and describe the fundamental rules that all investors need to practice. This process will help the serious reader avoid a large and varied number of pitfalls. Next we will take a closer look at the media and how they influence our decision process—usually for the worse. A visit to our friend and/or foe, the financial analyst, will identify what drives him or her, and why our interests are not always headed in a similar direction.

New and innovative systems for how to interpret financial statements will be unveiled. My aim for the book was always geared to connecting the things we do and see every day to financial markets. Paralleling something you do well (e.g., driving a car) to something you perhaps do poorly (e.g., investing) can often advance your skills in areas that need improvement.

A brief history and evolution of the stock market will be discussed as well. In it you will be introduced to new and innovative equity trading products.

In the final chapters, we will discuss recommendation-based strategies in detail. You will learn how to navigate and interpret these upgrades and downgrades to accomplish great returns and in the process beat the market. I hope you enjoy reading this book as much as I enjoyed writing it.

# 1

# LESSONS FROM CORPORATE AMERICA

Before we begin our journey we should differentiate speculators from investors. Typically speculators are gamblers. They approach the stock market like trips to the casino, often relying on the roll of the die instead of conducting appropriate due diligence. Occasionally they win, but since these triumphs are simply instances of lucky draws they always interpret them incorrectly. The longer speculators play the market the more chances that they will lose it all. Many unseasoned stock market participants begin their investment journeys as speculators. I was certainly a speculator before becoming an investor. Some eventually will evolve into investors while others will continue—not for long—to practice speculation. Unavoidably speculators lose on the stock market just like gamblers lose in casinos. Investors approach the stock market like a business endeavor. By controlling their impulses and instead focusing on data, fundamentals, and value, they inevitably succeed. Since our approach to investing will resemble a business process and not speculation, let's examine how the world's most successful companies run their business and why they continue to succeed.

## Research, Analysis, and Segmentation of Data

In July 1987 I started working as a programmer analyst with Chase Manhattan Bank. My department at the bank was called Credit Risk Management or, as we were better known internally, the CRM Group. The group was fairly small, roughly a dozen people; however, two and a half years later the group expanded to include 45 employees. This should be an indication of the importance our group had during those tenuous years for the banking industry and the economy as a whole. Downsizing was the business practice of the moment, but our group expanded by almost 400 percent. Many of the employees in this department had received their masters and doctorates in economics and statistics. Their assignment was to regularly monitor and examine the bank's credit card customer portfolio.

My job was to enhance and maintain a system that almost everyone in CRM used to make major credit card policy decisions. This system helped the bank decide who should receive a credit card from Chase and who should not. The system was called the portfolio monitoring system.

There I witnessed for the first time how large corporations use information about their clients and apply it to further their understanding of people's psychology. Today, there are fancy names for this technique, such as data mining, business intelligence, and what have you. For our business purposes, we were monitoring our customers' spending patterns and their ability to pay for purchases. If Chase Manhattan Bank ever solicited you for a new Visa or MasterCard, chances are your credit characteristics at one of the credit bureaus resembled the characteristics of a profitable credit card holder. This was a credit card holder who was paying his or her bills on time and, better yet, was habitually paying the minimum amount required.

## Similarly, Investors Who Take Advantage of Margin Accounts Are Most Desirable to a Brokerage House

In the next chapter, we will discuss margin accounts and why individual investors are better off avoiding them. They are the same reasons individuals should not pay just the minimum amount due on their credit card statements, bringing the overall cost of the purchase to another level.

The system we operated at Chase was very complex and produced a variety of reports for our senior management to scrutinize. Bar charts, line charts, and pie charts were plotted in vibrant colors to show various patterns that our portfolio of credit card customers exhibited. We knew if the number of customers who were not paying their bills was growing or shrinking. We knew if bankruptcies were on the rise or on the decline. Portfolio Monitoring System was like a hawk in flight, observing everyone and everything, which in turn gave our organization the ability to identify characteristics that our customers shared, which ones were fruitful, and those that were not. To succeed as an investor one must learn how to identify characteristics of good and bad companies as well.

Three to four times a year, the bank would embark on what was called a solicitation campaign. CRM would specify a set of traits that potential new customers must have for the bank to consider them for a credit card issue. We would then go to a credit bureau and ask them to run our selection criteria through their database. Those people who passed our standards were supplied with a letter inviting them to become our "most valued" customer. Different products were offered to different people. Some were eligible for a Visa, and others got a MasterCard. Some were offered better interest rates and/or frequent flier miles with their purchases. All the data were then thrown into the Portfolio Monitoring System to help us figure out how successful we were with our solicitations and how we could improve results even more for our next solicitation.

It helped us identify trends and formulate guiding principles for our policymakers. As a straightforward example, Portfolio Monitoring System would divide the portfolio into customers with one credit card in one segment, two credit cards in another segment, three in the next one, and so on. The patterns revealed were stunning. The more credit cards an individual held, the more likely he or she was to default on payment. This example illustrates a simple pattern teaching us, the creditor, to respond accordingly. If people have 10 credit cards in their wallet, let someone else give them another card. We, on the other hand, will look elsewhere; we should look for customers who only have one credit card or a maximum of two. From an investor's point of view a similar conclusion can be derived. For example, if a company began to aggressively pursue mergers and acquisitions, let someone else buy their stock; we, on the other hand, should stay away. By recognizing patterns, we were able to increase our ability to recognize people we considered to be "better" potential cardholders and weed out those who were more prone to bankruptcy, late payments, or nonpayment.

Let's not forget why successful companies stay successful. Their profits frequently grow due to their insatiable appetite to learn and their indisputable ability to know the habits of their existing customers, their marketplace, and their competitors. In their drive to succeed and not fall behind their competition, companies are always working on developing new solutions, testing them, and implementing them. It could be effected via a solicitation campaign using direct mail, such as the ones credit card companies send out, or through an ad campaign as seen on television, magazines, billboards, and so on. There is a multitude of avenues available to large corporations for product distribution and analysis. They study what consumers purchase and what they leave on the shelf. They continuously examine facets of their existing customers, such as money-spending patterns, how they come to be customers, and why some left to do business with our competitors. Investors need to follow the same principles. Understanding why certain stocks were a good investment and others were not is crucial.

Personally, the most enjoyable and valuable lesson learned while working for corporate America was my realization of how consistent and determined these companies are to improve their knowledge and understanding of the consumer and how willing they are to risk a portion of their pie—customers or profits—in exchange for innovative ideas.

## Champions and Challengers

Champions and Challengers is a money collection system that worked extremely well at Chase. Everyone knows how difficult it can be to collect money from habitual debtors. Needless to say, Chase, like any other creditor, wanted to see its money returned. To accomplish this, they have set up the Champion and Challenger system, which worked like this: Of all the defaulted accounts, 80 percent were turned over to the collection department that yielded the highest results in the previous year(s). This outperforming department was obviously employing the best strategy for collecting debt and, therefore, was known as the "champion." The remaining 20 percent of outstanding accounts were split evenly between two other collection departments that utilized two different collection strategies. They in turn were called "challenger I" and "challenger II." If by following a different (new) system, one of the challengers performed better than the champion, this challenger was promoted to the rank of the new champion until it was outperformed by a different collection strategy. If this was the case, this new top-performing challenger became the new champion and so on. Thus, the collection system with the best track record always became the new champion and retained its title until a different collection system prevailed. This rotating system of champions and challengers, which encourages competition and, consequently, progress, has a wide range of application in the investing arena.

Can we apply this collection system to our investment needs? Let's examine a hypothetical situation: It is 1992 and our asset management department was just entrusted with $1 million to invest in equity-based mutual funds. There is only one conditional stipulation from the people who have assigned to us this awesome responsibility: Do not underperform the market, which for the sake of comparison is the S&P 500 Index. It sounds easy. However, after investigating and examining the performance of all mutual funds out there, we found that 80 percent show a tendency to underperform the S&P 500. The 20 percent that outperform the index during any given year in most cases fail to fulfill this objective in the following year. That is, research showed that mutual funds either do worse than the market, or if they manage to beat the market, they cannot sustain their momentum.

Investing all the money into an index fund that tracks the S&P 500 will not justify our job. This can be done without the help of an asset management team. Therefore, our team decided to do the following: invest $800,000 of the available capital into the best performing system, the champion. Thus, we have picked the Vanguard S&P 500 Index Fund, which tracks the performance of the S&P 500 Index (VFINX). As we have said, it managed to outperform 80 percent of all actively managed mutual funds throughout its history. The remaining 20 percent, or $200,000, was divided between two different mutual funds, our challenger I and challenger II. For the sake of our demonstration, we chose the American Heritage Fund (AHERX) to represent the first challenger. In 1990 Heiko Theime, the fund's manager, caught investors' interest with an eye-catching return of more than 96 percent. This fund, by the way, proved to be one of the worst-performing mutual funds ever.

As challenger II we stopped our search on a more conservative Legg Mason Value Prime Fund (LMVTX), which beat the S&P 500 in 1990 by a modest 33 percent. This fund, by the way, proved to be one of the best-performing mutual funds ever.

After 5 years on the job, we are ready to show the results to our investors. Figure 1-1 is what our "report card" looked like for 1992 through 1996.

Our total return for 1992 to 1996, inclusively, produced a respectable 71.25 percent return, whereas the S&P 500 produced 66.37 percent. Not bad, considering our hypothetical asset manager spent only a few hours researching the mutual fund industry's performance over the last 5 years. As the table demonstrates, we were triumphant, outperforming the market by almost 5 percent. Nonetheless, we realized that there was room for improvement.

| Year | S&P 500 Index | VFINX Champion | AHERX Challenger I | LMVTX Challenger II | Total Investment Results for the Year (Using 80/10/10 Split) |
|---|---|---|---|---|---|
| 1992 | 5.18% | 8.07% | 14.33% | 12.11% | 9.10% |
| 1993 | 6.30% | 9.12% | 39.29% | 11.48% | 12.37% |
| 1994 | −1.54% | 1.20% | −36.90% | 1.33% | −2.60% |
| 1995 | 34.11% | 37.45% | −30.59% | 40.84% | 30.99% |
| 1996 | 22.32% | 22.81% | −6.76% | 38.20% | 21.39% |
| Total 5-year return | 66.37% | 78.65% | −20.63% | 103.96% | 71.25% |

Fig. 1-1.   Champion-Challenger scenario with VFINX as champion.

A mutual fund that is not sufficiently diversified, as was the case with AHERX, can be a sinker. Thus, we've learned our lesson and decided that Challenger I, occupied by Mr. Heiko's American Heritage Fund, should take a hike and be replaced with a new challenger. In addition we noticed that Challenger II, occupied by the Legg Mason Value Prime Fund, produced better results than the current champion.

What should our next logical step be? According to our champion-challenger theory, the reigning champion should be deposed, and the challenger that outperformed the competition should be crowned as the new monarch. It is a simple rule of capitalism, or as communists would call it the *jungle market* mentality, where the strongest survive while the weak fall into oblivion.

Our job as money managers is not over, however. On the contrary, we've just crowned a new champion, Legg Mason Value Prime, which has proven to have a better-performing system for picking stocks and which will be assigned 80 percent of the capital. Now we must immediately start thinking of finding new challengers to whom we will assign the rest of the business with 10 percent for each new mutual fund. As an investor or businessperson, you should never be lulled into a false sense of security. Perhaps you are satisfied with the new money management system that gets you market-beating results; however, you cannot stop here. As soon as you relax and stop innovating, someone else will think of a way to do it better and put you out of business.

To further illustrate how our strategy works, over the next 5 years our strategy may have been as follows. Challenger II, Legg Mason Value Prime Fund, became our new champion, attracting 80 percent of our capital. Challenger I was designated to carry a new mutual fund. Suppose we chose Fidelity Select Electronics (FSELX). The decision was based on its prior 5-year performance. The managers at this Fidelity fund produced stunning results. From 1992 through 1996, they outperformed the S&P 500 Index every year. In fact FSELX produced better results than our best performing fund, our new champion, LMVTX. For Challenger II we selected the top-notch performer: Growth Fund of America (AGTHX). This fund had very solid returns as well. For the period 1992 to 1996, it managed to outperform the S&P 500 Index on four of five occasions.

Chapter One

Results for the aforementioned mutual funds as applied to our investment strategy appear in Figure 1-2.

From 1997 through 2001 (our next 5-year period), our strategy beat the S&P 500 Index every year. The total return for the S&P 500 for the 5 years was 51.78 percent while our strategy produced a staggering 99.97 percent return. Our investors need not be brain surgeons to realize that for those 5 years this strategy outperformed the S&P 500 almost by a 2 to 1 margin.

But before we move ahead, let us go back to 1997, when we were selecting our new champion and challengers. Back then we selected Legg Mason Value Prime because of its solid performance in the previous years. However, if you recall, we noted that Fidelity Select Electronics had yielded better results than our newly elected champion from 1992 to 1996. This could have urged us to make FSELX our new champion instead of LMVTX. Let us look at Figure 1-3 for a demonstration of what would have happened had we chosen the other challenger.

Even though this strategy did not outperform the S&P 500 Index every year as did the strategy in which LMVTX was the champion,

| Year | S&P 500 Index | LMVTX Champion | AGTHX Challenger II | FSELX Challenger I | Total Investment Results for the Year (Using 80/10/10 Split) |
|---|---|---|---|---|---|
| 1997 | 28.73% | 37.06% | 26.67% | 13.22% | 33.64% |
| 1998 | 26.67% | 47.98% | 31.60% | 51.12% | 46.66% |
| 1999 | 19.53% | 26.79% | 44.76% | 105.71% | 36.48% |
| 2000 | −10.11% | −7.47% | 7.51% | −21.41% | −7.37% |
| 2001 | −13.04% | −8.73% | −11.39% | −13.17% | −9.44% |
| Total 5-year return | 51.78% | 95.63% | 99.15% | 135.47% | 99.97% |

Fig. 1-2. Champion–Challenger scenario with LMVTX as champion.

| Year | S&P 500 Index | FSELX Champion | AGTHX Challenger I | LMVTX Challenger II | Total Investment Results for the Year (Using 80/ 10/10 Split) | Results Against Market |
|------|------|------|------|------|------|------|
| 1997 | 28.73% | 13.22% | 26.67% | 37.06% | 16.95% | −12% |
| 1998 | 26.67% | 51.12% | 31.60% | 47.98% | 48.85% | 22% |
| 1999 | 19.53% | 105.71% | 44.76% | 26.79% | 91.72% | 70% |
| 2000 | −10.11% | −21.41% | 7.51% | −7.47% | −17.12% | −7% |
| 2001 | −13.04% | −13.17% | −11.39% | −8.73% | −12.55% | 0.5% |
| Total 5-year return | 51.78% | 135.47% | 99.15% | 95.63% | 127.85% | 76% |

**Fig. 1-3.   Champion-Challenger scenario with FSELX as champion.**

its overall 5-year return produced a positive 127.85 percent, compared to 51.78 percent for the market, and it had an almost 28 percent advantage over the results of the first scenario with LMVTX at the helm.

The message of our story is this: You cannot become stagnant in this business (or in any other business). Those who stop innovating, who become content with their current design no matter how superior it is today, will inevitably fail in the future. Investors should keep this simple rule in mind. No matter what your investment style is, you should always put a certain percentage of your portfolio into something slightly or radically different and at all times analyze your results against the market and/or other strategies you might practice. For those of you who were not able to outperform the market in the past or do not have an investment strategy in place, please do yourselves a favor and do the following right away: Allocate 80 percent of your stock funds to a mutual fund that tracks the S&P 500 Index. Most studies indicate that this index fund outperforms close to 80 percent of all actively managed mutual funds. Use this fund as your champion in the champion/challenger investment strategy. The other 20 percent should be split between challenger I and challenger II at 10 percent apiece. If you decide to use recommendation-based strategies, then Challenger I could consist of a group of stocks that, for example, Bear Stearns decided to upgrade, and Challenger II could be stocks that Lehman Brothers rates Market Perform. By using an approach like this, you are well diversified between many sectors and industries.

# 2

# RULES OF ENGAGEMENT

Improving and ultimately succeeding as an investor, as in any other activity, require discipline and following certain rules. Markets offer an investor a great many resources to gamble with, such as stocks, bonds, mutual funds, options, calls, puts, commodities, shorting, and so on. This surely can be an overwhelming experience. Many investors act like kids in a candy store and frequently go for the most popular item. If stocks have been performing well lately, they buy stocks. If it's bonds that are doing well, they buy bonds, and so on. The problem with this approach becomes clear when investors choose to assign most, if not all, of their money to stocks, bonds, or cash, often seeing the type of securities they avoided appreciate in value. Thus, diversification with different type of securities (e.g., cash, bonds, and stocks) is vital.

This book addresses stock investing only. It is very important to identify and learn the basic rules that all investors must follow if they want to prevail as stock purchasers. Profitable investing, without a doubt, can be learned. Despite popular belief, it is not some kind of clandestine operation, although it does use its own jargon, trying to protect its insular community. Stock markets have been around for a long time, and we dedicate Chapter 7 to the evolution of securities trading. And one pattern they habitually display is that uptrends are always followed by downtrends, and vice versa. In the future we will repeatedly continue to experience bull markets and bear markets. Similar to our own lives, in which we experience both good times and bad, slumps and booms in the stock market are inevitable. Everything is cyclical. And it is no wonder that people say, "The more things change, the more they remain the same."

Let us go over a few very important points. As we have said, what all stock investors need to improve their results is to follow some basic rules, which we call the "fundamental rules of investing" or simply "fundamental rules."

## Fundamental Rule 1: You Can Lose What You Don't Have.

The first and most important fundamental rule to remember is to make sure you do not lose more money than you have put in. For every dollar invested, you must make sure that in the absolutely worst-case scenario, you will lose that dollar only and not one penny more. The idea here, after all, is to see your money grow, not see you lose everything. Working on the assumption that you would not invest money you do not have, you also should not lose money you do not have.

## Fundamental Rule 2: Margin Threatens the Success of the Long-term Investor.

margin—*n*. an amount allowed beyond what is needed

### Reasons Not to Use Margin

Most books on investing advise you not to put money into the stock market that you cannot afford to lose (Fundamental Rule 1). By using margin you borrow money against the securities in your investment account, then you invest that money into more securities, and then you pay interest on the money you borrowed against the securities you own. If your securities drop in value by 50 percent or more, your broker will call you for additional cash to put into your account. The cash is in your checking, savings, or money market account. Remember that this is the cash you need for your other commitments. That is why it's not in your investment account in the first place. You cannot afford to lose any more money. You simply do not have it. However, your broker tells you to send more cash or he or she will have to sell the securities you own by 11 A.M. tomorrow. It's some choice you have. This is exactly why the dictionary defines the word *margin* as something beyond what is needed. In a situation like this, it is definitely beyond what is needed. So is margin. If the securities your broker sold do not cover the amount you borrowed, then you have a loan to pay off. And theoretically, you can end up with no securities, no money, and a debt.

Did you know that margin is one of the biggest and most profitable concerns at brokerage houses? Have you ever seen a prospectus from an online broker? Their entire business rests on customers who make use of margin. It is their objective to make you use your margin. They borrow money at a much better rate than you do, and just like the credit card companies, they make money on the difference between what they pay for funds and what they charge you for them. If this is good for them, it must be bad for us. There is no mutual benefit here. Margin is like a cancer eating away at your principal and substantially increasing the risk of your long-term survival as an investor.

## Fundamental Rule 3: Shorting Stocks Can, and Most Likely Will, Leave You Short.

Investors usually play the market hoping that the financial instruments (in our case stocks) they purchase will go up in price. This concept in the Wall Street jargon is called *going long*. Of course, there is an old practice of making bets against what most investors hope for. This practice is known as *shorting*, and theoretically, it can produce unlimited losses, as will be demonstrated in the following examples.

The best scenario: You borrow a stock from your broker that is currently valued at $10 per share, believing its price is outrageously high and absurd. You then sell this *borrowed* stock on the open market and collect your $10 minus the commission. You hope this stock will go down in price, and your dream comes true. Let's say that within 6 months the company declares bankruptcy, and you purchase the stock back for pennies. Literally and happily, you give it back to your broker, who lent you that stock when it was riding high at $10. When all is said and done, you have managed to make almost 100 percent profit minus commission. Let's estimate that at 95 percent, which is not bad for a 6-month return.

After this triumph, you feel smart and go hunting for the next overpriced stock, which brings us to our next point.

The worst scenario: You borrow a stock priced at $10, believing it to be overvalued. You then sell this stock on the open market and collect your $10 minus commission. Now you wait for your stock to drop in price. Only this time your dream crumbles. Within the next 6 months, the company declares record earnings (perhaps they have found a cure for cancer) and the stock soars. To safeguard yourself from the unlimited potential loss, you purchase this stock back for $100, at ten times what you have paid for it, and reluctantly give it back to your broker. In the end you lose 900 percent plus commission. These are dreadful numbers for only 6 months of activity.

Indubitably, these two examples are extreme, but they are educational nonetheless. When you short stocks, you expose yourself to a possible loss of astronomic proportions. There is no limit to how much you can lose. Do you still remember our rule 1: Never invest money that you cannot afford to lose? Now try to remember our rule 3: Shorting stocks is foolish. The odds are stacked against you. You might as well get in your car, drive to Atlantic City, and take your chances on blackjack.

## Fundamental Rule 4: Investing in IPOs Is a Trap.

Do you remember when your parents told you not to touch the stove when it's hot? Probably not, but nonetheless, you do know that if you touch it while it's hot, you will get burned. You can apply the same postulate to "hot" industries that create many IPOs.

During the late 1990s, many investors got burned buying hot IPOs. For example, Goldman Sachs underwrote PALM, a company that manufactures Palm Pilots, at $38 per share, and believe it or not, no individual investor was able to get PALM at that price. On that day alone, the stock closed at around $126 per share. A few days later, a PALM share reached $165. Its market cap that day surpassed General Motors. One year later PALM was trading at around $7 a share. Do you really want to end up stuck with stocks that have dropped in price 90 percent or more? This misfortune befalls IPOs quite often.

You should try to remember a very simple dictum: As an individual investor, your ability to make money in the IPO market is very limited. Just look at the current fallout. There are hundreds of lawsuits in addition to federal investigations into questionable IPO practices by major financial institutions. The plaintiffs' lawyers estimate that there will be hundreds of IPOs that could become subjects of lawsuits in the next year or so.

What is wrong with IPOs? The plaintiffs claim that brokerage firms involved in IPO underwriting used a very simple strategy to deceive investors. These investment banks allocated shares of the companies they underwrote to their good customers such as mutual funds, hedge funds, and so on. There is nothing wrong with that; however, these so-called good customers had to agree to buy more shares when these stocks began to trade. At the same time, they were not allowed to sell these shares on the open market. Although this alleged scheme works under an unwritten agreement rather than a company policy where your stockbroker refuses to sell your shares at your request, the result is the same, as artificially created low supply and high demand drive share prices up. And with the price so high and still climbing higher, less-experienced and less-informed investors flock to the feeding frenzy. Remember peer pressure and herding mentality?

Unfortunately, many individual investors are often at least one step behind. At this stage CNBC, CNNfn, and all the major newspapers have blown their horns so loudly that even the dead have heard about these stellar stocks. Everyone wants a piece of that pie and is eager to pay $165 for PALM, $170 for Ariba, $130 for Ivillage, and the list goes on. And now that the buying craze has hit its peak, agreements with the good customers, the ones who promised not to sell the IPO shares immediately, can be terminated, and they begin to sell their shares on the open market. Needless to say, when a large contingent of shareholders begins to sell, prices begin to drop.

According to IPO.com there were 996 IPOs issued during 1999 and 2000. The reason these lawsuits have any legal merit is that although it is not against the law to sell shares in hot IPOs to good customers, it is against the law to have any attachments these so-called good customers are obligated to fulfill. These agreements to buy more shares on the open market after trading has begun are illegal. All of these lawsuits are obviously expensive. Credit Suisse First Boston in the first quarter of its financial statement released in May 2001 states, "The results of such proceedings in the aggregate will not have a material adverse effect on our financial condition but might be material to operating results."

These cases will most likely be settled out of court. However, for our purposes the judgment should be issued right here and now. All of us should be aware that it is costly and foolish to pay only the minimum balance due on our credit card. We know that smoking cigarettes is hazardous to our health. We know that excessive drinking is not good for us either. Similarly, everyone should be aware that IPOs are bad for our pocketbooks and, therefore, our health. Remind yourself to stay away from IPOs unless you are one of those "good customers," which makes it a completely different story.

## Fundamental Rule 5: Things Are Not Always What They Seem; The Insiders Are Buying Shares.

The basic notion is that when insiders start buying shares of the company they work for, it is a signal of a bullish state of affairs. If anyone should know about how well a company is doing, it must be the insiders. This sounds logical and seems to make a lot of sense until you realize that some companies take this concept and use it to incite investors. Years ago high-ranking employees such as the CEO, CFO, and other directors would actually invest their own money by purchasing shares in their companies if they felt the shares were undervalued and believed that business was improving. Today it is frequently quite a different story. It is troubling to hear that the same CEOs, CFOs, and other highly positioned employees started to borrow money from the companies they are running and used it to buy their companies' shares. For instance, Michael Armstrong, a director, announced in April 2000 that he purchased 10,000 shares of AtHome (ATHM) at $17.52 per share plus commission at a total cost of $175,620. Within 18 months, AtHome went bankrupt and ceased to exist. In August 2001 Net2000 Communications (NTKK) announced that five of its executive officers purchased an aggregate of 58,500 shares. The price hovered around $0.90 per share. By March 2002 NTKK traded around $0.05 per share and issued a statement that it needs additional time to plan its Chapter 11 bankruptcy proceedings.

To the outside world the fact that the top brass is buying shares seems like a bullish sign, but in reality it can be a loan with forgiveness built into it. Knowing this should certainly alert us to the fact that things are not always what they seem to be, and just because the insiders are buying, it is not an indication that the business is rebounding.

## Fundamental Rule 6: The Risk May Not Justify the Reward.

### Acquisitions and What They Do for Investors

Management that decided to pursue an aggressive growth strategy can utilize two different available options. One way is through internal company growth. This involves hiring new employees, finding new clients, developing new products, and expanding operations within the limits of an existing organization. The other avenue for growth, which many organizations choose to pursue, is through the purchase of other companies. This is a very popular instrument for a quick infusion of new products and increased sales. On many occasions the buyers and sellers have been in a similar line of business and were competing for many years; thus, in many cases these mergers create a larger company with a more extensive product line and talented work force.

The other reason for an acquisition typically revolves around the model of diversifying the business into other sectors and/or industries of the economy. Acquisitions of this type should always be greeted with disapproval. Many successful companies put an end to their achievements when they start playing a highly risky mergers and acquisitions game. There are many instances when management has no experience or the faintest idea of what it takes to merge two companies. This is often the greatest risk for the shareholders of both the company being acquired and the one doing the acquiring.

The other risk is the company's loss of focus. Certainly, recent mergers between Chase Manhattan Bank and J. P. Morgan or America Online and Time Warner come to mind. Let's take a look at some other fairly recent mergers and acquisitions to ascertain whether shareholders have benefited from these transactions. In many instances the selling company benefits because the buyer pays a premium. However, it is our opinion that if you are holding shares in this company being acquired, now is the perfect time to sell them. Why wait? The risks, as discussed earlier, after this point do not justify the rewards. But we are running ahead of ourselves. Let's take a look at the mergers and acquisitions that have recently taken place involving companies we all know.

In 1999 Lucent Technologies (LU) acquired Ascend Communications for $24 billion. By July 2001 Lucent was in big trouble and announced that it would be laying off an additional 20,000 employees worldwide, cutting its staff by a total of 44,500 employees, or almost 50 percent. We are not pretending to blame all of Lucent's woes on its merger and acquisitions strategy. All we are saying is that if you took our advice and sold your shares the minute Ascend announced its merger with Lucent, you would not be stuck holding Lucent shares today. On June 28, 1999, just a few months after the merger, Ascend stopped trading forever. LU's closing price on the same date was $65.69. Today it is trading at around $6.

Here is another example, which will be discussed in greater detail later in the book. Exodus Communications acquired Global Center, a division of Global Crossing, for $6.5 billion. This deal was originally announced at the end of September 2000, when the price for Exodus was around $56 per share. By January 10, 2001, when the deal was completed, Exodus was trading at around $18. By mid-July 2001 Exodus was barely keeping its head above water, trading at just above $1. It was sinking under the burden of outstanding debt and its failure to generate enough cash flow. It is safe to say that Exodus would have been better off without this merger.

AtHome's (ATHM) market cap in 1999 was almost $40 billion when it purchased Excite for $6.6 billion. If this was not enough, it also purchased Blue Mountain for $800 million. By July 2001 AtHome's market cap was under $400 million. It is probably safe to say that without these mergers, ATHM would continue to survive today.

Figure 2-1 supports our rule. It is from Goldman Sachs's Web site and displays mergers and acquisitions transactions in which Goldman acted as an adviser and that were more than $100 million during year 2000. This list reminds us of a hospital room for the terminally ill. Some companies have died and are no longer around,

---

- Lucent Technologies' $24 billion acquisition of Ascend Communications
- Veritas' $20 billion acquisition of Seagate Technology and related sale of Seagate Technology's operating businesses to Silver Lake Partners'– Investment Dealers' Digest's Technology Deal of the Year (Goldman Sachs advised Silver Lake Partners)
- Motorola's $17 billion acquisition of General Instrument
- E-TEK Dynamics' $15.5 billion merger with JDS Uniphase
- Cap Gemini's $11.2 billion acquisition of the Global IT Consulting Business of Ernst & Young
- America Online's $10 billion acquisition of Netscape Communications Corporation
- i2 Technologies $9.3 billion acquisition of Aspect Development
- Exodus Communications' $6.5 billion acquisition of the Global Center division of Global Crossing
- ArrowPoint Communications' $5.5 billion acquisition by Cisco Systems
- Yahoo!'s $4.7 billion acquisition of broadcast.com inc
- LHS Groups' $4.7 billion acquisition by Sema Group
- Redback Networks' $4.3 billion acquisition of Siara Systems
- Kana Communications' $4.2 billion acquisition of Silknet Software
- Corning's $4 billion acquisition of the optical components and devices business of Pirelli
- Sterling Software's $4 billion acquisition by Computer Associates International
- Sterling Commerce's $3.9 billion acquisition by SBC Communications
- Marvell Technology Group's $2.7 billion acquisition of Galileo Technology
- Cisco Systems' $2.1 billion acquisition of Pirelli S.p.A.
- Genesys Telecommunications Laboratories' $1.5 billion sale to Alcatel

---

**Fig. 2-1.  Goldman's mergers and acquisitions deals.**

Source: Ranked by aggregate deal value. All mergers and acquisitions (M&A) deals, deal values (at announcement), and credit to advisers as reported from Securities Data Corporation (SDC), Thompson Financial Services, for high-technology universe of companies as defined by SDC; excludes all spinoffs to shareholders. Includes all other announced M&A transactions of over $100 million for high-technology targets reported in SDC from January 1, 2000, to December 31, 2000.

whereas others remain in critical condition and need major surgery and/or a miracle to survive.

On certain occasions mergers and acquisitions do make sense. Companies such as General Electric, Microsoft, IBM, Computer Associates, Citigroup, and many more have proven to have the ability and experience to integrate acquired firms into their existing structures and continue to grow. However, most companies that aggressively pursue growth through acquisitions will fail to provide their shareholders with positive returns. These companies are not dissimilar to the people who acquire more and more credit cards. Remember how the portfolio monitoring system identified a pattern about a credit card customer who possesses many cards as a potential candidate for bankruptcy or nonpayment? The same rule applies to mergers and acquisitions candidates. To the outsider they appear more affluent and prosperous, but in reality they expose themselves to more debt and to structures that become harder to manage and control. Often, this leads to unhappy customers and employees. And here we would like to reiterate our earlier advice: Do not hold on to your shares in companies that have just announced a merger because the risks do not justify the rewards.

## Fundamental Rule 7: Buyback Gets Companies on the Right Track.

When I took my first class in economics at Forest Hills High School in New York City, I learned about *supply and demand*. All prices, it seems, in our world rely on this simple formula. If there's more supply than demand, the price goes down. If the opposite is true, the price is driven up. The stock market is no different. There are only two ways to increase the price of company shares. One way is by increasing demand, and the other is by reducing supply. It has been proven that shares go up in price when a company has increased earnings. Earnings growth is the underlying reason that creates demand for shares while keeping the supply at the same level. That is why management is constantly trying to increase profit margins by cutting expenses and improving the flow of goods or services to its client base.

Another way to get your shares to grow is by reducing the supply of outstanding shares available to the markets. This is often effected through buyback or a share repurchase program. Whenever a company has excess cash on hand, one of the best ways to make use of this money is by embarking on a share repurchase program. Let's take a look at some of the recent announcements and how stock buyback programs affect the share price on the market.

On March 10, 2000, Alcoa Corporation (AA) announced that it intended to repurchase 20 million shares of its common stock. The company at the time had about 364 million shares outstanding. The closing price for Alcoa on March 10 was $32.83 on a split-adjusted basis. One year later the price was around $38. This represents a modest 15 percent increase, but let's not forget what happened to the S&P 500 during the same time frame. This most widely used index, which beats 80 percent of professionals, had declined by 15 percent during the same period.

Another example of a share repurchasing program that helped its shareholders achieve a positive return is with the Charlotte-based retailer Cato Corporation (CACOA). On February 25, 2000, Cato directors had approved the repurchase of up to 2 million of the retailer's class A common stock. The decision followed an earlier repurchase program in which the company bought nearly 4 million shares. Cato officials had also increased the company's quarterly cash dividend by 33 percent to 10 cents per share. This is what I call a "double blessing." Not only had the company announced an additional buyback program, but it also increased the dividend. This was certainly the stock to buy, but unfortunately, most people were actively buying Lucent, Cisco, Nortel, and the like. Yet Cato is what investors should have been looking for. Cato's closing price on February 25, 2000, was $9.50. On July 30, 2001, it rose to close at $16.22, which is a 70 percent return within an 18-month period. Even for technology junkies, this is a respectable return.

No one noticed this announcement, yet all an investor had to do was scan the Internet once a week for companies that make precisely this kind of announcement, buy their stock, and reap the rewards. Up to this day, Cato had only one financial institution, according to MarketPerform.com, following the retailer. Bank Boston Robertson Stephens has rated Cato as Attractive ever since March 14, 1999. The analysts could have and should have upgraded Cato immediately after such news hit the media. Unfortunately, they were engaged in upgrading many technology stocks that were actively involved in mergers and acquisitions only to tank shortly after that.

On February 23, 2000, Bloomington-based Toro Corp. (TTC) announced its board of directors' decision to purchase up to 1 million shares of Toro's outstanding stock. Toro does not have sexy products in the technology field such as Broadcast.com Inc., acquired by Yahoo! for $4.7 billion, or General Instruments, bought by Motorola for $17 billion. If we listen to CNBC or CNNfn, we are likely to be informed about Motorola and Yahoo!'s latest moves. These media giants do not care about Toro because their undemanding viewers do not care about Toro.

Toro is involved in the uninteresting business of designing, manufacturing, and marketing specialized turf maintenance equipment, irrigation systems, landscaping equipment, agricultural irrigation systems, and residential yard products. Now don't be surprised when we tell you that Toro, after announcing the buyback program, did extremely well. Its sales grew and so did the stock price. On February 23, 2000, Toro's stock closed at $32.58. By July 30, 2001, the stock managed to climb a respectable 43 percent to close at $46.80. No one on Wall Street noticed this one either. According to MarketPerform.com, only Bank of America was following this stock. It had had a Buy rating on Toro since December 12, 1999. They do have a Strong Buy rating, but it is our guess that they decided that a share repurchase program alone did not justify an upgrade.

On February 29, 2000, Troy Financial Corporation (TRYF), the parent of Troy Savings Bank, had received regulatory approval to repurchase an additional 10 percent of its common stock beginning March 31, 2000. The statement revealed that approximately 1.1 million shares will be purchased from time to time in open market transactions. In October 1999 the company launched its first buyback plan, which called for the purchase of about 1 million shares. As we have illustrated in previous examples, it is strongly advisable to purchase shares in companies that announce share buybacks. Of the company's outstanding stock, 10 percent (an enormous quantity) will disappear from the float. If Troy can further increase earnings, they will be applied to a much smaller number of outstanding shares, which in turn will increase its earnings per share. This is what you need to look for because experience has taught us that programs like this benefit the stock price. On February 29, 2000, Troy Financial's stock price closed at $9.16. By July 30, 2001, again almost 18 months later, the stock climbed a respectable 113 percent to close at $19.52. Individuals who bought Troy at the time of its buyback announcement should be very proud of their ability to pick stocks. Not surprisingly, such stock-picking ability is not so much luck as knowing what to look for.

On March 20, 2000, a technology company announced that its board of directors had approved a program to repurchase up to 8 million shares. Autodesk Inc. (ADSK) is located in San Rafael, California, and is involved in the software design and digital content for the architectural design and land development, manufacturing, utilities, telecommunications, and media and entertainment industries. Autodesk's management said that its board of directors is always looking to enhance shareholder value. One of the ways to achieve this goal is to repurchase shares. Carol Bartz, chairman and CEO of Autodesk, said, "We believe having the authority to repurchase an additional 8 million shares is an opportunity to provide significant value to our shareholders." Little did Carol Bartz know about the tough times that lay ahead for the industry and the technology sector.

The performance by Autodesk, while disappointing, has nevertheless outperformed many of its peers and was consistent with others that announced considerable buyback programs. In March 2000 Autodesk's closing price was $48.41. By July 30, 2001, it was $36.34. This time, had you purchased this company stock, you would have lost 25 percent of your original investment. Although this is disappointing, you would have still managed to outperform many professional money managers in the technology sector overall.

This fundamental rule about share buyback or repurchase, or any other rule, does not work all the time, as you have seen from previous examples, but it will not fail you in the long run. Whenever you find an announcement about a share buyback program, you should consider it as the ultimate catalyst that spurs additional investigation and research.

On August 5, 2000, *Financial Times* published an article in which its author, Andrew Hill, discussed the wisdom of share repurchases by the oil giants. "The Big Buyback Is Back" read the headline. Two of the world's largest oil companies, Exxon Mobil (XOM) and the Anglo-Dutch group the Royal Dutch/Shell (currently Royal Dutch Petroleum Company (RD)), declared large share repurchase plans. Exxon Mobil was setting up to resume the share buyback program, which returned a massive $26 billion to its shareholders between 1983 and 1999. Shell also planned to take advantage of the new Dutch legislation that would allow a multiyear repurchase of its shares worth between $1.5 and $4.8 billion annually.

Why do it? A new study, sponsored by the Financial Executives Research Foundation (Ferf), a New York–based financial research organization, looked at 200 companies that announced and completed share repurchase programs between 1991 and 1996. It concludes that there are five main reasons for buybacks:

1. To increase the share price.
2. To rationalize the capital structure—the company believes it can sustain a higher debt-equity ratio.
3. To substitute dividend payouts with share repurchases (because capital gains may be taxed at rates lower than dividend income).
4. To prevent dilution of earnings caused, for example, by the issue of new shares to meet the exercise of stock option grants.
5. To deploy excess cash flow.

You should understand that companies that benefit from this rule tend to increase their sales and earnings as well. Do not consider purchasing any shares in a company that has slowing sales and declining earnings, as that will always offset any other benefits the management may throw at you.

The Ferf study of 200 companies took a closer look at whether open-market buybacks achieved the companies' longer-term objectives. In general the companies examined have benefited from repurchase plans. The study paints a picture of misunderstood and thus undervalued companies with above-average sales growth and returns on equity but below-average share price growth. Distraught, they undertake share repurchase, and in the 3 years after completing the program, share price growth improves until it almost falls in line with industry averages.

Thus, according to the study, a repurchase of shares program is a sure sign of a company's turnaround and heralds a rise in that company's stock price.

## Fundamental Rule 8: Beware of Stock Dividends.

Sometimes companies issue dividends in stock rather than in cash. The typical sales pitch to investors for justifying such a move revolves around a theme that the company saves cash for future expansion and at the same time rewards its shareholders with more shares. However, the procedure is a device that rarely, if ever, produces positive results for shareholders. In reality this is just a stock split and nothing more. During a bull market, companies that split shares get a short-term boost in their stock price by creating higher demand because of the lower share price. The conventional accepted wisdom proclaims that investors buy stocks in lots of 100; thus, splitting shares might entice someone who wants to invest $2000 to buy 100 shares at $20 while passing up 50 shares at $40. Those who believe this conventional wisdom should look at Warren Buffet's Berkshires shares. To my knowledge they have not split and currently trade around $70,000.

Issuing stock dividends is not dissimilar to the winemaking process in Moldova, a former Soviet republic. Many wineries diluted the wine by adding a little water to the carafe, which sold for a ruble. With a bit of watering down, they still made their ruble but sold a reduced amount of alcohol. Similarly, stock dividend programs give us more paper but with the same value. Stock dividends are a sign of trouble and should be viewed with caution.

## Fundamental Rule 9: The Magic of Diversification Is That You Do It Every Day.

Harry Markowitz introduced the modern portfolio theory in his paper "Portfolio Selection" in the 1952 *Journal of Finance*. In 1990 he shared the Nobel Prize with Merton Miller and William Sharpe for what has become a wide-ranging theory for portfolio selection and corporate finance. The theme of the paper can be summarized by the following formula:

$$\text{Diversification} = \text{Risk Management} = \text{Safety}$$

To most investors, diversification seems intuitively obvious: Don't put all your eggs in one basket. Diversification helps spread risk between areas of the world, securities, and markets. It can facilitate an advantage from opportunities as they occur around the globe. It offers a method of hedging our bets against catastrophes (e.g., warfare or natural disasters) and unforeseen events (e.g., collapsing stock markets or oil embargoes). Diversification surely reduces risk. Modern portfolio analysis has revealed that even an unsystematic blend of investments can reduce risk compared to putting all your money in a single stock. For the identical amount of risk, diversification can add to returns.

The scientific details of modern portfolio theory are complicated in themselves, taken from mountains of financial data and by applying statistical theory and probability. Many financial publications confirm why this strategy works, and it is supported by numerous examples from the financial world. We, however, wanted to present an example of diversification that everyone, including you, applies to everyday life.

Let us assume that you drive. The first thing you learned about driving a car, believe it or not, is diversification. Think about it for a moment. When you drive, you have to look through your windshield to see what is ahead. You also need to look into the rearview mirror to know what is happening in the back. Sideview mirrors alert you of what is occurring on the driver and passenger sides of your vehicle. With all these mirrors at your disposal, there are still blind spots that you need to manage. When you change lanes, you must turn your head to make sure there is no one inside your blind zone. Only then do you change lanes.

What was just described is risk management through diversification. Most of us do perform this task on a daily basis without even thinking about its simplest form. But although we can almost be sure of our safety precautions while driving, we have no control whatsoever over the actions of other people driving around us.

Peter Bernstein's book on the history of risk, *Against the Gods*, says: "The essence of risk management lies in maximizing the areas where we have some control over the outcome, while minimizing the areas where we have absolutely no control over the outcome." Think of the aforementioned driving scenario in terms of diversifying your actions—looking in front, in the rear, to the left, to the right, and turning your head to manage the blind spots. You diversify your attention and maximize the area where you have some control over the outcome while minimizing the area where you have no control whatsoever (other drivers).

Imagine if you could look only through the windshield while driving. Disaster would catch up with you pretty quickly. The same thing could happen to you with investing. The problem with buying stocks in one sector or industry resembles looking only in your rearview mirror, and it doesn't take long for an accident to occur. To manage risk, use common sense: Diversify! Diversify! Diversify!

Another analogy on the subject of diversification involves our diet. We all know that our bodies function best when we receive the right mix of nutrients and minerals. We all need some carbohydrate, protein, and fat. Most of us are not medical doctors, but we know the importance of food diversification. Recently, a friend invested most of his funds in technology stocks, such as CSCO, JDSU, NT, and ORCL, believing this was diversification. He was surely mistaken. This type of diversification is on a par with eating spaghetti with tomato sauce, ziti with tomato sauce, and angel hair pasta with oil and garlic. This is not diversification. Diversification means spreading your investments across different sectors, not one with different products.

Peter Lynch, the successful money manager and author, has owned approximately 1400 various stocks while managing the Magellan Mutual Fund. He says that of these 1400 stocks, there were many he wished he did not own; however, his overall results were phenomenal. He speaks about the fundamentals as the underlying reason for a company's stock going up or down, and who can argue with that? In his book, *One Up on Wall Street*, Lynch says, "to make a spectacular showing, you only have to find one big winner out of eleven. The more right you are about any one stock, the more wrong you can be on all the others and still triumph as an investor." These are words of advice we must all remember. We too can build our own mutual funds, but the question is "How?" Someone who manages a huge mutual fund has many resources at his or her disposal. Analysts meet with CEOs and CFOs to discuss their plans for expansion and cost-cutting programs. Individual investors surely do not have the resources or time to do all this. There are, however, advantages that we do have.

We do not need to buy a million shares in a company and we don't need to sell them all at once either. When you take into account all the pluses and minuses of being an individual investor, it acts as an equalizer between individuals and professional investors when it comes to executing a successful investment strategy.

Another example that converges with the concept of antidiversification is the practice by many investors to purchase more shares of a stock they already own if the price of that stock declines. This type of purchase does not contribute to the diversification of investor's portfolio, and it should be avoided. If a financial adviser tells you to buy more shares that you already own because the price dropped, he or she should be released as your financial adviser immediately.

## Fundamental Rule 10: Investigate Before You Invest.

Invest

Invest-igate

What do these two words have in common besides sharing the same first six letters? In the dictionary you will find *invest* first. Its meaning is to commit money or capital in order to gain profit or interest as, for example, in purchasing property, security, or bonds. Following the word *invest*, you will find the word *investigate*, which means to observe or inquire in detail; to examine systematically. However, before you commit your money (*invest*), you should observe in detail (*investigate*). Please switch these two words around and investigate *before* you invest. On the other hand, if the process of financial investigation does not excite you, I suggest that you consult an index fund, which tracks the S&P 500.

# 3

# MEDIA AND THE INVESTOR

Most investors make their decisions based on knowledge and guidance they obtain from others. This guidance can be received from a multitude of sources: a friend or a family member, a stockbroker, a financial newsletter, a message board, or the Internet, to name just a few. It makes most investors feel more comfortable when someone else who in their eyes is more knowledgeable informs them what stock to buy and when to buy it. A large number of investors are inexperienced and in need of sound advice. This need for someone else to guide us, to let us know what to do and when, is in most cases the manifest seed of the herd mentality planted deep inside us and instinctive to most people. But how reliable is this advice? Can we trust it blindly or should we get a second opinion?

Television is the most convincing medium of all. When we see a person who is articulate, seemingly educated, and with a long list of qualifications in the subject tell us what stocks he or she finds attractive and why, we very often are persuaded to follow the recommendations. Every day we listen to investors, who are usually professional money managers or analysts, pick several of their favorite stocks. But how do we really know if they practice what they preach? How confident are we that the stocks they "praise" or suggest we buy are not the ones they are desperate to sell?

In 1995 one of the fund managers at Fidelity Magellan had been pushing Micron Technology (MU) on his unsuspecting audience. MU stock had been in a relentless slide from its peak of $45 per share on a split-adjusted basis to approximately $25. The fund manager was "pounding on the table," as Wall Street likes to say, about MU shares being oversold and undervalued. He stressed that this decline in price presented a rare and wonderful opportunity for the investment community to get in and buy MU shares at unprecedented discount. However, rumors started circulating that this manager was actually unloading his stake in MU as quickly as he possibly could. In fact the stock went down to $9, and our so-called adviser had to resign soon after that disgrace. One of the reasons for this fund manager's forced resignation was the continued embarrassment caused to Fidelity by the fact that one of its most prominent money experts had deliberately deceived his listeners by leading them into a trap with the Micron stock. The other reason was his unfortunate decision to swap a huge portion of equity holdings for bonds just when most equities started a bull run, thus causing his fund to miss out on huge profits. (We will discuss market-timing models later, as well as why they do not perform consistently.) This fund manager never owned up to his deceitful and self-serving ways and was forced to look for another job.

Such lessons are not to be found solely in the major media. For people who get their stock picks from message boards on the Internet, we refer you to the story of Mr. Jonathan Lebed, a 15-year-old boy from New Jersey. This young man was trading stocks from his computer at home. As the story unfolded, it was revealed that the SEC determined that on 11 occasions between August 23, 1999, and February 4, 2000, Lebed acquired a considerable number of shares in thinly traded microcap stocks through his brokerage account. Within hours of making a purchase, Lebed sent off thousands of fabricated and deceptive messages hyping the stock he had just bought. In addition to spam, the teen also placed messages on numerous Yahoo! finance message boards.

Lebed's messages and postings were made by means of invented names. His announcements included groundless price predictions and other fabricated and deceitful statements. For example, one of his messages stated that a company trading at $2 per share would be trading at more than $20 per share "very soon." He endorsed one stock as the "most undervalued stock ever" and expected another to become the "next stock to gain 1000 percent." The SEC classified the case as a "large pump and dump scheme."

These stories are by no means rare occurrences. Like everything else in the media, the reason we know about these stories is because they were sensational. Throughout this book, we will come across numerous advisers whose suggestions should be dismissed and on occasion whose suggestions actually dictate when the opposite action should be taken.

With the advent of the Internet, the number of sources giving investment advice either free or for a fee has mushroomed to unprecedented levels. Viewing television, you have CNBC, CNNfn, Bloomberg, and other 24-hour, 7-days-a-week business news and financial analysis. There are publications such as *Money, Smart Money, Worth, Forbes, Fortune,* and many more. All major newspapers have a business section that has grown throughout the years. A friend pointed out that even fashion magazines offer "smart money management" sections. Most business publications and media houses adhere to a simple rule of economics. There is a huge demand for advice, and they will supply this advice and give their customers what they want.

Having said that, we need to remember one simple fact: Most of the advice out there comes with baggage and different agendas on every table. There is an interesting comment about CNBC's Maria Bartiromo in *Fortune Tellers,* a book by Howard Kurtz: "Bartiromo didn't worry about whether the analysts issuing their upgrades and downgrades were right about the companies involved; that was beyond her purview." The book goes on to say, "She delivers the calls of the major firms she really cares about, Goldman Sachs, Morgan Stanley, Merrill Lynch, and Donaldson Lufkin & Jenrette. These are the impact calls, the companies with thousands of brokers, the ones most likely to move stock prices." To the contrary, the data show that many of these so-called "impact calls" delivered by big firms do not commonly produce market-beating results. The claim "most likely to move stock prices" is wrong again, both in the short run and especially in the long run. Most of these stocks can be bought the following day or the day after without a statistically significant price differential. There are many small firms with very few brokers or no brokers at all whose recommendations tend to outperform the recommendations issued by the big firms that media love to cite. Many financial journalists unfortunately do not compile, study, or present the data in any form from which an investor can benefit. On the contrary, the more you watch programs that deal with excitement and sensationalism, the more likely your investment losses will increase.

Investors need to realize that success can be achieved only if an investment strategy and discipline are followed. They need to evaluate transactions carefully, study the performance of a targeted overall strategy, detailed tactics, stock, company, and so on over a period of time, and then make their decision objectively, without emotional involvement. Just like in any branch of science (even though it's debatable whether money management is a science), you need to amass evidence, then form a hypothesis, and then test it against a result. It is called "making an educated guess." And even if following this formula, or any other, there are no guarantees. However, if investors succeed in being patient, objective, and methodical in their approach, then they have planted a seed that is guaranteed to grow and reap great rewards for years to come.

If your stock investment excursions so far have been filled with emotional judgment calls and failure, you need to make the first and, in many cases, the hardest adjustment. You need to acknowledge that you need to change your investment strategy.

## Top-Rated Stocks

No discussion on stock tips would be complete without addressing the upgrades and downgrades issued daily by financial institutions. The convoluted rating system that financial institutions use to evaluate stocks can be confusing and frustrating, but it does not have to be that way. One point all investors must remember is that not all recommendations are created equal. The root of the problem for this disparity lies either in the conflicting interests or poor stock-picking ability of the so-called professionals.

## The Rating System in Abstract

Most financial institutions that make stock recommendations to their clients and the public have research departments that employ two types of *market professionals*. The first group that most individual investors come into contact with are often called stockbrokers or certified financial consultants. Their job is to help build a sound investment strategy such as a 401(k) plan for retirement needs, estate planning, saving for a child's education, and building a diversified portfolio. Simply put, they are the qualified experts whose job is to help us see our money grow. When they make stock recommendations, they usually tap into their counterparts' research for information.

These counterparts are a group of employees called security analysts, or financial analysts. They investigate public companies, analyze their business models, and make projections on the future. Many of them develop cozy relationships with the management of a company being researched. They customarily have access to the top brass of the firm such as the CEO and CFO. The function of a security analyst, who tends to practice fundamental analysis as opposed to technical analysis, is to prepare a detailed report on the basis of an assessment of the company's financial health. This involves an analysis of the income statement, balance sheet, and cash flow statements. These research professionals are often required to meet with clients and vendors of the firm, as well as with their competitors, to paint an accurate picture of the stability the firm represents in terms of investment. The analyst must also be aware of any governmental legislation and regulations that may have an adverse effect on the company's business development and prevent it from moving forward. The opposite could also be true: The government may issue new regulations that would directly or indirectly end up helping the company's future earnings growth.

The analysts must also determine what they perceive to be the "intrinsic value" a particular company represents. If the current market cap is below that intrinsic value, a Buy or Strong Buy recommendation is issued. On the other hand, if the current market cap is above this intrinsic value, the outcome is a Neutral or Hold recommendation. In some rare instances, when the security analyst believes there are major problems facing the company, the consequence is a Sell or Underperform recommendation. During the exuberant 1990s, less than 1 percent of analyst recommendations were a Sell. By February 2002, during a bear market, Sell recommendations represented slightly more than 2 percent. This is an increase from the bull market times of the 1990s but not a dramatic change by any means.

The value of security analysts largely depends on their ability to discern this intrinsic value derived from their examination of the security at hand. They also must take into consideration current market conditions. This is not an easy task because there are so many variables, such a multitude of details, and so many people that it is beyond any human being's reach to consider them all. Market analysis is a very uncertain business, yet some excel at this challenge, whereas others inevitably fail. Let us examine this a little more closely.

The rating system that financial institutions have in place gives them a certain degree of flexibility. Why do so many utilize two types of Buy recommendations, distinguished by terms such as Strong Buy and Buy? This at first seems confusing because investors can only buy, hold, or sell stocks. We cannot call our broker and say, "Do me a favor and *strong buy* me 200 shares of IBM." How would this differ from "Do me a favor and buy me 200 shares of IBM?" To us, as investors who are purely transaction oriented, the difference relating to a Strong Buy and Buy is meaningless. Nevertheless, for an analyst there is a world of difference. And as you will shortly discover, you only have to learn how to read it. The security analyst has to walk a fine line in serving both the clients who are desperately in need of advice and the management of the company under analysis.

Recently, there were headlines on how management at some firms refused to talk with analysts who have made negative statements about their business decisions or their companies in general. No one likes to be criticized. Some disgruntled shareholders have gone so far as to threaten security analysts with physical violence, according to Andrew H. West in the article, "A Stern Opinion—Kill the Analysts."

In 1999 there was an article on Motley Fool's Web site (www.motleyfool.com) called "The Fribble," by T. Allen Grider. His assessment of recommendations by financial institutions is as follows:

Then I noticed that a lot of the analysts who issued these upgrades/downgrades mostly worked for brokerages that also market mutual funds. Putting all this together with what I learned in The Fool's School and The Truth About Mutual Funds, I think I can finally define these terms:

When an analyst says, "Strong Buy," he actually means, "Many of our funds have just acquired a large position in this stock and we need a large upswing to improve our quarterly returns."

When an analyst says, "Buy," he actually means, "Our funds have had this stock for a while and it's down a little. Bid it up so that we can improve our quarterly returns."

When an analyst says "Hold," he actually means, "We have very little of this stock in our funds, so we do not care what happens to it."

When an analyst says "Moderate Sell," he actually means, "We sold this stock from our funds yesterday. Please sell it down some more so we can buy it back cheap."

When an analyst says, "Strong Sell," he actually means, "We are uncovered shorting this stock. Please sell it down quickly so we can improve our quarterly returns."

This article gives a perfect example of how silly and ridiculous the media can be. This assessment of financial institutions' rating systems certainly does not educate the investor nor does it reveal the truth. Even academics acknowledge that recently upgraded stocks tend to perform better than stocks that were recently downgraded.

The question an independent investor should ask is, "Can I make money listening to financial analysts or not?" The answer to this question is both yes and no. Following recommendations is comparable to eating fish. People need to learn how to eat fish by picking out the flesh and leaving the bones on the plate. Similarly, investors need to learn how to read recommendations, how to extract data that are hidden between the lines, and how to use this information to their advantage by making their own picks and discarding the bones.

Here is another example of analysis gone astray. In the June 2001 issue of *Kiplinger* magazine, there is an interview with a prominent money manager. The *Kiplinger* editor—the interviewer—asks this financial expert a number of questions including one that piqued my interest: "Do you use Wall Street research at all?" The reply was, "I do. Some of the analysis is very good. But the recommendations should get chopped off and used as kindling." He then gives an example of a Piper Jaffray's Buy rating for Intel (INTC) and Dell Computer Corporation (DELL) in August and September 2000. Both of these stocks went south shortly thereafter. The money manager points out that had investors listened to recommendations alone—both stocks were rated Buy—they would have lost a substantial amount of money. However, this manager discerned negative statements from the body of the report made by the analysts at Piper Jaffray, which alerted him to avoid buying or holding Intel and Dell shares in his portfolio. Yet our money expert conveniently ignores the fact that on these reports Piper Jaffray downgraded both stocks from its Strong Buy rating to a Buy.

A downgrade for any equity issue should always alert the investor to the possibility of trouble for that stock. Any downgrade, as the word itself suggests, is a move down; it is a negative move. To illustrate, let us dissect a simple rating system (see Figure 3-1). The left side of the figure represents all upgrades, and the right side represents all downgrades.

We will compare two scenarios. First is Piper Jaffray's upgrades in the computer and technology sector. Stocks that have been

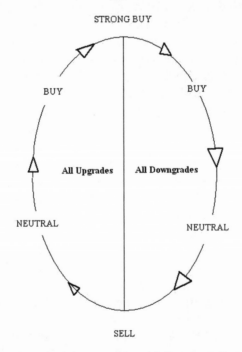

**Fig. 3-1.  Rating system for upgrades and downgrades.**

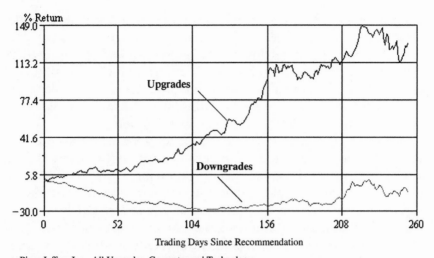

**Fig. 3-2. Piper Jaffray's upgrades and downgrades in the computer and technology sector.**

upgraded represent a change for the better. For instance, from Sell to Neutral, from Neutral to Buy, or from Buy to Strong Buy all represent an upgrade, or a positive revision. The second scenario is their downgrades in the same sector. Stocks that have been downgraded represent a change for the worse. For example, from Strong Buy to Buy, from Buy to Neutral, or from Neutral to Sell all represent a negative revision.

As you can see from Figure 3-2, when Piper Jaffray downgraded a stock in the technology sector, these stocks lost on average 25 percent of their value within a 6-month period. On the other hand, stocks that have been upgraded increased in value by 50 percent within the same time frame.

With this kind of information at your disposal, it becomes clear that when a stock is downgraded to a Buy (lowered from a Strong Buy), it really means *Sell.* A case in point was broached by the aforementioned money expert in the article we looked at earlier. Piper Jaffray downgraded Dell on August 2, 2000, when Dell's stock closed at $39.56. And even though by this date the stock declined substantially, a further plunge still lay ahead. A year and a half later, as recently as January 2002, Dell traded at around $26, which is an additional drop of 32 percent. Similarly, on September

5, 2000, Piper Jaffray downgraded Intel as well. On that day Intel closed at $69.25. In February 2002 Intel was down to $30, which is roughly a 60 percent decline in a little over a year. Both these cases confirm our theory. Even though Piper Jaffray recommended Dell and Intel as a Buy, the fact remains that both these companies were *downgraded* from a Strong Buy rating, a detail that should have alerted the investor to consider a Sell transaction.

Investors should not use recommendations as firewood; this would be too expensive. However, it is important to learn to read between the lines. Investors need to remember that security analysts are constantly walking that fine line, sandwiched between the companies they cover, their clients, and, last but not least, their investment banking–division bosses who are breathing down their necks and pursuing their own agendas. We will address this topic in Chapter 4.

After reading the article in *Kiplinger,* I decided to do some research on the star of the article himself. How did his recommendations pan out? Let's take a closer look at what this research revealed.

Our money manager runs a few very successful mutual funds within the Kemper family of funds and is known to favor value stocks that appear to be out of favor. A value stock often has a price-earnings (P/E) ratio lower than the S&P 500 and thus is more often than not less volatile and risky. During the bull market of 1999, value stocks were out of fashion, and his funds did not perform well, losing more than 13 percent of their value. However, in March 2000, when markets started to decline, his funds rose more than 41 percent in value per share, easily beating the S&P 500 Index. Even after the 5.75 percent front-end load (an amount the fund charges investors), his funds were still outperforming the S&P 500 Index by one tenth of 1 percent over the past 5 years according to Morningstar.

In addition to running mutual funds, he often appears as a guest on CNBC and makes his views known, describing the current situation and how investors can take advantage of the existing climate to navigate financial markets. He is often asked what stocks he prefers and does not shy away from making stock recommendations. I was curious to see if he ever made negative comments about any stocks and, if he did, when? The answer was found on a

Web site called www.validea.com. This Web site tracks stock recommendations made by individuals who appear on television and/or in print. During April 2001, this fund manager identified eight stocks he considered to be undervalued and presented them as "pick-of-the-litter investments" (Figure 3-3). Their total average return 3 months later was a negative 2.95 percent.

On April 23, 2001, he recommended Intel (INTC). The closing price for INTC on that date was $30.32. By July 19, 2001, the date these results were tabulated, the stock price fell to $29.93, representing a 1.29 percent loss. And so it continued. Only two of the eight stocks endorsed with a positive recommendation in April were up in price. The other six were down.

During the same month, this money manager made pessimistic comments on five stocks as well. April 2001 was used as the month for comparing his stock selection because I wanted to aggregate both positive and negative stock recommendations. The performance of his negative selections appears in Figure 3-4. Of these five stocks, two were down by July 19 once again, but three were up and their total average return was 5.18 percent.

These examples are not intended as an attack on this fund manager or on anyone in particular. Three months is not enough time to determine a good indication of strategic vision and stock-picking ability. Rather, it is only an observation. Mutual fund and other professional money managers who speak of stock recommendations as an unnecessary part of research could be saying this only to protect their interests. After all, the more informed and successful an investor becomes, the less he or she requires the services

| Symbol | Company Name | Comment | Date | Price | Price on 7/19/01 | % Return |
|--------|--------------|---------|------|-------|---------|----------|
| INTC | Intel Corp | Positive | 4/23/2001 | $30.32 | $ 29.93 | (1.29) |
| AAPL | Apple Computer | Positive | 4/23/2001 | $24.25 | $ 19.98 | (17.61) |
| HWP | Hewlett-Packard Co | Positive | 4/23/2001 | $30.96 | $ 26.42 | (14.66) |
| CHV | Chevron Corp | Positive | 4/23/2001 | $94.06 | $ 88.95 | (5.43) |
| FRE | Freddie Mac | Positive | 4/23/2001 | $62.61 | $ 67.56 | 7.91 |
| MO | Philip Morris | Positive | 4/23/2001 | $47.43 | $ 46.00 | (3.01) |
| COCB | Conoco Inc Cl B | Positive | 4/12/2001 | $28.45 | $ 27.85 | (2.11) |
| FNM | Fannie Mae | Positive | 4/12/2001 | $74.17 | $ 83.50 | 12.58 |

**Fig. 3-3. Return on money manager's "pick-of-the-litter investments."**

| Symbol | Company Name | Comment | Date | Price | Price on 7/19/01 | % Return |
|--------|--------------|---------|------|-------|------------------|----------|
| ET | E Trade Group Inc | Negative | 4/12/2001 | $ 8.77 | $ 6.75 | (23.03) |
| Q | Qwest Comm Intl | Negative | 4/12/2001 | $35.70 | $ 28.23 | (20.92) |
| AMZN | Amazon.Com Inc | Negative | 4/12/2001 | $14.67 | $ 16.49 | 12.41 |
| YHOO | Yahoo Inc | Negative | 4/12/2001 | $16.96 | $ 17.43 | 2.77 |
| EBAY | eBay Inc | Negative | 4/12/2001 | $41.63 | $ 64.40 | 54.70 |

**Fig. 3-4.   Return on money manager's downgrades.**

of a money manager. And without money to manage because investors are taking responsibility for their own stock selection, professional money managers may soon find themselves professionally unemployed.

Let us continue analyzing the performance of Piper Jaffray recommendations, which are good for kindling, according to our fund manager. In April 2001, the same month as he made his recommendations, Piper Jaffray had revised its ratings on a certain number of stocks, and by July 19, or approximately 3 months later, we see the results shown in Figure 3-5.

Of the 10 stocks that were upgraded in April 2001, only American Express (AXP) and Electronics for Imaging, Inc. (EFII) showed a price decline 3 months after the date the upgrade was issued. Eight other stocks climbed higher, and their total average return was 29.31 percent within this time period, beating our fund manager's picks by 32 percent.

Figure 3-6 lists all stocks whose outlook according to Piper Jaffray analysts had turned negative during April 2001, which caused the brokerage house to downgrade them.

Of 25 stocks that were downgraded by Piper Jaffray in April, only 7 went up in price within the following 3 months. Eighteen other stocks fell, just as predicted, and their total average return was a negative 10.12 percent within 3 months. This is not a bad performance for something our fund manager dismissed as useless, and frankly, it's better than his own track record during the same time period.

This example should not leave investors with a notion that buying a stock after an upgrade guarantees them a profit. Other factors should be taken into consideration, and further analysis should be carried out. On numerous occasions we noticed that some financial

| Piper Jaffray Upgrades | During April 2001 | 7/19/0 | Return | |
|---|---|---|---|---|
| DLTR Dollar Tree Store | 4/25/2001 | $21.36 | $33.20 | 55.43% |
| THQI THQ Inc | 4/25/2001 | $37.00 | $54.92 | 48.43% |
| AXP American Express | 4/24/2001 | $40.75 | $38.00 | -6.75% |
| DRRADura Automotive | 4/24/2001 | $12.16 | $17.60 | 44.74% |
| GWWW.W. Grainger In | 4/24/2001 | $37.50 | $42.18 | 12.48% |
| TWR Tower Automotive | 4/20/2001 | $9.67 | $13.30 | 37.54% |
| HNCSHNC Software In | 4/19/2001 | $22.69 | $25.61 | 12.87% |
| EFII Electronics For Imag | 4/18/2001 | $26.68 | $22.89 | -14.21% |
| ANSI Advanced Neuro | 4/5/2001 | $14.75 | $23.31 | 58.03% |
| IDPH Idec Pharmaceutics | 4/3/2001 | $35.69 | $51.60 | 44.58% |

**Fig. 3-5.  Return on Piper Jaffray upgrades from April 2001 to July 19, 2001.**

institutions have a poor track record with their upgrades and downgrades. To cite an instance, look at the two figures that follow. Figure 3-7 compares Prudential Securities' upgrades and downgrades. As you can see, the general trend for stocks that Prudential upgrades has an upward momentum, and within 6 months after the upgrade, returns are at a positive 4 percent. On the other hand, the general trend for stocks that have been downgraded by Prudential Securities has shown a downward movement and an average loss of 8 percent of their original value. In terms of percentages, these results are not as dramatic as Piper Jaffray's, but they certainly illustrate that a downgrade continues a downward trend, and an upgrade continues an upward trend. There is some value to be derived from Prudential's ability to discern the intrinsic value of stocks they follow. The upgrades still tend to bring in a profit, whereas the downgrades bring on a loss.

However, when we start to dig into individual sectors, we find a disturbing picture in their basic materials sector (Figure 3-8). Here Prudential Securities performs rather poorly. As you can see, the downgrades outperform the upgrades. Within 6 months after receiving an upgrade, upgraded stocks averaged a 5 percent drop, whereas downgraded stocks averaged a 9 percent increase. In this particular instance, it perhaps would be prudent to disregard

| Piper Jaffray Downgrades in April 2001 | | 7/19/2001 | Return |
|---|---|---|---|
| NUFO New Focus Incorporated | 4/26/2001 14.31 | 6.27 | -56.18% |
| PSFT PeopleSoft Inc | 4/26/2001 36.62 | 35.81 | -2.21% |
| SLTC Selectica Incorporated | 4/25/2001 3.99 | 3.34 | -16.29% |
| ARBA Ariba Inc | 4/23/2001 6.91 | 4.37 | -36.76% |
| EMLX Emulex Corp | 4/23/2001 28 | 23.3 | -16.79% |
| EXDS Exodus Communications | 4/23/2001 9.87 | 1.2 | -87.84% |
| ECL Ecolab Inc | 4/20/2001 40.13 | 39.54 | -1.47% |
| AUDC AudioCodes Ltd | 4/19/2001 9.17 | 6.88 | -24.97% |
| ITWO I2 Technologies Inc | 4/19/2001 19.95 | 11.55 | -42.11% |
| LVLT Level 3 Communict | 4/19/2001 14.43 | 4.01 | -72.21% |
| DGLH Digital Lighthouse Corp | 4/17/2001 0.43 | 0.01 | -97.67% |
| RAS RAIT Investment Trust | 4/17/2001 14.02 | 16.35 | 16.62% |
| EAGL EGL Incorporated | 4/12/2001 20.3 | 14.7 | -27.59% |
| FAST Fastenal Co | 4/12/2001 55.13 | 64.55 | 17.09% |
| RIMM Research In Motion Ltd | 4/12/2001 28.27 | 27.55 | -2.55% |
| AETH Aether Systems Incorporated | 4/11/2001 13.72 | 9.22 | -32.80% |
| APRS Apropos Technology | 4/11/2001 2.98 | 2.8 | -6.04% |
| ARDI At Road Inc | 4/11/2001 1.7 | 1.9 | 11.76% |
| GOAM GoAmerica Incorporated | 4/11/2001 2.11 | 1.68 | -20.38% |
| SAWS Sawtek Inc | 4/10/2001 16.04 | 24.86 | 54.99% |
| TMPW TMP Worldwide Inc | 4/9/2001 36.93 | 51.65 | 39.86% |
| RVSN RADVision Ltd | 4/6/2001 6.19 | 5.43 | -12.28% |
| ACXM Acxiom Corp | 4/4/2001 12.75 | 10.87 | -14.75% |
| MTWV Metawave Communications Corp | 4/4/2001 2.5 | 3.75 | 50.00% |
| ZOLL Zoll Medical | 4/4/2001 17.94 | 30.76 | 71.46% |

**Fig. 3-6.    Return on Piper Jaffray downgrades from April 2001 to July 19, 2001.**

Prudential's research and use their recommendations in the basic materials sector as kindling, as our fund manager likes to call it.

Knowing what we do now, we can draw a few conclusions. The most important is that we must differentiate among our sources of investment advice. Although two different brokerage houses (bulletin boards, magazines, financial networks) may issue the same sounding Buy recommendation, we should protect ourselves by doing a little research of our own and investigate that broker's

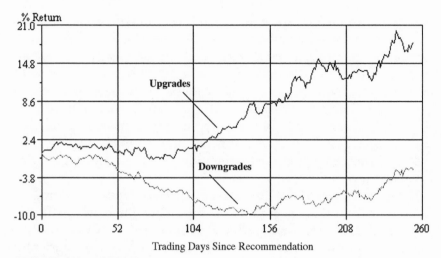

– Prudial Securities, All Upgrades
– Prudial Securities, All Downgrades

**Fig. 3-7.   Prudential Securities' upgrades and downgrades.**

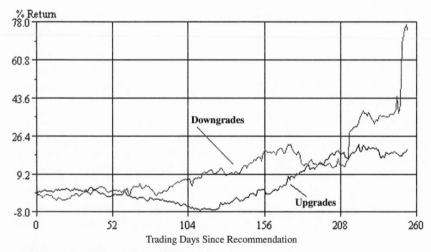

– Prudial Securities, All Upgrades, Basic Materials
– Prudial Securities, All Downgrades, Basic Materials

**Fig. 3-8.   Prudential Securities' upgrades and downgrades in the basic materials sector.**

performance history. After all, not all recommendations are created equal because not all analysts are created equal; therefore, it would not be prudent to treat them all as equal. Only after we are certain of the integrity and objectives of the research department, after its competence and qualifications have been thoroughly investigated and established, and after the financials have been thoroughly examined should any investor consider making a transaction based on a recommendation. We should only take advice from professional experts with a solid and thoroughly researched reputation.

This is a very powerful concept indeed. The first thing an investor should do is identify a reputable financial institution whose advice in the past produced positive results. Once this hurdle has been overcome, the investor should learn how to identify characteristics shared by stocks that go up in price and those of stocks that do not. This will be a true work in progress. With time you will gain tremendous knowledge and experience that will result in success, which in turn will provide you with something even more important: a belief in your ability to triumph as an investor. Many of these characteristics will be addressed in later chapters.

On the other hand, if you buy stocks just because someone else tells you to do so, you will most likely experience many failures and disappointments. It is strongly recommended that investors take the time to study the financial statements of companies they would like to purchase. In the long run, the stock of companies with earnings growth will appreciate in price.

# 4

# WHO ARE THE ANALYSTS?

Research departments on Wall Street hire and maintain a group of people called security or financial analysts. These individuals follow and analyze a group of companies in a particular industry or sector. Some analysts follow the banking industry, others specialize in the semiconductor industry, and so on. The specialization within an industry familiarizes the analysts with products and services this industry delivers. It also allows analysts to speak the same language as employees in the companies they cover. They get to know the major players and their personalities. This process allows analysts to mirror the insiders, even though they work for a different industry in most cases.

Day after day analysts initiate or adjust ratings on particular stocks. Rating or recommending stocks is an essential component of the brokerage business. Wall Street analysts claim to have the wisdom and means to predict when stocks are undervalued and conversely when they are overvalued. Let's look at what the analysts do and what they produce.

## The Analyst Report

A typical analyst report will include the following items:

1. A comprehensive depiction of the company along with its industry group.
2. An accurate story of a company, as the analyst understands it, and not the story the companies necessarily want to tell.
3. A performance prediction for the stock within a relatively short time frame of usually 1 year.
4. Recommendations to buy, sell, or hold the stock.

The majority of analysts put an ample amount of effort into these reports, frequently traveling to the company's headquarters, meeting its senior management, and receiving a personal tour of the business. After collecting and processing the data, the analysts will typically disseminate their conclusions to their institutional clients. Usually, this distribution appears in a report, which will normally include buy, hold, and sell recommendations and other pertinent information such as earnings forecasts and target price.

### Conflict of Interest 1

Every company tries to work to develop strong relationships with analysts to ensure they understand the business, the products, and the industry. A company's management is always anxious to make certain that the analysts and the financial markets value their shares appropriately. To do that, every company must demonstrate to the analyst the ability to execute its business plan and meet or beat internal projections. Furthermore, the company must realistically state when it will turn cash flow positive. Nonfinancial metrics are just as important as financial ones in demonstrating to the security analyst that the vigor and knowledge of the company's management team is one of the key essentials and, therefore, that the company's stock is worthy of the analyst's Buy recommendation.

The analyst, on the other hand, assumes that insiders, or the managers of the company they cover, are better informed than outsiders. These assumptions suggest that the analyst values this relationship as extremely important. Therefore, this association cuts both ways. Just like management values its relationship with prominent analysts, so does the analyst value his or her relationship with company's management. During this process, management and analysts often build formal and informal long-term business relationships.

And so, the first conflict of interest is set. What begins as an objective review of a company can turn into something more—a relationship between an analyst and key members of management or other insiders within the firm.

### Conflict of Interest 2

On January 10, 1993, an article in *The Wall Street Journal* stated:

> a funny thing usually happens about a month after a hot new stock offering (IPO). Almost like clockwork, a prominent Wall Street brokerage firm will issue a "buy" recommendation. In response, an already highflying stock frequently rises even more during the following days or weeks. Traders have a name for this. It's the postoffering "booster shot." What many investors do not realize is that these postoffering buy recommendations are coming from the underwriters—the very Wall Street firms that sold the stock to the public in the first place.

Underwriters recommending the stocks they helped bring to the market raise the question of conflict of interest. One example of this conflict is the initial public offering of Alteon, Inc. (ALT). According to *The Wall Street Journal*, the biotechnology company became public in 1991. Stock was presented to the market at $15 per share and performed rather well. Alex Brown & Sons was the lead underwriter and, shortly after trading began, issued a Buy recommendation at $24 per share. Within 2 years after the initial public offering, Alteon stock was trading at $10. This case illustrates the typical existence of a conflict of interest between the functions of the security analyst and their coworkers, the investment bankers, across the hall.

The conflict of interest between analysts and investment bankers has the following consequences. Financial analysts are expected and frequently appear to be the sales force for the investment banking department. This is in direct conflict with analysts' roles as objective industry outsiders examining the financial health and profitability a company demonstrates.

The title *investment banker* is given to an organization that is engaged in the process of bringing a private company into public markets. This process is usually called underwriting and consists of selling a certain percentage of shares of the private company to the public. Investment bankers work closely with the client (usually a private company) and its own internal legal and compliance professionals. They draft a prospectus, or official document, linking a description of the offering and generating a detailed financial examination. The underwriters clear internal hurdles of legal, regulatory, and risk-management compliance groups. But they also need to obtain the endorsement of the firm's senior management to gain their approval for the underwriting. The other internal groups that get involved in the process are institutional sales, trading, research, and retail sales. After all in-house groups have been briefed, the investment banker prepares registration with appropriate governmental and regulatory entities such as Securities and Exchange Commission, prints the prospectus, and makes the offering to the public. More often than not, a majority of the shares go to institutional clients. When demand for that particular offering is smaller than supply, the balance is sold through the investment banker's retail sales force to individual investors.

Typically, within a short period after this process is complete, the financial institution(s) involved in underwriting the security asks its research department to issue a Buy recommendation to create greater demand for the security in the public markets.

Hardly anyone has overlooked the debacle with Henry Blodget of Merrill Lynch and Mary Meeker of Morgan Stanley. There has been much written about these two analysts. During the bull market of the 1990s, they virtually became celebrities overnight. Blodget's rise to fame rested on his prediction in 1998 that Amazon (AMZN) would be worth $400 per share in 3 years. In fact it got there in 3 weeks. Mary Meeker was made famous with her new valuation models, which argued that it was the number of page views generated by the Web site—any Web site—and not cash flows that was the number one priority for a typical Internet company. A good analogy to this concept may perhaps be along these lines: Being popular is more important than breathing air. But how long does that last? Meeker's nickname became "Queen of the Net."

Blodget and Meeker made many headlines. But their rise to the top was just as phenomenal as their downfall. In one appearance after another, they pushed the Internet companies their employers underwrote to the public. The result of this biased research was detrimental to the investment community and, in the long run, to investment banks as well.

This conflict of interest between investment banking and research departments at financial institutions gained prominence during the stock market decline of 2000. Many well-known analysts remained extremely optimistic and bullish, particularly on technology stocks that were sinking faster than the *Titanic*. How could this phenomenon be explained? Either the analysts were totally brainless or someone was twisting their arm. It seems that the latter was the case. Merrill Lynch acknowledged that analysts' compensation comes from a pool that includes investment banking profit. On top of that mess, many analysts were also shareholders of the companies they rated Strong Buy or Buy. Not surprisingly, all of this feeding frenzy has been at someone else's expense—usually the individual investor—and it has eventually led to a backlash.

One reaction to this conflict of interest came in the form of a New York doctor who claimed he lost $600,000 he invested for his children's education after following Blodget's stock recommendations. He sued Merrill Lynch and Henry Blodget, alleging that the high-profile analyst recommended stocks in which the investment bank had a financial interest. Dr. Debasis Kanjalil purchased shares in Infospace (INSP) on the recommendation of his Merrill Lynch stockbroker, who in turn had relied on Mr. Blodget's recommendation. His lawyers claimed that Mr. Blodget did not disclose a conflict of interest, namely, that Merrill Lynch represented a company that was being acquired by Infospace. The issue at stake was whether security analysts at investment banks were recommending shares for unethical or immoral reasons. For this reason and his monetary loss, Dr. Kanjalil requested $10 million in damages.

However, Merrill Lynch quickly requested that the case be dismissed and claimed, "Dr. Kanjalil is a sophisticated, experienced investor who sought high-risk investments and made his own decisions."

It is hard to agree with Merrill's assertion that Dr. Kanjalil was a sophisticated, experienced investor. Nothing could be further from the truth. When people invest most of their money in one stock, they obviously have no experience or understanding of the stock market. The stockbroker who sold Infospace shares to his client should have warned him about the dangers of putting all his eggs in one basket, because one of the keys to successful investing is diversification.

As these pages were written, Merrill Lynch decided to settle with Dr. Kanjalil for $400,000. After all was said and done, the biggest winners here as usual were the attorneys. Dr. Kanjalil did not recover all of his losses, and Merrill Lynch embarrassed itself, may I add, for not the first time.

Wall Street's main purpose in life is to raise capital. The practice of upgrading recent hatchlings is one way financial institutions try to boost the prices of the new issues. Another custom consistently practiced on Wall Street is to have a prominent analyst upgrade the stock of an existing company to get new or additional investment banking business such as secondary offerings, fixed-income products, spinoffs, and the like.

Perhaps you are familiar with the story of how Salomon Smith Barney's star telecom analyst, Jack B. Grubman, upgraded AT&T (T) to a Buy rating on November 29, 1999. AT&T stock closed at $60.13 that day. Three months later Salomon Smith Barney obtained a lucrative underwriting job from AT&T to take its wireless unit public. In early October of the following year, after AT&T stock lost over 50 percent of its value, Grubman at last had no alternative and downgraded the stock to Smith Barney's less enthusiastic Outperform rating. Within 1 month Grubman downgraded AT&T again, this time to Smith Barney's Neutral rating. These are the games business partners play.

Although stories like this receive exposure in the press, one must keep in mind the simple fact that Wall Street's main purpose is to raise capital. This is especially true with new and fast moving industries. During their early existence, many companies yearn for capital and other resources to assemble their ideas, develop sales and marketing teams to promote their services, and put their intended business models into practice. Unfortunately, many of these start-ups fail. We often see a similar process in nature. For example, a sea turtle produces many eggs after the mating season; however, most young sea turtles will perish as hatchlings and never reach adulthood. The same holds true for newly created companies that go public, especially with new industries. Many will fail miserably and leave their investors, who anticipated making a quick dollar, in the dust. Those that do their utmost to survive will grow and eventually enrich their shareholders immensely. This is economic Darwinism.

In 1999 associate finance professors at Cornell University, Kevin Womack and Roni Michaely, produced a paper called "Conflict of Interest and the Credibility of Underwriter Analyst Recommendations." They noted that analysts who help draw underwriting to their firms might be given "bonuses that are two to four times those of analysts without underwriting contributions." Thus, the second conflict of interest is set: In many cases, analysts are rewarded for participating in this dangerous game.

Womack and Michaely deciphered 391 initial public offerings from 1990 and 1991 and, not surprisingly, found that analysts had a tendency to be more optimistic about the prospects for stocks underwritten by their company than about stocks underwritten by competitors.

During the first month in which underwriters are officially permitted to remark on their new IPO issues, analysts for underwriters made 50 percent more Buy recommendations on their IPO stocks than did other analysts. Typically, stocks recommended by underwriter analysts had decreased in price ahead of the recommendations, suggesting that some recommendations were booster shots to push stock prices up. By contrast the standard stock recommended by nonunderwriting analysts was already going up in the month before the Buy recommendations were made, suggesting these analysts were making more impartial assessments.

Were the underwriting analysts' optimistic observations due to their superior knowledge gleaned from unique access as lead underwriters? Evidently, they were not. According to this study, in the 2 years after the IPOs, stocks pushed by underwriting analysts returned 15.5 percentage points fewer than those recommended by nonunderwriters. Were the underwriting analysts just poor performers? The answer is no. Analysts who made weak recommendations on stocks their firms underwrote had superior records when analyzing other stocks. The researchers concluded that poor recommendations by underwriting analysts were consequently rooted in biased opinion and not lack of skill.

Analysts cannot repeatedly give poor counsel without damaging the reputation that makes them valuable to the firm. They should be expected to do their finest work when there are no major conflicts.

A recent study by Brad Barber of the graduate school of management at the University of California, Davis, looked at 360,000 analyst recommendations from 269 brokerage houses between 1986 and 1996. He concluded that stocks getting strong positive recommendations beat the average stock by a healthy 4.13 percentage points a year, indicating that analysts are indeed capable of identifying good stocks.

Regrettably, the study found the average investor could not match these results, which would require ownership of large quantities of stock and would have individual investors buying or selling when the latest recommendations were issued. The consequence would be a yearly portfolio turnover of 400 percent, causing colossal transaction costs, such as taxes and commissions. The extra gains would be shattered.

Although stock predictions can be flawed, many researchers think investors should examine reports by analysts who have first-class track records. The book will address this issue in the chapters that follow, describing how an investor can identify which recommendations and analysts perform well and which do not. That, however, will still not be enough to generate market-beating results. Further fine-tuning will be necessary. The system that will be laid out will make this job much easier. For example, we already described our fundamental rules in Chapter 2 such as staying clear of IPOs. If you follow this fundamental rule as one of your guiding principles, you will undoubtedly avoid many pitfalls along the way, thereby improving your overall investment results.

As seen from previous examples, conflicts of interests on Wall Street are not a product of the dot com craze that rained supreme during the late 1990s. Articles from *The Wall Street Journal* on the subject date back to the early 1990s. They clearly illustrate instances of how Wall Street professionals have been abusing their power and continue to do so; after all, they are only human. Power invariably corrupts. It makes no difference who the abusers are; they could be analysts, investment bankers, or whatever. Unfortunately, it seems that very few investors have cared to focus on these conflicts. When markets were performing well, they did not bother many people. Investors were making money, and during those wonderful years, they turned their backs on this puzzle. But when the dot coms crashed and the markets went south, investors started looking for reasons why analysts were able to tell them when to buy but could not tell them when to sell. Many people started revealing tales of shattered dreams. Their early retirement or children's education funds vanished with the collapse of the NASDAQ. Lawsuits against analysts and financial institutions became plentiful. And although many of these lawsuits were thrown out of court, the damage to the financial industry's image was enormous.

## Government Intervention

Time and again, when many people are being hurt, the government steps in and congressional hearings begin. This time was not different. The Securities and Exchange Commission, whose mission is to protect investors and maintain the integrity of the securities markets, was the first on the scene. After analyzing the issues, it came up with a protective contraption called Regulation Fair Disclosure.

## Regulation Fair Disclosure: Why Is the SEC Troubled with Selective Disclosure to Analysts?

The Securities and Exchange Commission recognized that analysts and management at companies they cover have a very cozy relationship. Ideas started to appear on how to deal with this thorny issue. As part of this information campaign, SEC Chairman Arthur Levitt focused his efforts on the topic of selective disclosure. Selective disclosure occurs when a public company provides private, behind-closed-doors significant information with reference to the corporate business to chosen individuals, such as securities analysts and/or institutional investors, prior to revealing that information to the general marketplace. In many cases this is considered to be material nonpublic information. These means of communication are assumed to take place in discussions among company representatives, analysts, or institutional investors in advance of making this information freely available by the company to the public or in certain cases without the company ever publicly announcing the information at all.

It became clear to the SEC that selective disclosure was chipping away at the integrity of the markets. The SEC said in its findings that selective disclosure to analysts and institutional investors is no different from insider trading. It is wrong, the SEC concluded, when a minority of privileged individuals profit from their greater entree to corporate insiders rather than from their ability, good judgment, or diligence. Selective disclosure produces conflicts of interest for securities analysts who have an incentive to steer clear of making negative statements with reference to a company out of fear of losing access to selectively disclosed information. Once the Securities and Exchange Commission recognized that individual investors did not have the same access to vital and time-sensitive information as the analysts, a proposal to change the landscape was initiated. This proposal stipulated that all investors, big and small, should have access to vital information at the same time. This "dysfunctional relationship" between analysts and the companies they deal with must end, noted Mr. Levitt.

There is the continuing question of precisely how much independent analysis the typical analyst actually performs, with some people describing them as glorified stenographers who restate conference calls and disclosure statements.

The extensive use of code words permits analysts to pass on information without ever visiting the negative aspects of the companies they cover. In many cases Strong Buy means Buy, Buy means Hold, and Hold means Sell. This is the simple explanation of the code words, which are commonly referred to as the rating system. A number of people have complained, and rightly so, that you rarely hear the term *Sell*. More likely, an analyst would simply stop covering a stock, which is referred to as terminating coverage, rather than issue a Sell recommendation. During the exuberant 90s, fewer than 1 percent of analyst recommendations are Sell signals. Louis Thompson, Jr., president of the National Investor Relations Institute, has described the status quo as "sheer madness."

To combat this dreadful syndrome, the SEC enacted Regulation FD. This document states that information is material "if there is a considerable probability that a rational shareholder would deem it significant in making an investment decision." Furthermore, there must be a "considerable probability that the information would have been viewed by the rational investors as having significantly altered the 'overall blend' of information available." In addition the SEC points out that the subsequent information, which is commonly considered to be material information in the context of other SEC rules, could be considered material for purposes of Regulation FD. Here are some examples of what SEC deems "material information":

- Earnings information
- Mergers, acquisitions, tender offers, joint ventures, or changes in assets
- New products or discoveries or progress concerning customers or provisions, such as the loss or attainment of a new contract
- Changes in management or in control of the company
- Change in auditors or statement by the examiner that the company may not rely on the auditors' audit report
- Proceedings with reference to the company's securities such as stock splits, dividends, defaults on securities for redemption, stock or bond repurchase plans, changes to the privileges of securities holders, or public or private offerings of securities
- Bankruptcies

The most evident path for distributing this information to all investors will be open-access conference calls on the Internet. Thompson proposed that the SEC's anticipated rules would enhance the reputation of analysts and financial institutions by making open conference calls as companies use them to "immunize" against accusation of selective disclosure.

In addition, the public disclosure requirement of Regulation FD is satisfied by:

- Filing Form 8-K with the SEC when there is a change in control of the company or the company has changed its certifying accountant, a director resigned, and so on. In other words there are internal changes the company deems important.

- Other alternative resources realistically intended to give wide-ranging, nonexclusionary distribution of the information to the public. The SEC considers that satisfactory procedures consist of:
  - Issuance of a press release containing the information disseminated through commonly circulated news or wire services; or
  - Holding a press conference call by which interested members of the public have access, provided that the public is given sufficient notice of the conference or call and the means for accessing it. This notice could be made by Web site posting or press release.

In addition to individual investors, Regulation FD stipulates that companies should invite business journalists to join their analyst conference calls. Some have suggested that this created a state of affairs in which analysts and the press are in direct competition with one another. Media and financial analysts are stumbling over each other to be the first to announce timely and sensitive investment information. Presumably, if it is true that analysts pass along what they hear from management during the conference call, there is little difference between an analyst and a journalist. This could lead to the hypothesis that competition will arise between the analysts and the press. The press's source of revenue is surely not endangered by this situation. However, the same could not be said for analysts. Will Regulation FD make the stock analyst the ultimate casualty of this campaign? It may, especially for those analysts who continue to perform the following functions:

1. Downgrade stocks following management's caution concerning upcoming sales, profit, and so forth.
2. Upgrade stocks following management's good news about upcoming sales, profit, and so forth.
3. Adjust their recommendation from Strong Buy to Hold once a stock has decreased on average 70 percent.
4. Change their recommendation from Hold to Strong Buy after a stock has already risen 60 percent and has been at or near its 52-week high for about 3 months.

Unfortunately, while Regulation FD has addressed issues concerning the first conflict of interest, it did not do anything to tackle the issues surrounding the second conflict of interest. The analysts' issue has become such a hot topic that even the U.S. Congress and state prosecutors started examining it. On May 17, 2001, a congressional subcommittee opened hearings on how analysts carry out their business practices.

The Securities Industry Association brings together the shared interests of nearly 700 securities firms (including investment banks, broker-dealers, and mutual fund companies) and pledges to earn, inspire, and maintain the public's trust and confidence in the securities industry and the U.S. capital markets. On June 12, 2001, the association implemented "best practices" procedures designed to increase the independence of analysts and rid the conflict of interest from investment banking pressures.

The National Association of Securities Dealers (NASD) is a self-regulatory association of the securities industry accountable for the regulation of the NASDAQ Stock Market as well as the immense over-the-counter securities market and the many products traded in it. On July 2, 2001, the association proposed rules mandating that analysts and financial institutions disclose ownership or investment banking relationships with companies under research coverage. This served to help further limit any conflict of interest between analysts, investment bankers, and the companies with which they do business.

By July 10, 2001, Merrill Lynch adopted the NASD-proposed rule prohibiting its analysts from buying shares in companies they cover. But could this implementation be sidestepped? For example, if analyst X covers energy stocks and analyst Y covers semiconductors stocks, what is to prevent them from making a deal? Analyst X buys semiconductors stocks and Y rates them as a Buy while analyst Y buys energy stocks and X rates them as a Buy. No rules are broken, and yet nothing has changed. The status quo is maintained through friendship and networking. It may be unlikely that situations like that will happen, but the fact remains that if there is a will to beat a system, there is a way.

In another attempt to limit conflicts of interest, some institutional investors believe that analysts should be required to own stocks they cover and should be required to buy and sell them in accordance with their recommendations on the stock. Peter Siris, a columnist and a hedge fund manager, wrote an article in *Wall Street Letter* arguing: "Instead of restricting analysts, brokers should force them to invest their bonuses in stocks they follow. Their ratings would have to be the same as their most recent actions. They could only have buys on stocks they were buying and would be forced to have sells on stocks they were selling." Obviously, this type of regulation in which the analysts' own wealth is at stake would force them to be more prudent with their research. This is equivalent to the "put your money where your mouth is" concept. Surely, this would work much better than the policy Merrill instituted. The restrictions that Merrill has implemented very likely will not in any way reduce the inherent conflict of interest. Then again, perhaps it is not in Merrill's interest to change anything. Siris makes a case that analysts should be treated like corporate insiders and be required to file registration statements whenever buying and selling the companies they cover. This is an interesting idea. They also have to make sure that their employer and/or the company does not lend them money to carry out such a transaction.

In the end we must hold financial institutions and analysts accountable. This can be accomplished not so much by establishing procedures, though they surely can't hurt, but by educating investors and analyzing the credibility and performance of their past recommendations. Similar to what Morningstar is doing for the fund industry, perhaps a company like MarketPerform.com or Investars.com can answer this type of calling. Only performance monitoring of each financial institution individually can change the recommendations' returns. Only when they understand that their performance is closely followed, compared to competitors, and then widely distributed will analysts and especially their employers become more accountable and more interested in recommending stocks that truly represent value. Otherwise nothing will change. As soon as markets recover, greed will outperform fear, and the trap will be set again.

## "Their" Side of the Story

Throughout the process of creating this book, repeated efforts were made to invite analysts and research directors to participate and discuss the pressures they face in the workplace. Although most of them were willing to speak "off the record," many felt uncomfortable to participate in this project openly. Some approached their supervisors for permission but were requested not to participate because of the negative atmosphere. Others referred to their legal departments, who advised them not to discuss these matters. Nevertheless, many felt compelled to answer my questions anonymously.

Our goal was to search for an honest response from the analytical community. The questions were asked in a manner similar to that of an interview. Each analyst and/or research director was asked a number of questions. Of the 37 professionals invited to participate, 21 thought it was worth their time and effort. There were 3 research directors and 18 sell-side[1] analysts. It would be beyond the scope of this book to repeat their answers word for word to every question. The most noteworthy and controversial answers are summarized for the reader.

1. How do you feel about the current environment that surrounds the analytical community?

The answers to this first question, not surprisingly, were very similar. The forces that steer all markets (fear and greed) drove the Internet bubble to unsustainable heights. To assign responsibility for the collapse of the Internet stocks to the analysts appears unfair. It is a well-known fact, probably referring to the study by Brad Barber mentioned earlier, that stocks with positive recommendations (e.g., Buy rating) outperform those that have less favorable recommendations. And while the period following March 2000 has been excruciatingly painful for most analysts and investors, we again see the performance of Buy recommendations continue to outperform stocks rated less favorably. Several analysts felt somewhat responsible for not moving more quickly with downgrades. Many admitted that they had not experienced a major bear market in their careers. Some were prone as other investors to irrational exuberance, which prevailed throughout the 1990s.

As an example to back up this claim of how investment professionals can be foolish and bow to peer pressure just like anybody else, one analyst pointed to the now defunct Merrill Lynch Internet fund.

---

[1]Used to describe the research departments that sell securities and issue BUY HOLD SELL recommendations. Mutual funds are considered buy-side.

The firm mulled over launching an Internet fund in the summer of 1999. According to Merrill's official, who has asked to remain anonymous, there was considerable debate about launching such a fund. Interestingly, there were voices of reason in Merrill's investment group. Those who were against the fund argued with good reason that Merrill already had a Global Technology Fund and that Internet shares could be incorporated into that fund as part of a well-diversified technology portfolio. But peer pressure kept mounting as Internet stocks kept soaring and Merrill's brokers were handing over their clients' assets to competing firms that carried Internet-based funds. This, of course, could not go on for much longer. The pain became very acute. Something had to give, and as is very often the case, reason and wisdom gave way to ignorance and greed. Speculation in Merrill's highest echelons was now steaming full speed ahead. And in Internet fashion, the road show promoting the fund was online. *The Wall Street Journal* reported that Paul Meeks, the fund's manager, in one of his public appearances in San Francisco, took the microphone and yelled, "Let's get ready to ruuuumble!" And *ruuuumble he did!*

With the NASDAQ reaching new heights almost every day and with Merrill's name, reputation, and marketing know-how, it is no wonder that the Internet fund was a huge success. The fund was launched on March 22, 2000, with $1.1 billion in assets. There was so much interest in the fund that new investors were barred from the fund for a month to give Mr. Meeks time to get invested.

Within 13 months, more than $700 million, or 70 percent of the $1 billion originally raised, had evaporated. With losses mounting, Merrill's top brass decided to ask shareholders of the Internet Strategies Fund to merge with the Global Technology Fund, which was the original argument of the more conservative colleagues at Merrill. Merrill's spokeswoman Christine Walton came out with the following statement:

> Now that most technology companies have moved into Internet space, it no longer makes sense to have two mutual funds with similar objectives. Combining the Internet Strategies and Global Technology funds will eliminate redundant holdings, reduce expenses to shareholders, and provide exposure to the Internet

sector as part of a more broadly diversified technology investment. (*The Wall Street Journal*, May 4, 2001)

The statement by Christine should be considered in light of two very interesting points. First, it probably had been taken from one of those Merrill officials who a little more than a year earlier had preached against the wisdom of opening such a fund in the first place.

The second, somewhat more disturbing point is the remark "Now that most technology companies have moved into Internet space . . . " I for one have been running a computer consulting firm since 1989, and even before 1997, we were already to some degree involved in developing Internet applications. I keep wondering which technology companies were not greatly involved in the Internet space in March 2000 but had moved into that space by April 2001. Perhaps such companies included Microsoft, Intel, Dell, IBM, etc. In the final analysis, a mutual fund should provide an investor with a diversified portfolio that has professionals selecting undervalued stocks. But in this particular case, it did not accomplish any of those objectives. Instead, it supplied investors with something as volatile as owning one stock.

Investors who lost most of their money by following Merrill's Buy recommendations did not perform much worse than Merrill itself. All their know-how and timely research reports did not seem to help. Money that Paul Meeks was managing for Merrill's clients, together with money from millions of faceless individual investors, went to the same slaughterhouse and practically disappeared. Even the most experienced could not withstand the burden of peer pressure that existed during the exuberant 1990s.

2. Is there a spoken and/or unspoken insistence within financial institutions to issue positive recommendations?

One analyst pointed out an article in *The Wall Street Journal* dated July 14, 1992. It referred to a Morgan Stanley internal memorandum that stated the firm considers analysts' pessimistic coverage in regard to their clients a poor business practice. It went on to state that Morgan Stanley's intent is to create, practice, and if need be enforce these guiding principles. The entire firm, together with the research department, has to understand our objective.

There are what analysts describe as political pressures as well as financial incentives built into the brokerage environment that keep employees in line to project a kinder and gentler outlook about the firm they work for and its clients. The analysts said that most people, no matter what they do for a living, tend to protect their sources of revenue in the analogous manner. If people are confused about where our loyalty lies, they should ask themselves a simple question: What do you do for a living? Did you ever make a decision knowing it would cause someone financial discomfort to benefit yourself?

It is obvious from these statements why most analysts would not disclose such testimonials on the record. Nevertheless, they continue to express a desire to achieve the best results possible within the existing framework that does not jeopardize their career and/or alienate them from their coworkers. It is often in their own personal interest that they produce the best possible analyses and issue the right recommendation. Only in this way can they build a reputation for excellence and distinction. However, not all analysts have such strong integrity. Some lack the moral fiber to stand up to their supervisors and do what they believe is right. They equate this process with a juggling act. With so many interests pulling them in different directions, analysts must please them all to survive. Some will undoubtedly succeed, but many will fail. Many of those who come to the job with the romantic notion of doing their best, regardless of the politics involved, ultimately do not last. Most often they leave quietly. Sometimes you hear about it in the news.

There are examples of analysts who tried to tell the truth. While at Donaldson Lufkin & Jenrette, Tom Brown was an unrelenting critic of First Union's insatiable acquisition strategy, prompting the anger of the company. Brown left DLJ in 1998 in the midst of the controversy and soon after that joined Tiger Management. After Tiger he started his own investment firm, Second Curve Capital. In 1998 First Union ultimately sagged under the burden of its acquisition spree and had a period of weak performance.

As a Merrill Lynch Internet analyst, Jonathan Cohen was suspicious of the high valuations provided to Web stocks such as Amazon.com all through the tech-stock mania of 1999. Amazon and other Web favorites kept moving higher. After voicing his suspicion in 1999, Cohen was replaced by Internet bull Henry Blodget. Since then, Cohen's skepticism has been justified. He later became director of research at Wit Soundview but has since moved on.

Marvin Roffman published a research report while working for Janney Montgomery Scott in 1990 anticipating that Donald Trump's Taj Mahal would go bankrupt. Taj Mahal did indeed go bankrupt before long, but not before Trump threatened a lawsuit, and Janney released Roffman. Currently, he is a partner in Roffman-Miller, a research firm in Philadelphia.

As a Crédit Suisse First Boston analyst, Michael Mayo issued an across-the-board recommendation to sell bank stocks in May 1999. The call proved timely, as bank shares weakened throughout that year. But when his firm acquired Donaldson Lufkin & Jenrette, he lost his job to his DLJ counterpart. Mayo says it's because of the Sell call, but the firm denies that. Mayo is now the bank analyst for Prudential Securities.

As you can see, going against the grain on Wall Street does not always put bread on the table for analysts. This is one of the primary reasons we see approximately only 1 percent of all recommendations designated as Sell.

3. Could analysts do a better job if there was no investment banking division breathing down their necks?

Analysts acknowledge that pressures do exist from the investment banking side, but the overall improvement in performance might not be statistically significant. They argue that they would continue to be prisoners of their own environment even if investment banking became obsolete. Certain things will never change, such as the need to work with corporate management. These important business relationships must be maintained at all times. Analysts continue to stress that the upper management at companies they analyze must view them as allies. The moment analysts harshly criticize their firms or their decision-making process (presumably through a Sell recommendation in public), the rapport between analysts and company management can and often does change dramatically for the worse. A delicate balance must be preserved at all costs. Quite often, analysts take on the role of the diplomat trying to bridge two factions together. One faction is management of the firm they analyze, and the other is the investment community at large. At the same time, analysts are also well aware—and so are their institutional clients—that biases and absurdities are inherent in the forecasting process. The reasons for this partiality are largely driven to encourage trading and to guard access to private information. Frequently, as we have seen, analysts are asked to take on the responsibility of a salesperson rather than an impartial financial specialist, thus creating a conflict of interest.

On a final note, we should realize that conflicts of interest exist in many, if not all, other industries. The financial industry is by no means the only abuser of this art but rather just another practitioner. The key for investors is to realize the existence of the problem, to design a strategy that limits their exposure to this syndrome, and to adjust their investments accordingly. In following chapters, we will explore various strategies for how to achieve this seemingly insurmountable task.

# 5

# TYPES OF ANALYSIS: FUNDAMENTAL VERSUS TECHNICAL

## What Is Fundamental Analysis?

*Fundamental analysis* describes the process of investigating essential elements that have an effect on the health of the economy, sectors, and companies. The goal of this investigation is to obtain and sustain an edge in predicting and profiting from opportunities available to investors. On the company level, fundamental analysis entails assessment of financial data, management's competence, business models, and competition. On the sector level, there is an assessment of supply and demand for the products and services offered. For the economy as a whole, fundamental analysis focuses on economic data such as consumer confidence levels, unemployment, inflation, and other statistical data. Alan Greenspan, chairman of the Federal Reserve, is the most important fundamental analyst who evaluates the current and future expansion of the economy.

To predict future stock movements, fundamental analysis combines economic, sector, and company analysis to obtain a stock's present fair value and anticipate potential movements in stock price. If the current fair value of a particular stock is not equivalent to its current price, fundamental analysts will adjust their opinion

—upgrade or downgrade the stock—until the stock's price ultimately gravitates toward perceived fair value. At that point, in
theory, fundamental analysts will adjust their opinion again.

Fundamental analysts in general do not agree with the academics and their view of the efficient markets theory[1] and as a result
believe there is no natural random walk inherent in the markets. In
fact fundamental analysts believe that stock prices do not accurately reflect all available information. This conviction typically
stems from their doubt in investors' ability to interpret all available
information correctly. Thus, analysts must anticipate to get the
most out of assumed price discrepancy between current market
price and fair value of stock.

The one factor of utmost importance in fundamental analysis is
the ability to read and interpret a company's financial statements.
In the next few pages, we will decode financial statements taken
from three different companies. For people who find this subject
interesting, I recommend an informative book entitled *Security
Analysis* by Benjamin Graham and David Dodd. This highly
notable book pays particular attention to the interpretation of
financial statements. Many people use this book as a learning tool,
and others use it to reexamine their knowledge and understanding
of financial statements, including someone most of you are familiar with—the most successful investor of all, Omaha's Warren
Buffett.

A few words should be said about obtaining financial statements
on the Internet. There is a multitude of sources out there and finding one that works for you is a matter of personal choice, although
Edgar Online at www.edgar-online.com gets my personal vote. In
the past it was possible to download most of the financials into
popular programs such as Microsoft Excel or Microsoft Word for
free; however, at the time of this writing, Edgar has changed its
policy and is charging for these services. Other services we found
to be comprehensive and user-friendly for evaluating financial
statements can be found at www.msn.com and www.zacks.com.

---

[1]The efficient markets theory is a highly contentious hypothesis. Followers of
this model consider it is useless to look for undervalued stocks or attempt to fore-
cast trends in the market through any modus operandi from fundamental to technical analysis. They also argue and offer much evidence that supports their view.
The efficient markets theory is also associated with the "Random Walk Theory."

Financial statements can be foreign terrain to many people. For those who are not accountants or financial analysts, the next few pages may be of benefit in the understanding of these reports and will help make them better investors. Financial statements are similar to the report cards high school students receive during the year. They contain information on whether the company was successful in executing its plan to increase earnings, cut costs, increase profit margins, and so forth. This information is quite important. Even though these reports analyze the past, they often can tell a potential investor whether the company and its management have the ability to perform well in the future. As we have mentioned, the economy plays a crucial role and is often the most important variable that contributes positively or negatively to the success of a company's financial performance. Nevertheless, companies in the same industry and during the same time frame have been known to yield different performance results. Surely, this type of disparity depends on the ability and accomplishments of the company's management.

The financial statements from three different companies we'll shortly evaluate certainly can assist us in confirming one truly important factor: value. If there is value to the company, it will undoubtedly appear in these reports, as will any indications that a company is in trouble.

Every publicly traded company has to file financial statements with the Securities and Exchange Commission on a quarterly basis. Most of the filed documents include the following: a letter to shareholders, the business review, and the financial review followed by management's discussion and analysis (MD&A).

The letter to shareholders and the business review often provide details about changes in the management structure, and many people read these reports because they like to evaluate and be informed about top management. For example, if a new chief executive officer has been appointed to run a company, investors would like to know everything available on this person, including his or her background, where the person came from, and what kind of results he or she delivered on the last job. Many on Wall Street consider the company's management a catalyst for its future and a determinant in its success or failure. There is a famous expression on Wall Street that describes investors who follow management changes: "Bet on the jockey, not on the horse." An example of this practice is the "second marriage" of Steve Jobs to Apple Computer Inc. (AAPL) in 1997 or Lou Gerstner's arrival at IBM. Both Apple and IBM performed very well after these managers took the helm. We, however, will focus on the financial review portion of the reports because it is here that we find the balance sheet, income statement, and cash flow statement, which encompass the financial performance and health of a given company. Occasionally, it will be very helpful to turn to managements' discussions section to find terminology that might be unfamiliar and requires further clarifications.

## The Balance Sheet

We start our evaluation of financial statements with the balance sheet. This statement illustrates the financial position of a company by summarizing what the company owns and what it owes at a specific time.

The balance sheet gets its name because it represents the following expression, which must always remain equal:

Assets (what the company owns) = Liabilities (what the company owes) + Equity (the company's net worth)

If your friend tells you that he has $1000 (assets) and no debts (liability), you can draw a conclusion that his assets are $1000 and his net worth, or equity, equals $1000 as well. If your friend were to generate a balance sheet, it would look like this:

Assets ($1000) = Liabilities ($0) + Equity ($1000)

On the other hand, another friend who also has $1000 owes $500 of this money to the bank. This friend would produce a balance sheet that looks like this:

Assets ($1000) = Liabilities ($500) + Equity ($500)

Thus, although each friend owns $1000, your first friend is better off financially than your second.

In the real world, of course, it's not that simple. Individuals and companies alike hold assets that constantly increase or decrease as resources are purchased, disposed of, become less valuable, or become used up in the course of operations. Liabilities also increase or decrease as debts are incurred or liquidated. In some cases liabilities may need to be projected and are subject to adjustment (upward or downward) in later periods. Equity increases or decreases primarily as a result of income or loss from operations of the business. It also increases when the owners contribute capital to the business, and it decreases when the capital is withdrawn or dividends are paid.

Let's move on to the analysis of real financial reports. The examples chosen provide reports of the following three companies: Exodus Communications (EXDSQ), Idec Pharmaceuticals (IDPH), and Dollar Tree Stores (DLTR). The reason for choosing these companies is somewhat deliberate. As you may remember, in Chapter 3 we discussed Piper Jaffray's upgrades and downgrades and how an investor could have profited by following these recommendations. However, it is important to understand and make a personal judgment on whether you agree or disagree with these changes (upgrades or downgrades) recommended by Piper Jaffray or any other analyst.

Exodus Communications was a company Piper Jaffray downgraded, albeit later than need be. At approximately the same time, Idec Pharmaceuticals and Dollar Tree Stores were upgraded.

### Exodus Communications

Let us start by evaluating the balance sheet for EXDSQ as it was available for analysis to the individual investors at the time these opinions were issued. Exodus was a company many on Wall Street loved and respected. Armies of analysts were singing praises for the company's management and its business model. The principal activities of Exodus were to provide Internet hosting for enterprises with mission-critical Internet operations, sophisticated systems and network management solutions, and technology professional services. There is no question that these services were in demand. As Internet use grew, many well-established organizations were looking to outsource this function due to its complexity and fast-moving changes in technology and personnel. Not every company wanted or was able to perform this job. Exodus, on the other hand, was able to build and deliver the technology and people who understood how to take advantage of economies of scale to create a large, "well-run," and well-funded organization.

Only one thing eluded Exodus time and time again: profitability. But this was the Internet bubble and, frankly, no one cared. During the Internet boom, profit was not important. In fact, by looking at Exodus's price chart (see Figure 5-1), we find there were many who made millions by owning its stock. Nevertheless, those who got in at the tail end or simply did not get out in time (a process discussed in detail in future chapters) were eventually wiped out. It is beyond any doubt that there were trouble signs for Exodus's investors. All one had to do was take a closer look at their financial statements.

Before we start analyzing the statements, here is an excerpt from Exodus's annual report, followed by the balance sheet. This report was prepared for the fiscal year ending December 31, 2000.

> We have incurred operating losses each fiscal quarter and year since 1995. Our accumulated deficit was approximately $484.6 million at December 31, 2000. We anticipate continuing our investments in new Internet Data Centers and network infrastructure, product development, sales and marketing programs, and personnel. We believe that we will continue to experience net losses on a quarterly and annual basis for the foreseeable future. We may also use significant amounts of cash or equity to acquire complementary businesses, products, services, or technologies. Although we have experienced significant growth in revenue in recent periods, this growth rate is not necessarily indicative of future operating results. It is possible that we may never achieve profitability on a quarterly or an annual basis.

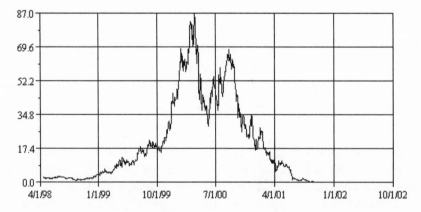

**Fig. 5-1.  Price chart for Internet startup Exodus Communications.**

**The Balance Sheet: Exodus Communications**    Let's try to simplify the review of financial statements because the process can be full of twists and turns. The interpretation of these statements, as you will see, can be quick and simple. Here is how it works. Given that all financial statements have at least two columns next to each other, with each displaying typically a year's worth of data, it will be useful to designate and flag each line of the balance sheet and the income statement. Two types of flags will be used. Every line marked with a P flag represents positive directional change from last year to this year, and every line marked with an N represents a negative change from last year to this year. After labeling every line of the balance sheet and the income statement with positive and negative flags, we will go ahead and sum up the P and N flags. This process, which I named *directional progress report*, will aid us in the interpretation of financial statements. For example, the balance sheet in Figure 5-2 for Exodus has sixteen negative (N) flags and eight positive (P) flags. This is not a good ratio. Obviously, when a company's balance sheet has twice as many negative as positive flags, it will be difficult to make this stock move higher in the future.

The first line of the balance sheet for Exodus has $805 million in cash for the year 2000. This represents a $210 million decline in the cash position from a previous year (1015 − 805 = 210). Unmistakably, a decline in cash represents a negative development, and thus, an N flag demarcates this line of the balance sheet. On the other hand, Receivables—money due to Exodus from clients—have increased from $61 million in 1999 to $175 million in 2000. This represents a positive development, and thus, we will label that line with a P flag and so on. Total Assets increased from $1742 as on December 31, 1999, to $3894 as on December 31 2000, which we again will label with a P flag.

In most cases, when a line item increases on the assets side of the balance sheet, it stands for a positive development. Nonetheless, there are instances when the opposite is true. One such line is called Intangibles or Goodwill. Whenever this line increases, you should label it with a negative flag. In Exodus's case in 1999, Intangibles stood at $156 million, and by the end of 2000, they increased to $181 million. Hence, an N flag demarcates this line.

What are the Intangibles or Goodwill, and why do we label it with the N flag when it increases? This line is often used as a

| | Flag | 12/31/2000 | 12/31/1999 |
|---|---|---|---|
| **Assets** | | | |
| Cash & Equivalents | N | 805.03 | 1015.96 |
| Receivables | P | 175.64 | 61.91 |
| Other Current Assets | P | 65.15 | 15.33 |
| **Total Current Assets** | N | **1045.83** | **1093.20** |
| Net Property & Equipment | P | 1760.70 | 368.23 |
| Investments & Advances | P | 413.5 | 0 |
| Intangibles | N | 181.28 | 156 |
| Deposits & Other Assets | P | 493.03 | 125.44 |
| **Total Assets** | P | **3894.35** | **1742.89** |
| **Liabilities & Shareholders' Equity** | | | |
| Notes Payable | N | 7.24 | 0 |
| Accounts Payable | N | 395.18 | 60.2 |
| Current Portion Long-term Debt | P | 0 | 6.89 |
| Current Portion Capital Leases | N | 48.25 | 17.16 |
| Accrued Expenses | N | 184.53 | 66.28 |
| **Total Current Liabilities** | N | **635.2** | **150.54** |
| Convertible Debt | N | 552.83 | 749.8 |
| Long-term Debt | N | 2167.82 | 784.58 |
| Noncurrent Capital Leases | N | 64.95 | 40.34 |
| Other Noncurrent Liabilities | N | 9.63 | 0 |
| **Total Liabilities** | N | **3430.44** | **1725.27** |
| **Shareholders' Equity** | | | |
| Common Stock (Par) | | 0.42 | 0.17 |
| Additional Paid-in Capital | N | 938.14 | 247.98 |
| Accumulated Deficit | N | −(484.55) | −(228.21) |
| Total Shareholders' Equity | P | 463.9 | 17.61 |
| **Total Liabilities &** | **3894.35** | **1742.89** | |
| **Shareholders' Equity** | | | |
| **Shares Outstanding** | N | **405.704** | **335.848** |

Fig. 5-2.   Annual balance sheet for Exodus Communications.

bookkeeping device where overpayment for an acquired company can be recorded. For instance, if a hardware store has assets of $40,000 (lamps, sledge hammers, nails, etc.) and someone happens to come along and buy it for $100,000, the difference of $60,000 has to be applied somewhere, and the Intangibles or Goodwill line is where it goes. Eventually, the business has to reduce Goodwill or Intangibles to zero on the assets side of the balance sheet. This reduction always drags down the equity side of the balance sheet, not the liability portion, which is clearly a negative occurrence.

The reason a buyer overpays for the acquisition has to do with anticipated future profits. But what happens if the business does not generate desired profits or stops functioning altogether? This might force the new owner to liquidate the assets to pay off debts or just get as much cash back as possible. Intangibles and/or Goodwill immediately become worthless because creditors and/or the owner will not be able to turn it into cash; hence, they become useless.

It can be argued, and not without merit, that an increase in Receivables and/or Inventory can be regarded as a negative development. The general rule of thumb regarding this particular issue should be as follows. If Sales during past year have expanded, then an increase in Accounts Receivable is a positive development. However, if Sales did not increase or perhaps even decreased, then a rise in Receivables should be viewed as a negative. A similar concept can be applied to Inventory.

We have learned from the preceding pages that an increase on the assets side of the balance sheet must be accompanied by an equal amount of increase on the liability and/or equity side. As we continue the process of marking each line of the Exodus balance sheet with a P or an N flag, you will notice that Liabilities increased almost twofold. In 1999 they stood at 1725 and by end of 2000 they increased to 3430. We should label this increase in debt with an N flag. Every line on the liability side of the balance sheet should be marked with the N flag if it increased and with the P flag if it decreased. This particular line unfortunately represents an unpromising sign for Exodus and its investors. Whenever a company or an individual takes on a lot of new debt, an alarm bell should start ringing. Why does a company need to increase debt to such levels? One must remember that debt eventually must be paid back, and interest must be paid as well. This will certainly eat away future anticipated profits. And since profitability continues to elude Exodus up to this point, where will the money to pay this interest come from? To realize this objective of continued expansion and making interest payments, Exodus had to take on more debt, which was immediately added on the liability side of the balance sheet equation.

Many prudent money managers would end their analysis right here. Most educated investors, after seeing this portion of the balance sheet, would agree that Exodus's management acted irresponsibly and exercised poor judgment. How can anyone, except the federal government, which can print money, take such burden on its shoulders? This is what many would call "financial suicide." The question one should pose is: Where were the accountants and financial advisers? The answer, of course, is that they were only interested in charging exuberant fees for these underwriting activities.

But let's move on and tackle the final portion of the balance sheet, the part called Equity. The good news, or at least it may seem this way initially, is that Total Equity increased from $17 million in 1999 to almost $463 million by the end 2000. Unfortunately, at this juncture Exodus fails to deliver yet again. As we break down the equity side of the balance sheet, we notice a very important line item called Additional Paid-in Capital. This line is of utmost importance because it warns the investor that Exodus, besides taking on more debt, was also selling more shares of its stock to raise additional capital. A directional increase in the Additional Paid-in Capital line should always be treated as a negative (N) flag because it informs potential investors that the company has sold more shares to the public.

To predict future stock prices, we must remember one basic rule of economics: Prices go up for any product, including stocks, when demand is greater than supply. Conversely, prices drop when supply exceeds demand. By increasing the circulation of additional shares in the public markets, the supply of Exodus stock increased. Since earnings continue to elude this company, the demand will most likely decline. Increased supply and smaller demand indeed resulted in Exodus's stock spiraling down out of control.

One line below Additional Paid-in Capital we find a row called Accumulated Deficit. This particular line is essentially a bucket where losses or profits accumulate throughout the years the company is in business. This bucket is continually filled or drained with the bottom line—net income—from the income statement, which we will break down next.

The Accumulated Deficit line informs the investigator/investor that Exodus Communications continues to lose money as cumulative loss has increased from a negative $228 million in 1999 to a negative $484 million by the end of 2000. This means that during 2000 Exodus has produced a loss that amounted to $256 million.

The loss in 2000 was greater than all previous losses since the inception of the company in 1995 and up to the end of 1999 combined. Hence, this line again will bear the N flag.

On the final line of the balance sheet, Shares Outstanding, it is painfully clear to see, for those who owned the stock, that the number of shares outstanding increased from 335 million in 1999 to 405 million by the end of 2000. This may be viewed as an additional nail in the coffin. After careful objective analysis of the Exodus balance sheet, you must agree that it is filled with numbers that convey financial irresponsibility, disappointment, and failure.

## The Income Statement

The key financial report used by scores of financial investigators and would-be investors is the income statement (see Figure 5-3 for an example). It illustrates how much the company earned or lost throughout the year. A helpful analogy here would be your salary minus all your expenses. If you earn more than you spend, you will have money left over for savings, investments, and so forth.

| | Flag | 2000 | 1999 |
|---|---|---|---|
| Sales | P | 818.44 | 242.14 |
| Cost of Goods | N | 565.95 | 197.23 |
| **Gross Profit** | **P** | **252.49** | **44.9** |
| **Gross Profit Percentage** | **P** | **30.85%** | **18.54%** |
| Selling & Administrative Expenses | N | 329.07 | 118.76 |
| **Income Before Depreciation &** | **N** | **(90.2)** | **(82.72)** |
| **Amortization** | | | |
| Nonoperating Income | P | 70.04 | 10.87 |
| Interest Expense | N | 192.27 | 49.03 |
| **Pretax Income** | **N** | **(247.23)** | **(130.32)** |
| Income Taxes | N | 0.75 | 0 |
| **Income from Cont. Operations** | **N** | **(247.98)** | **(130.32)** |
| Extras & Discontinued Operations | N | (8.35) | 0 |
| **Net Income** | **N** | **(256.33)** | **(130.32)** |
| Income Before Depreciation Amortization | N | (90.2) | (82.72) |
| Depreciation & Amortization (Cash Flow) | | 34.79 | 9.43 |
| **Income After Depreciation & Amortization** | **N** | **(124.99)** | **(92.15)** |

**Fig. 5-3.  Annual income statement for Exodus Communications.**

However, if you spend more than you earn, then . . . But perhaps that is best left to the individual's imagination.

An income statement summarizes the revenues earned from selling merchandise or services and other activities against all expenditures and outlays sustained in operating the business. The costs sustained by and large consist of cost of merchandise or services, salaries of employees and consultants, rent, utilities, marketing, interest on money borrowed, taxes, and so on.

The difference is the net income (or loss) for that period of time. The income statement serves as an indispensable tool in helping investors anticipate how the company may perform in the future. Just like the balance sheet, the income statement for one year alone does not tell an investigator the complete story. However, a chronological record of a number of years might shed some light on the overall financial picture of the company.

**The Income Statement: Exodus Communications**   Exodus's income statement (see Figure 5-3) once again is marked with a helpful directional progress report showing P and N flags. After they were totaled, the result was not more impressive than Exodus's balance sheet. There were eleven N flags and four P flags. For the second time, we see that the negative flags outweigh the positive ones by a ratio of more than 2:1.

Sales is typically the first item on the income statement. It signifies the key source of revenue from the clients received by the business for goods or services provided. Sometimes this line is called the Top Line because of its position at the top of the income statement. For Exodus sales have increased from 1999 to 2000, which is undoubtedly a positive development, and therefore, a P flag was placed on this line.

The Cost of Goods line typically represents all the costs and expenditures the company incurs in connection with the production of its final products or service. Since it increased from $197 million in 1999 to $565 million in 2000, we must mark it with an N flag. Gross Profit usually comes on the next line and represents the actual direct profit from sales after subtracting the cost of goods. Because it increased from $44 million in 1999 to $252 million in 2000, a P flag was attached. Gross Margin Percentage is an investigative tool that helps would-be investors assess whether or not the business has been able to expand profit margins. The formula for deriving gross margin is computed by dividing Gross Profit by Sales. A bigger Gross Margin is always a good sign, and for that reason, a P flag has been placed.

In Exodus's case this particular portion of the income statement looks very good. Sales increased from $242 million in 1999 to $818 million in 2000. Gross Profit Margin, on line four, has also increased from 18.5 to 30.85 percent. So far so good, one might say. Yet in spite of this, as we continue our directional progress account down the lines and mark each with either a P or an N flag, it becomes clear that almost everything else following this portion of the income statement turns out to be negative.

Selling and Administrative Expenses, which often include expenses such as advertising and promotions, travel and entertainment, officers' salaries, and other office expenses, have grown from $118 million to $329 million, almost tripling in size. For this an N flag is deservedly attached. Interest Expense has swollen to $192 million from $49 million. This is an almost fivefold increase. Perhaps this line should have five N flags next to it instead of one. But since our task is to track directional movements only without assigning weight, we will stick to only one. This particular item, as you may recall seeing on the balance sheet, comes from aggressive borrowing to acquire other companies, which may or may not ever justify themselves by contributing to the Exodus's bottom line.

At last, we reach the line called Net Income, which is at negative $256 million. Bingo! But this time you didn't hit the jackpot. This is what we call the bottom line, and this number is very troubling indeed. You may remember this number from our analysis of the balance sheet. This is the number that contributes to the continued expansion of the accumulated deficit line. Furthermore, we are reminded again that the number of shares available for trading, sometimes referred to as float, has increased.

Many educated investors agree that in the long run earnings growth is the biggest, if not the only, catalyst in creating demand with regard to any stock. As far as this income statement is concerned, there is no earnings growth and only a growing earnings loss. On top of this injury, there is insult in the form of increased supply in available shares.

For all intents and purposes, Exodus's balance sheet and income statement paint an unattractive picture. There are 27 negative flags and only 12 positive flags so far. Anyone who owned the stock when this annual report was issued was obligated to sell and do so immediately. Anyone who bought the stock hoping to average down or something to that effect obviously did not look at these financial statements or know what they were doing.

## The Cash Flow Statement

Every business exists for one purpose and one purpose only: to generate cash and enrich its shareholders. The products or services offered are essentially by-products. Without cash a business is out of business. And that is where the cash flow statement comes in.

The cash flow statement measures the money a company generates from its business activities. Every publicly traded company is required by the Securities and Exchange Commission to produce this statement.

Cash flows, even though interconnected with net income, are not the same. This is because of the *accrual method of accounting.* By and large, with the accrual method of accounting, a transaction is recorded on the income statement as soon as it is executed. To paraphrase, after the goods and/or services have been provided or rendered or an expense has been incurred, it is recorded. This does not happen automatically at the same time as the actual exchange of cash. Frequently, there is a gap between when services are performed and when cash is received from customers, vendors, suppliers, and so on. However, in spite the time lag between delivery of goods or services and the actual payment, the sale is usually recorded right away on the income statement. Therefore, sales increase and the balance sheet account receivables increase. The transaction is later reconciled on the cash flow statement. Here is an illustration that makes it easier to understand. (See Figure 5-4.)

Remember our two friends with assets of $1000 each? Let's take it one step further and imagine that neither of them earned any money, yet both bought $500 worth of furniture. One paid in cash, and the other paid with a credit card. From the cash flow statements in Figure 5-4, can you identify which statement refers to which friend?

You are right if you guessed that friend 1 bought the furniture on credit. As you can see, it is extremely important to consider and compare Cash at Beginning of Period and Cash at End of Period.

Friend 1

| | |
|---|---|
| Net Gain (Loss) | $(500) |
| Net Change from Liabilities | $500 |
| Net Cash from Operating Activities | $0 |
| Cash at Beginning of Period | $1000 |
| Cash at End of Period | $1000 |

Friend 2

| | |
|---|---|
| Net Gain (Loss) | $(500) |
| Net Change from Liabilities | $ 0 |
| Net Cash from Operating Activities | $(500) |
| Cash at Beginning of Period | $1000 |
| Cash at End of Period | $500 |

**Fig. 5-4.   Comparing two cash flow statements.**

These two lines inform the investigator whether the amount of cold hard cash has increased or decreased during the period analyzed.

Moreover, cash flows are also categorized by business activity. This breakdown is of no small significance and typically consists of three parts: operating activity, investing activity, and financing activity. There is a lot of information on this statement that is not relevant for our purposes and which we will skip here. However, there is also information essential to our exercise, and it is this: Did the company generate or consume cash from its operations (we know this from the balance sheet) and how did it happen? We examine operating activities first, followed by investing activities, and then wrap up our analysis of cash flow statements with financing activities.

**The Cash Flow Statement: Exodus Communications**   Since the cash flow statement is a reconciliation of the balance sheet and the income statement, we do not need to mark it with P and N flags. However, if you were to perform this task anyway, your results will have been 14 N flags and 7 P flags, the already familiar 2:1 ratio of N to P flags for Exodus (see Figure 5-5).

Every cash flow statement, as its starting point, takes a number from its sibling, the income statement. That is why the first line on Exodus's cash flow statement starts with negative $256 million.

| Cash Flow from Op. Inv. & Fin. Activities | 2000 | 1999 |
|---|---|---|
| Net Income (Loss) | −(256) | −(130) |
| Depreciation/Amortization & Depletion | 188 | 54 |
| Net Change from Assets/Liabilities | 136 | 30 |
| Net Cash from Discontinued Operations | 8 | 0 |
| Other Operating Activities | −(2) | −(1) |
| **Net Cash from Operating Activities** | **74** | **−(46)** |
| Net Property & Equipment | −(1284) | −(283) |
| Acquisition/Disposition of Subsidiaries | −(3) | −(77) |
| Investments | −(90) | 0 |
| Other Investing Activities | −(336) | −(29) |
| **Net Cash from Investing Activities** | **−(1714)** | **−(390)** |
| **Uses of Funds** | | |
| Issuance (Repurchase) of Capital Stock | 133 | 35 |
| Issuance (Repayment) of Debt | 1140 | 1271 |
| Increase (Decrease) Short-Term Debt | 170 | −(11) |
| Other Financing Activities | 0 | 1 |
| **Net Cash from Financing Activities** | **1444** | **1296** |
| Effect of Exchange Rate Changes | −(15) | 0 |
| **Net Change in Cash & Equivalents** | **−(210)** | **859** |
| **Cash and Equivalents** | | |
| Cash at Beginning of Period | 1015 | 156 |
| Cash at End of Period | 805 | 1015 |
| **Diluted Net EPS** | **−(0.63)** | **−(0.39)** |

Fig. 5-5.   Annual cash flow statement for Exodus Communications.

Please keep in mind that this number came from an income statement that was produced on an accrual basis. However, on a cash basis, the company claims it made $74 million. This important number is found on the line called Net Cash from Operating Activities. How can something like this happen? Upon closer examination, the cash flow statement reveals that Exodus either did not pay cash for goods/services it bought and/or did not receive cash for goods/services it sold. All this amounted to $136 million displayed on the Net Change from Assets/Liabilities line. In addition Exodus depreciated the value of its existing equipment by $188 million. Depreciation is a noncash transaction that reduces the net income but in reality does not affect the cash position. In any case Exodus, like many other companies who have aggressive capital expenditures budgets, produced negative earnings but positive cash flow from operations. Many accountants will tell you that this type of operational positive cash flow should be treated with suspicion.

The Net Property & Equipment line tells us that Exodus was aggressively purchasing new computers, property, and plants (again we see aggressive capital expenditure), and that activity has reduced Exodus's cash coffers by $1.284 billion. Furthermore, other investment activities were also quite aggressive, and when all was said and done, Exodus's Net Cash from Investing Activities were computed at negative $1.714 billion. Where did this money come from? Clearly, this enormous amount of money could not have come from profit (i.e., operating cash flow). But it had to come from somewhere. And so this leads us to the final portion of the cash flow statement, which is Net Cash from Financing Activities. Here we can see how all these aggressive expenditures were financed. In addition to selling more stock to the public, Exodus took on additional long-term debt and increased its short-term debt. These particular frivolities will without a doubt come to haunt this company and its shareholders. The only question is when? Unfortunately, it did not take too long to find out. On Wednesday, September 26, 2001, Exodus filed for Chapter 11 bankruptcy. Word of the pending bankruptcy leaked out on Tuesday, September 25, sending the company's stock into a 55 percent drop prior to halting its trading on the NASDAQ.

Exodus CEO William Krause, who replaced his long-time boss Ellen Hancock, said, "Bankruptcy reorganization would facilitate the company to concentrate on long-term growth." In the bankruptcy filing statement, the company recognized that its dependence on debt and the assumption that the Internet will grow much faster than it did were the main reasons for its downfall.

Cary Robinson, Piper Jaffray's senior research analyst, who downgraded the stock back in April, said, "They had so much debt, they were planning on a significant growth in the Internet demand, and when that ended, so did their company." Breakdown of the Exodus balance sheet, income statement, and cash flow statement revealed a picture of a company so burdened by debt that it was forced into closure.

But let's move on to greener pastures, as other financial statements are waiting to be investigated. Let's look at financial statements that seem to be healthier and of better quality. They are by no means perfect (by that I mean all positive flags and not one negative flag), because financial statements and, consequently, companies never are. Finding a perfect financial statement is like finding a perfect human being. The quest to find one is always desirable, but the outcome of locating one is until the end of time unattainable. The most we can hope for is that after producing a directional progress report, we will see more P flags than N flags. Having done this, the decision whether to buy stock becomes perfectly clear.

**Idec Pharmaceuticals** On April 3, 2001, Piper Jaffray upgraded Idec Pharmaceuticals (IDPH) to its top rating of Strong Buy. For a fundamental analyst like myself, this is a perfect time to sit down and perform a quick 10-minute directional progress report and thus make a personal determination of whether I agree or disagree with the analysts at Piper Jaffray.

First, here is a summary of the company's business. IDPH is a biotechnology company engaged in the research and development of targeted therapies for the treatment of cancer and autoimmune and inflammatory diseases. After the upgrade—prior to this I had never heard of the company—the balance sheet was quickly and systematically analyzed.

**The Balance Sheet: Idec Pharmaceuticals** The first line of the balance sheet should stir any potential investor's interest immediately (see Figure 5-6). Cash & Equivalents increased sixfold. As a consequence, the now infamous P flag decorates this line. Once again the temptation of putting multiple Ps was rejected due to our objective of keeping the process directional only. Total Current Assets more than doubled, and Total Assets almost tripled in size. From examples given through our analysis of the previous balance sheet, you may recall that an increase in assets must be accompanied by equal increases on the liabilities/equity portion of the balance sheet. And although the liability portion did increase from $147 million to $161 million, it is obvious that the biggest share of increases fell into the equity portion of the statement.

This is not a perfect statement by any means, with 10 positive and 10 negative flags. Negative flags notwithstanding, this is a much better statement than that of Exodus. That statement, as you

|                                           | FLAG | 12/31/2000 | 12/31/1999 |
|-------------------------------------------|------|------------|------------|
| **Assets**                                |      |            |            |
| Cash & Equivalents                        | P    | 401.05     | 61.4       |
| Receivables                               | P    | 1.69       | 1.31       |
| Inventories                               | N    | 0          | 23.65      |
| Other Current Assets                      | P    | 48.22      | 7.26       |
| **Total Current Assets**                  | **P** | **631.25** | **278.51** |
| Net Property & Equipment                  | P    | 47.51      | 20.82      |
| Investments & Advances                    | P    | 177.63     | 7.73       |
| Total Assets                              | P    | 856.4      | 307.07     |
| **Liabilities & Shareholders' Equity**    |      |            |            |
| Notes Payable                             | P    | 0.74       | 1.51       |
| Accounts Payable                          | N    | 1.73       | 1.26       |
| Accrued Expenses                          | N    | 16.07      | 12.83      |
| Other Current Liabilities                 | N    | 4.49       | 0          |
| **Total Current Liabilities**             | **N** | **23.04** | **15.61**  |
| Mortgages                                 |      | 0          | 0          |
| Deferred Taxes/Income                     | N    | 9.85       | 8.57       |
| Long-term Debt                            | N    | 128.88     | 122.91     |
| **Total Liabilities**                     | **N** | **161.78** | **147.09** |
| Shareholders' Equity                      |      |            |            |
| Common Stock (Par)                        |      | 0.07       | 0.02       |
| Additional Paid-in Capital                | N    | 680.6      | 195.21     |
| Retained Earnings (Accumulated Deficit)   | P    | 13.42      | −(34.71)   |
| Total Shareholders' Equity                | P    | 694.61     | 159.97     |
| **Total Liabilities &**                   |      |            |            |
| **Shareholders' Equity**                  |      | 856.4      | 307.07     |
| **Shares Outstanding**                    | **N** | **159.31** | **151.29** |

**Fig. 5-6.  Annual balance sheet for Idec Pharmaceuticals.**

may recall, had 16 negative flags and only 8 positives. Again, we see that outstanding shares have increased through Additional Paid-in Capital; however, most of this extra cash has stayed within the firm and, therefore, increased shareholders' equity.

The Accumulated Deficit line has been renamed Retained Earnings, and this change in name signals that, cumulatively, the company became profitable at last. All losses from previous years have finally been offset by profits generated by Idec. I imagine that this particular line on the balance sheet gave Idec's management good reason for celebration. To mark this positive name change from Accumulated Deficit to Retained Earnings, we will mark this line with a P flag.

**The Income Statement: Idec Pharmaceuticals**   Idec Pharmaceuticals' income statement looks excellent (see Figure 5-7). This time there are ten P flags and only five Ns, making this a positive 2:1 ratio, as opposed to the Exodus statements examined earlier. The Sales, or top line growth, increased nicely from $118 million to $154 million during 2000. The Gross Profit and Gross Profit Percentage lines have shown increases as well. And although the company's expenses have also increased, they did not have a significant effect on the growth of the bottom line. As a result the bottom line, or Net Income, has grown to $48 million, which in turn kept the company on good footing to move forward.

**The Cash Flow Statement: Idec Pharmaceuticals**   The cash flow statement for Idec Pharmaceuticals (see Figure 5-8), again, looks much better than the one for Exodus Corporation, which we subjected to close scrutiny earlier.

| | FLAG | 12/31/2000 | 12/31/1999 |
|---|---|---|---|
| Cash & Equivalents | P | 401.05 | 61.4 |
| Sales | P | 154.68 | 118 |
| Cost of Goods | P | 2.13 | 14.27 |
| **Gross Profit** | **P** | **152.54** | **103.72** |
| **Gross Profit Percentage** | **P** | **98.62%** | **87.90%** |
| Selling & Administrative Expenses | N | 27.76 | 19.47 |
| **Income Before Depreciation &** | **P** | **55.85** | **41.41** |
| **Amortization** | | | |
| Nonoperating Income | P | 20.54 | 10.24 |
| Interest Expense | N | 7.05 | 6.05 |
| **Pretax Income** | **P** | **69.34** | **45.6** |
| Income Taxes | N | 11.93 | 2.44 |
| **Income from Cont. Operations** | **P** | **57.4** | **43.15** |
| Extras & Discontinued Operations | N | −9.26 | 0 |
| **Net Income** | **P** | **48.14** | **43.15** |
| **Earnings Per Share Data** | | | |
| Average Shares | N | 159.31 | 151.29 |
| Diluted Net EPS | P | 0.3 | 0.29 |

**Fig. 5-7.   Annual income statement for Idec Pharmaceuticals.**

| | 12/31/2000 | 12/31/1999 |
|---|---|---|
| Cash & Equivalents | 401.05 | 61.4 |
| **Cash Flow from Op. Inv. & Fin. Activities** | | |
| Net Income (Loss) | 57 | 43 |
| Depreciation/Amortization & Depletion | 4 | 4 |
| Net Change from Assets/Liabilities | −(10) | −(3) |
| Net Cash from Discontinued Operations | −9 | 0 |
| Other Operating Activities | 19 | 8 |
| **Net Cash from Operating Activities** | **61** | **52** |
| Net Property & Equipment | −(31) | −(4) |
| Acquisition/Disposition of Subsidiaries | 0 | 0 |
| Investments | −(163) | −(138) |
| Other Investing Activities | 0 | 0 |
| **Net Cash from Investing Activities** | **−(194)** | **−(143)** |
| **Uses of Funds** | | |
| Issuance (Repurchase) of Capital Stock | 474 | 14 |
| Issuance (Repayment) of Debt | 0 | 0 |
| Increase (Decrease) Short-Term Debt | −(1) | 110 |
| Payment of Dividends & Other Distributions | 0 | 0 |
| Other Financing Activities | 0 | 0 |
| Net Cash from Financing Activities | 472 | 125 |
| Effect of Exchange Rate Changes | 0 | 0 |
| **Net Change in Cash & Equivalents** | **339** | **34** |
| **Cash and Equivalents** | | |
| Cash at Beginning of Period | 61 | 26 |
| Cash at End of Period | 401 | 61 |
| **Diluted Net EPS** | **0.3** | **0.29** |

**Fig. 5-8.   Annual cash flow statement for Idec Pharmaceuticals.**

Net Cash from Operating Activities is showing an increase as a consequence of generated cash rather than delays in settling outstanding bills and/or outstanding invoices. If there is one major negative ingredient in this statement, it is obviously the company's issuance of more stock. However, even in spite of this negative development, average earnings per share have managed to grow from 29 cents to 30 cents. Furthermore, cash received from the sale of additional shares has stayed within the firm. Ideally, it will be used smartly by paying off their debts first. This stock closed at $35.69 on April 3 when the upgrade was issued and by November 30 had increased to $70.30.

## Dollar Tree Stores

The final company to be analyzed in this chapter is Dollar Tree Stores (DLTR). This company does what its name implies: It sells products for $1 or less. Here is an abbreviated profile description for Dollar Tree Stores that was copied from Yahoo!'s Web site.

> Dollar Tree Stores, Inc. is an operator of discount variety stores offering merchandise at the fixed price of $1.00. The Company's stores offer a wide selection of core and changing products within traditional categories, including candy and food, housewares, seasonal goods, health and beauty care, toys, party goods, gifts, stationery, and other consumer items.

On April 25, 2001, Piper Jaffray upgraded Dollar Tree Stores to its Strong Buy recommendation. The closing price for this stock on that date was $21.36. By the end of November, it closed at $28.04, delivering a respectable 31 percent increase to its shareholders, even if you take into consideration your trading fees, which on the current market can be as low as $5 or in some cases even lower. This is a subject we will touch on briefly in Chapter 7. If you then proceed to subtract the impact of ask-bid disparity,[2] you would have still gotten out with a conservative 25 percent profit. During the same time span, the S&P 500 Index, which 80 percent of professional money managers can't beat, had lost in excess of 89 points, or slightly more than a 7 percent decline.

**The Balance Sheet: Dollar Tree Stores**   The balance sheet for Dollar Tree Stores also underwent a directional progress report and thus was marked with positive and negative flags for a quick overview of the company (see Figure 5-9). This time the P flags

---

[2]To buy or sell a stock on the open market, people typically need to use the services of an agent sometimes also referred to as a market maker. These individuals are always prepared to sell you that specific security for a certain asking price (the "ask") if you are interested in buying it. The opposite is also true. If you possess the stock and would be interested in selling it, they will purchase the stock from you for a certain price (the "bid"). The disparity between the bid and ask is called the spread. Stocks that are heavily traded are likely to have very narrow spreads, for example, 5 cents per share. However, stocks that are thinly traded can have spreads that are substantial, sometimes reaching a price of a few dollars.

| | Flag | 12/31/2000 | 12/31/1999 |
|---|---|---|---|
| **Assets** | | | |
| Cash & Equivalents | N | 181.55 | 181,58 |
| Receivables | | 0 | 0 |
| Notes Receivable | | 0 | 0 |
| Inventories | P | 258.68 | 192,84 |
| Other Current Assets | P | 37.67 | 20.5 |
| **Total Current Assets** | **P** | **477.9** | **395.1** |
| Net Property & Equipment | P | 211.63 | 157.36 |
| Investments & Advances | | 0 | 0 |
| Other Noncurrent Assets | | 0 | 0 |
| Deferred Charges | P | 1.56 | .4 |
| Intangibles/Goodwill | P | 40.37 | 42.39 |
| Deposits & Other Assets | N | 15.38 | 15.89 |
| **Total Assets** | **P** | **746.85** | **611.23** |
| **Liabilities & Shareholders' Equity** | | | |
| Notes Payable | | 0 | 0 |
| Accounts Payable | N | 75.4 | 71.75 |
| Current Portion Long-Term Debt | P | 25 | 28.1 |
| Current Portion Capital Leases | N | 3.54 | 3.18 |
| Accrued Expenses | | 0 | 0 |
| Income Taxes Payable | P | 23.44 | 29.19 |
| Other Current Liabilities | N | 46.9 | 36.19 |
| **Total Current Liabilities** | **N** | **174.3** | **168.40** |
| Mortgages | 0 | 0 | |
| Deferred Taxes/Income | | 0 | 0 |
| Convertible Debt | P | 0 | 4.39 |
| Long-Term Debt | P | 18.0 | 49.14 |
| Noncurrent Capital Leases | P | 25.18 | 28.37 |
| Other Noncurrent Liabilities | N | 10.71 | 9.51 |
| Minority Interest (Liabilities) | | 0 | 0 |
| **Total Liabilities** | **P** | **228.2** | **259.8** |
| Cumulative Convertible Mandatory Redeemable Preferred | | | |
| **Shareholders' Equity** | **P** | **0** | **35.17** |
| Additional Paid-in Capital | N | 156.78 | 75.03 |
| Other Equity | P | 360.75 | 240.54 |
| Treasury Stock | | 0 | 0 |
| Total Shareholders' Equity | P | 518.65 | 316.24 |
| **Total Liabilities & Shareholders' Equity** | | **746.85** | **611.23** |
| **Shares Outstanding** | **N** | **111.81** | **107.96** |

**Fig. 5-9. Annual balance sheet for Dollar Tree Stores.**

outnumbered the N flags by 16 to 9. This unquestionably represents a healthy improvement from 1999 to 2000. It is gratifying to note that Goodwill, an asset we like to see reduced, has been; therefore, we mark this line with a positive flag. Total Assets increased, and Total Liabilities decreased during the year. All together these excellent bits of improvement notably translate into enhanced shareholder value. All of these changes are a positive development, and, as a consequence, many P flags grace this balance sheet.

**The Income Statement: Dollar Tree Stores**   Let's quickly perform this analysis of directional progress report for the income statement as well (see Figure 5-10).

The income statement does not disappoint either. Again, when we tally the P and N flags, we find 10 positives and 6 negatives. This income statement, together with the very solid balance sheet and an upgrade from a financial institution with the reputation for providing investors with good recommendations, would be enough to convince me to buy Dollar Tree Stores stock in April 2001.

|  |  | 12/31/2000 | 12/31/1999 |
|---|---|---|---|
| Sales | P | 1688.10 | 1351.82 |
| Cost of Goods | N | 1064.51 | 854.56 |
| **Gross Profit** | **P** | **623.58** | **497.26** |
| **Gross Profit Percentage** | **P** | **36.94%** | **36.78%** |
| Selling & Administrative Expenses | N | 420.55 | 321.65 |
| **Income Before Depreciation &** | **P** | **203.03** | **175.61** |
| **Amortization** |  |  |  |
| Nonoperating Income | P | 4.27 | 1.74 |
| Interest Expense | N | 7.81 | 7.43 |
| **Pretax Income** | **P** | **199.48** | **169.90** |
| Income Taxes | N | (77.47) | (63.33) |
| **Income from Cont. Operations** | **P** | **122** | **106.57** |
| Extras & Discontinued Operations | N | −(0.38) | 0 |
| Preferred Stock Dividends | P | (1.41) | (7.02) |
| **Net Income** | **P** | **120.21** | **99.55** |
| **Earnings Per Share Data** |  |  |  |
| Average Shares | N | 111.89 | 98.84 |
| **Diluted Net EPS** | **P** | **1.08** | **0.92** |

**Fig. 5-10.   Annual income statement for Dollar Tree Stores.**

The cash flow statement for DLTR looked very healthy. The company made money as we have seen from the income statement and Net Cash from Operating Activities was plus $107.65. Operations continued to grow. Growth—as we all know—requires money (e.g. opening new stores). Thus, Net Cash from Investing Activities had a negative ($94.76). Finally, Net Cash from Financing Activities was a negative ($12.91). Negative cash flow from financing activities is typically a positive detail. It means the company either is reducing debt, buys back outstanding shares, or pays dividends. In this case DLTR reduced its long-term and short-term debt.

Before we end the discussion of directional progress reports and marking each line of the balance sheet and the income statement with a P or N flag, investors should keep in mind that neither this process nor any other is foolproof. There will be instances where you will lose money no matter what your strategy. Whether it is fundamental analysis, technical analysis, or another approach, no strategy works each and every time. All I can say from my own experience is that the directional progress report strategy has proved to be very successful.

## What Is Technical Analysis?

Technical analysts, unlike fundamental analysts, concentrate on how stock prices and share volumes that are bought and sold change on a day-to-day basis. Technical analysts rarely familiarize themselves with the company's past earnings, assets, liabilities, and so forth. The management's brilliance or foolishness is beyond their purview as well. Typically, they believe that future stock prices are not random (see random walk theory and efficient markets hypothesis) but can be predicted by analyzing price charts from the past. By looking at the pattern of these historical movements, skillful technical analysts occasionally can anticipate future price trends.

One needs to understand that there are almost no pure fundamental or technical analysts. Fundamental analysts occasionally employ a number of technical analysis tools, and vice versa. In this section, we cover a number of tools technical analysts use to make their predictions.

## Support and Resistance

The price for every stock—or anything else in life—is the result of a confrontation between demand and supply. The bulls (buyers) create demand for the stock at a certain price, and the bears (sellers) supply it. Thus, the bulls push prices higher, and the bears push prices lower. Because bears and bulls are not patriotic, they often change sides. Politicians would call this "shifting alliances," and this is how it typically works: When the price of a particular stock rises, there are clearly more bulls than bears, and we can, accordingly, draw a conclusion that bulls emerge victorious in this confrontation. However, this rise often precipitates defections from the bulls' camp into the bears' camp. As more and more bulls cross the line and join forces with the bears, the pendulum swings in the opposite direction, making the bears victorious. The same process is repeated when prices head lower.

For example, let's compare this parallel to the change in prices for Fannie Mae (FNM) in Figure 5-11.

In 2001 the daily price has bounced roughly between $74 on the low end and $85 on the high end. From this vantage point, a technical analyst was able to deduce that when prices fell to the $74 level, many bears switched sides and became bulls (i.e., sellers became buyers), seizing control and prohibiting prices from declining further. Judging by this example, we can say that the price of $74 attracted additional buyers of Fannie Mae and reduced the number of bears who were willing to sell this stock for less than $74. Thus, $74 is referred to as *support level*, or sometimes as the

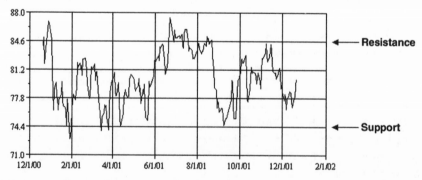

Fig. 5-11.   Price chart for Fannie Mae.

*floor.* Similarly, the price of $85 has produced the resistance level for this stock. This time the bulls started switching sides and joining the ranks of the bears. This process creates what technicians call the *resistance level,* or sometimes the *ceiling.* The area between support level and resistance level is called the *trading range.*

However, the support and resistance levels are not set in stone and change quite often. Usually this happens suddenly and unexpectedly (see Figure 5-12).

Figure 5-12 displays daily closing prices for Minnesota Mining & Manufacturing (MMM). As you can see, for most of 2000 (the box on the left), the prices fluctuated at the support level of around $80 per share, and the resistance level established around the mid-$90s. Then, all of a sudden, there was a huge upswing in volumes (see the bottom section of the figure) in early December 2000, and the stock gathered enough momentum from this action to propel itself into the next trading range of $100 to $120 per share. The drop out of the box on the right represents the tragic events of September 11, 2001. However, the stock quickly recovered and got back into the ring to continue its path. This graph clearly represents an example of how a huge pickup in volume can propel the stock into its next trading range. The average number of shares traded for MMM was

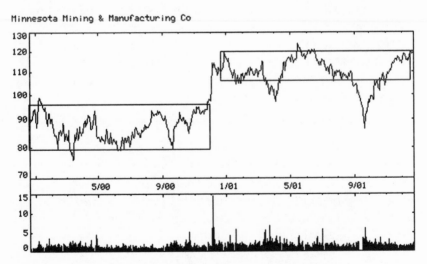

**Fig. 5-12. Daily closing prices for Minnesota Mining & Manufacturing.**

hovering slightly above 1 million per day; however, on December 4, 2000, more than 6 million shares changed hands, and the stock closed just over $99 per share. On the following day, 14.5 million shares changed hands, creating a new trading range for 2001.

The reason for high trading volumes in early December was due to the election of W. James McNerney, Jr., as the new MMM chairman and chief executive officer. A technical analyst might decide that December 4, when trading volume increased sixfold and the stock price moved higher closing at $99 per share, is the day to purchase this stock. This in turn would let the analyst take advantage of the 16 percent upswing that occurred on the following day when the price closed above $116 per share.

A fundamental analyst might point out the fact that MMM announced record sales and earnings on October 23 and, to top that off, a share repurchase program on November 15. With these announcements preceding the big upswing in the volume traded, the overall return could have been close to 25 percent.

## Moving Averages

Moving averages are one of the oldest and most popular tools available to the technical analyst. Moving averages tend to smooth out daily volatility; therefore, it is easier to spot trends. Finding the average price of a security over a set number of trading days shapes a simple moving average. In the majority of cases, a closing price is used to calculate the moving average. For example, a 5-day moving average is calculated by adding closing prices for the past 5 days and dividing the sum by 5:

$$5 + 6 + 7 + 8 + 9 = 35$$
$$35/5 = 7$$

A moving average changes because as the latest closing price is added, and the oldest closing price is dropped. If the next closing price in the average is 10, then this new price must be added, and the oldest one, which is 5, is then dropped. The new 5-day moving average will be calculated as follows:

$$6 + 7 + 8 + 9 + 1 = 40$$
$$40/5 = 8$$

In the past 2 days, the moving average changed from 7 to 8. As new prices are added and oldest prices are dropped, the moving average continues to change all the time.

The preceding example is for a 5-day moving average. Most technical analysts concentrate on longer moving averages. The 50-day, 100-day, and 200-day moving averages are industry standards and often can reveal interesting trading strategies. Contrary to intuitive thinking, technical analysts believe you should consider purchasing stock when its price closes above the moving average and sell the stock when its price falls below the moving average. For instance, the chart for Enron Corporation (ENE) could have generated the following buy and sell transactions (see Figure 5-13).

Let's say you always buy $1000 worth of stock. On January 3, 2000, you bought 23 shares of Enron at $43 per share, which equals roughly $1000. The stock was trading above the 200-day moving average until the end of November 2000. At this point the stock price slid below the moving average line, resulting in a sell transaction at roughly $70 per share. Your profit at this point would have been $610. However, by December 15 Enron again crossed over the 200-day moving average, forcing you to purchase 13 shares at $77 per share. (Again we adhere to the $1000 per purchase transaction rule.) By January 5, 2001, the stock again dipped below the 200-day moving average, generating a sell transaction. Your loss would have been around $90. By the end of January, the stock again closed above the moving average, which created another buy

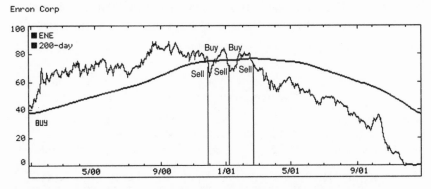

**Fig. 5-13.  Chart comparing Enron price with ongoing moving averages.**

transaction for 12 shares of Enron at $80 per share. Unfortunately, this transaction is short lived, and the stock permanently closes below the moving average by the middle of February 2001. This generated a final sell transaction for Enron stock at approximately $77 per share. This time you would have lost an additional $36 dollars. In total you have generated six transactions that cost you $30 ($5 commission per each trade) and your cumulative return for Enron would have been approximately $450. Undeniably, this is not a bad performance for a stock that went from most favored to most despised in such a short time. Figure 5-14 presents a list of hypothetical trades for Enron.

### Pros and Cons of Moving Averages

The pros of utilizing the moving average system (i.e., buying and selling when prices break through their moving average) can be achieved only when there is a long-term trend such as the one for Enron between January and November 2000. A benefit for the investor who observes and practices the moving average system is that it forces the investor to take action and not be caught dumbfounded like a mouse in front of a snake. You do not want to watch motionlessly as the stock price keeps plummeting and hold on to it until the bitter end. Enron's demise is a perfect example of the benefits the moving average system can bring.

The drawback of this system becomes apparent when a stock starts to trade between the support and resistance levels—as we have seen in Enron's case between November of 2000 and February of 2001—leaving the investor paying trading fees and accumulating losses.

|                   | # Shares | Bought | Sold | Profit | Commission $5 Each |
|-------------------|----------|--------|------|--------|--------------------|
| January 3, 2000   | 23       | $43    | $70  | $610   | $10                |
| December 15, 2000 | 13       | $77    | $70  | –$91   | $10                |
| January 24, 2001  | 12       | $80    | $77  | –$36   | $10                |
| **TOTAL RETURN**  |          |        |      | **$483** | **$453**         |

**Fig. 5-14.   Enron trades.**

Technical analysts employ many tools. The most popular Web sites such as www.msn.com, www.yahoo.com, and many others help investors with tools such as Bollinger Bands, Money Flow, MACD, RSI, Fast Stochastic Oscillator, Slow Stochastic Oscillator, and so on.

Technical analysis methodology has developed a huge investor following over the years. Wall Street employs an army of technical analysts who manage assets and assist institutional and individual investors alike. They often appear on popular TV programs and make stock price predictions. For people who wish to learn more about this subject, there is a multitude of sources of information. Very popular books include *Technical Analysis Explained* by Martin J. Pring, *A Complete Guide to the Futures Markets* by Jack D. Schwager, as well as numerous others.

With regard to technical analysis, it is probably safe to say that it all depends on the individual's preferences. Many are skeptical in regard to the merits of technical analysis, yet many others swear by it. Whether you agree with the merits of technical analysis or not, the bottom line is this: Technical analysis is better than no analysis at all. If you would like to try it, then study it, understand it, create a challenger system (with a small portion of your funds allocated for stocks) as described in Chapter 2, and measure its performance against your champion system, whatever it may be.

# 6

# THE FOOD CHAIN OF CAPITAL MARKETS

## Lions, Zebras, Grass, and Vultures

Understanding the forces and interdependencies that exist among various sectors and industries can often help investors recognize the big picture. This awareness frequently leads the investor to make better and more profitable trading decisions.

A resemblance to this concept can be found in nature. In nature, where the existence of various food chains is well understood, scientists have shown that, for example, on the Serengeti Plain in Tanzania, zebras and other herbivores' health and diet largely depend on grass, whereas the health and diet of lions largely depend on the zebras. Therefore, the scientific community proved that lions ultimately depend on the grass even though they do not directly use it for their survival. Throughout the rainy season, when grass grows in abundance, zebras flourish. The food is plentiful, and this contributes to an explosion in the zebra population on the Serengeti Plain. An abundant supply of zebras always benefits the lions' population due to an expanded food supply.

However, when fortunes change and drought arrives, the hardships in this food chain begin to show. As grass slows down its growth, the zebra population shrinks due to a smaller food supply.

Less grass often means fewer zebras. This transformation typically has a detrimental effect on the lions' population. As the zebra population dwindles down to a minimum, lions begin to suffer shortly after that. Fewer zebras often mean fewer lions.

Our Serengeti example is not far off from the food chain on Wall Street. The capital market follows a very similar pattern. Interdependencies among companies, sectors, industries, and the economy exist in a similar way. If we go back to the story earlier in the book describing the downgrade of Dell in August 2000, we'd notice an interesting pattern. During that month, Piper Jaffray had downgraded Dell Computer from its Strong Buy rating to a Buy rating. The report associated with this downgrade concluded that PC sales growth was declining at Dell and earnings would not meet analysts' expectations. The report was alarming and, frankly, unexpected. For almost a decade, PC sales growth at Dell was hovering around 40 to 50 percent per year, and then all of a sudden, the most successful, innovative PC manufacturer and distributor of them all blinked. What went wrong? Was it an isolated case affecting only Dell Computer or was it an industrywide slowdown?

It is well known throughout the computer industry and the financial industry that Dell by the end of the 1990s became an undisputed leader among PC manufacturers. Dell's prowess in marketing, handling of inventory, and business execution was unmatched by any of its competitors. In fact, Dell was instrumental in putting many of its early competitors out of business. After that feast, Dell began its unstoppable march by encroaching into the territory of Compaq, IBM, and Hewlett-Packard. The march was so successful that by the end of the exuberant 1990s, Dell took the number one spot in total PC desktop shipments throughout the world.

However, in early 2000, when the technology drought started rearing its ugly head and the economy started to unfold, Dell and many other computer makers began to lose their footing. The NASDAQ had received a heavy blow in early April 2000, and even though it managed to recover somewhat from the setbacks during that summer, things were not going well. The economy and the stock market were shaken to the core. It became clear toward the end of the summer that Dell was not losing any market share to any of its competitors.

Piper Jaffray's report contained troubling notes such as "current revenue growth guidance of 30 percent is unsustainable" and "The

Company is fast approaching a brick wall." The report later added, "More worrisome is the fact that even though component prices are falling, the company's gross margins are negative due to a tough pricing environment and weak demand."

This turn of events unfortunately was not a seasonal slowdown either. It was the beginning of back-to-school season, usually a time of robust sales in the PC industry. And yet that did not seem to be of any help. All signs were pointing to one thing and one thing only: Apparently, there was an industrywide slowdown in demand for PC products. What were the contributing factors to this decline?

As corporations were preparing for Y2K throughout the late nineties, they were busy buying new software and hardware to make sure that every technology component throughout the organization was Y2K compliant. Large corporations would order thousands of new PCs at a time to address and resolve this problem. This buying spree had a terrific effect on companies such as Dell, Gateway, Compaq, and others. They were shipping new computers in droves. Unfortunately, as the Y2K project came to an end, so did the astonishing growth at Dell Computer.

The company in its quarterly report cited weaker-than-expected government sales, as agencies stepped up their purchases in 1999 on Y2K worries. Unfortunately, the report omitted the fact that private and public companies made similar purchases in 1999 as well. Many industry observers noticed this trend and began to worry that PC demand would fall from historical levels. Shortly after that, Piper Jaffray analyst Ashok Kumar, who had continued to follow Dell, said, "Their growth has shrunk quite dramatically, very quickly." He then added, "Will they keep going down or sustain stronger growth? We continue to believe there's downside risk."

As soon as this troubling trend in the PC manufacturing food chain was recognized, it should be of no surprise to what transpired next. Take a look at Figure 6-1. In it you will see industry gears and how each wheel depends on the other to keep things rolling. If one of the wheels sputters and shows a strain, the others will follow rather quickly. In terms of our story, the domino effect had begun, and the PC food chain was quickly getting knocked off balance. The question educated investors started asking was: Who will be next? It did not take long to find out the answer.

In September 2000 the same analyst who downgraded Dell in August downgraded Intel (INTC) as well. This insight was based

Micron Technology

Intel

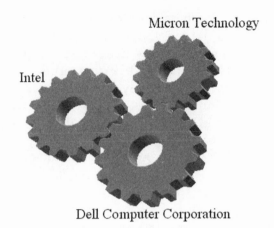

Dell Computer Corporation

**Fig. 6-1.    Interdependence of companies involved in PC manufacturing.**

on logical thinking and common sense. By looking at the big picture—the PC food chain in this case—Kumar was able to make better trading decisions than many of his peers. Less than 1 month before this downgrade, Dell Computer Corporation, the leader in PC manufacturing, had said something that was not heard before. Expectations for growth in the PC industry on Wall Street were too optimistic. They needed to be lowered substantially.

This is a story of the inevitable. When sales at companies such as Dell, Compaq, and Gateway become sluggish, the impact on companies that supply these firms with chips, monitors, and other products will undergo a similar experience. As PC orders dwindled down to a minimum, the companies down this food chain started showing their pain and suffering as well.

On September 5, the day of Kumar's insightful downgrade, Intel lost more than 6 percent of its value and closed at $69.25 per share. Within a few months after that, it was trading below $40 per share, and by July 2001 it dipped to the mid-$20s.

As this awful story for technology companies was unfolding—especially in the PC and chip manufacturing businesses—and gaining momentum, some analysts continued to dispatch Strong Buy recommendations in this food chain/industry group. The fact that the most commonly used indicators, such as sales growth, gross profit margins, and inventory buildup, were all pointing toward a rough road ahead was not enough to deter certain Wall Street professionals from hanging on to their Buy calls. In particular Sudeep Balain, a senior analyst with Hambrecht & Quist (currently part of J.P. Morgan Chase Corporation), steadfastly continued to issue such advice. During September 2000, when Dell, Intel, and others saw tremendous declines in their share prices and publicly conceded, albeit timidly, that business trends were not leaning in the direction that made them comfortable, it regrettably did not stop this particular analyst from issuing a positive endorsement for Micron Technology (MU). Why? PC sales growth was declining so rapidly during these months that any endorsement of a large company in the business of supplying PC manufacturers was surely to suffer, and Micron Technology, which produces dynamic RAM (DRAM) chips, was no exception. On September 19, 2000, when Hambrecht & Quist initiated Micron Technology with an untimely Strong Buy recommendation, the stock was trading at $65.25 per share. Yet within a little more than 1 month, Hambrecht & Quist was forced to reconsider its initial decision and downgraded the stock from a Strong Buy rating to a Buy. However, by the time this downgrade was issued, Micron Technology was trading at approximately $30 per share. As readers can easily observe, this represented more than a 50 percent decline from the original Strong Buy recommendation. The note next to the downgrade had the following remark: "decrease price target; decrease rating; decrease earnings estimates; downgrade based on 'current market dynamics'; reduce target to $65 from $120." But this was not the end of the story because on December 8, 2000, Hambrecht & Quist downgraded Micron Technology for a second time. Once more the reason for the downgrade was phrased in the similar manner: "decrease price target; decrease rating; decrease earnings estimates; downgrade based on 'continued weak PC sales'; reduce target to $50 from $65." This is a classic example of when Buy means Sell. Micron Technology, like Dell, started crumbling together with other industry peers. The entire computer industry food chain was at risk. Once an investor appreciates the fact that companies within a specific industry live their lives and perform similarly to animals within a specific food chain, the big picture becomes clearer than ever before. Neither companies nor animals operate in a vacuum. Companies that belong to a particular industry, or food chain, often depend on the economy and the hierarchy of that industry. When leaders within this group all of a sudden falter without someone else loudly claiming that they are taking away market share, an investor should become suspicious and alert to the possibility that there are fundamental problems in this particular industry and avoid investing in this area altogether.

It is important for investors to appreciate that Dell was, in this particular case, the first victim or sign of trouble brewing. Of course, it does not always have to be that way. Trouble can come from a different angle. For example, Intel can also be the first to address a slowdown in demand for its products. If that were to happen, companies such as Dell, Compaq, and Gateway should be viewed with caution as well because Intel is their primary supplier for microprocessors. Figure 6-1, illustrating industry gears, still applies.

Looking again at the tumble Dell took in 2000, after Intel and Micron were identified as Dell's potential (and probably actual) vendors, it was only a matter of time until their own vendors would start feeling the business squeeze as well. In particular, let's look at Applied Materials (AMAT). This company manufactures, markets, and services semiconductor wafer fabrication gear and associated spare components for the global semiconductor industry. Clientele for these products consists of semiconductor wafer producers and semiconductor integrated circuit manufacturers that either use the integrated circuits they produce in their own products or sell them to other companies. Thus, Applied Materials' customers include companies such as Intel, Micron Technology, and others. Referring to the previous examples and understanding of food chain scenarios, it becomes clear that trouble was set to start brewing in these quarters as well.

If we take our grass-zebra-lion food chain example and apply it to the Dell-Intel-Applied Materials example, we will undoubtedly notice many interdependencies and similarities. During economic expansion, there is a great demand for all kinds of semiconductor gear. Companies that sell electronics to hungry consumers such as Dell must purchase large quantities of semiconductors to build, and then they must ship their merchandise. Therefore, companies like Intel and Micron Technology must produce chips at ever-greater speed to satisfy the demand of their customers such as Dell, Compaq, and so on. This path eventually leads to companies that build equipment to produce all types of chips. Applied Materials is one of those companies. It creates and builds new and innovative state-of-the-art tools that enable companies such as Intel and Micron Technology to produce semiconductors at faster speed. However, when economic growth slows down, it becomes inevitably clear that demand for these tools will decline as well. To see this concept in the real-world stock prices, see Figure 6-2. The values populating Figure 6-2 consist of closing daily prices during 2000 and 2001 for four securities: Micron Technology (MU), Intel (INTC), Dell Computer Corporation (DELL), and Applied Materials (AMAT).

All four companies that were analyzed adhere to similar patterns in terms of performance and direction. This graphic representation answers another important question that many investors frequently ask: Is my portfolio diversified? You can find an answer to this question by looking again at Figure 6-2. Certainly, investors who purchased these four stocks for diversification purposes would not attain their goal. Why? By evaluating this chart, it is simple to notice that prices for all four stocks in general move up and down in concert with each other.

So from a diversification standpoint, investors should pay close attention to companies whose stocks move in tandem with peers in

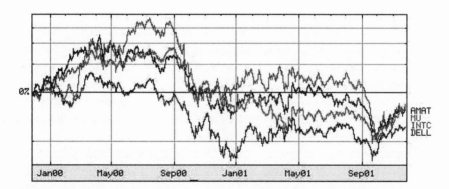

**Fig. 6-2.  Daily closing prices for four PC-sector manufacturers/ suppliers.**

their industry groups. And it is important to monitor the analysts who focus on those industry groups. It is likely that a downgrade from, for instance, Strong Buy to Buy or Hold on Dell could soon be followed by a similar recommendation for other companies in the industry food chain, such as Intel, Micron Technology, and others.

## The Automotive Industry

As in the previous example, the auto industry also has a multitude of connections and interdependencies that make it move in tandem. When General Motors sells a large number of cars, companies that supply auto chassis, for instance, benefit as well. One helps the other grow in times of plenty and suffer in times of famine. To make an educated investment decision, the investor has to know and understand how the gears in this particular industry turn as well.

Throughout the 1990s, as gas prices continued to trend lower and the overall economy was booming, large trucks, luxury cars, and spacious minivans became the vehicles of choice. Big 4- and 5-liter engines running on eight cylinders were extremely popular. This turn of events gave Detroit a much-needed boost. After the terrible recession of the early 1990s, American auto manufacturers were finally on the road to recovery and revival. They needed to produce a large number of vehicles to satisfy the growing consumer demand. This was unquestionably the best of times for automakers. Regrettably, good times do not last forever. Fortunately, the same can be said for bad times as well. The beginning of a rough road ahead for the auto industry can be traced back to 1999. As the Federal Reserve began to tighten the money supply by raising the federal funds discount interest rates, the economy started showing signs of distress. On five different occasions between August 1999 and May 2000, Fed Chairman Alan Greenspan increased the discount rate. This aggressive attempt to slow growth to tame possible inflation resulted in the discount rate reaching the 6 percent mark by May 2000.

These increases regularly translate into a higher cost of borrowing for the consumer. And as loans become more expensive, the auto industry starts to suffer. Again, we can equate this picture to our grass-zebra-lion food chain scenario. In this scenario loans are like grass and auto manufacturers are like zebras. As it becomes harder and more expensive for the consumer to borrow money, it will undoubtedly result in declining demand for cars. Therefore, it becomes as clear as day that as the economy begins to undergo a slowdown, auto manufacturers will start showing signs of significant wear and tear in parallel.

By the end of June 2000, Ford (F) came out with the following statement: "As general unemployment in the United States continued its rise, our company saw a decline of 12 percent in its unit shipments of cars and light trucks as compared to May of 2000." Clearly, as the economy slowed, year-on-year sales fell.

Besides rising unemployment and higher interest rates, gas prices rose as well, and that obviously did not bode well with auto manufacturers. For years large 4 x 4 sport utilities were major contributors of profits to Ford and other automakers. With interest rates going up, with unemployment going up, with gas prices going up . . . , well, you get the picture. Ford was also involved in a brutal dispute and litigation with Firestone regarding the tires used on its popular Ford Explorer SUV. Major litigation never helps any stock, and this was no exception. Ford stock took a terrible beating, nosediving from around $29 in May 2000 to $17 in October 2001, a hefty 41 percent decline. For people who were heavily invested in the Internet stocks, a 41 percent decline would seem like a blessing. Nevertheless, for conservative people who usually invest in companies like Ford, this decline was brutal.

If Ford was hurting, it makes sense that other automakers were too. Subsequently, the time came to evaluate General Motors (GM). General Motors had also seen its stock price, like Ford's, peak in May 2000, reaching $93 per share. However, in June, when it became obviously clear that the American economy was slowing, the stock started a quick descent. Within 1 month it traded down to the mid-$50s. By October 2001 it did not manage to provide investors with any better results than Ford. GM's stock price was hovering below $50 per share.

Interestingly, most analysts managed to downgrade GM in time. Prudential Securities downgraded GM to its Hold recommendation on May 3, 2000. The stock closed at $88.06 that day. No doubt this was a timely downgrade. Merrill Lynch followed up on May 10, and the stock closed at 81.94. When J.P. Morgan Chase made a similar call on May 15, the price was $86.44. Goldman Sachs, on the other hand, continued to keep GM on its Recommended List, and whoever followed Goldman's advice suffered. This is not the first time that Goldman's analysts in the auto sector blundered. If we look at an average trend for stocks rated Recommended List *across all sectors,* we see a fairly convincing picture (see Figure 6-3). It is clear that stocks rated Recommended List outperform stocks rated Market Perform. However, after drilling down to the auto industry, the opposite trend emerges (see Figure 6-4). Here Market Perform produced better results than Recommended List.

This clearly illustrates that Gary Lapidus, Goldman's analyst covering the auto industry, is missing a bit with timely upgrades and downgrades.

If we look at the economy and interest rates as grasslands and auto manufacturers such as Ford and General Motors as zebras, there must be companies in the auto industry that are comparable to the lions. If we acknowledge and agree to the existence of food chain theory in capital markets, it seems rational and consistent

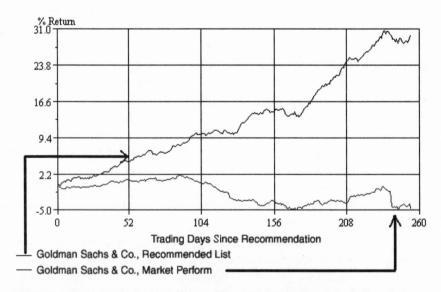

**Fig. 6-3.** **Performance of Goldman Sachs's Recommended List and Market Perform stocks over a 260-day trading period.**

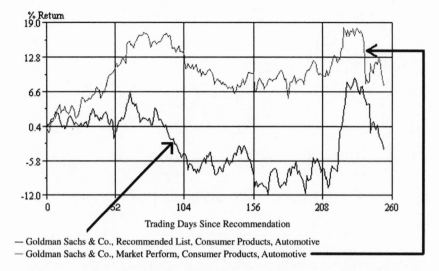

Fig. 6-4. **Performance of Goldman Sachs's Recommended List and Market Perform stocks in the automotive sector over a 260-day trading period.**

with this view that companies who produce and sell products to automakers will depend and undergo a similar fate as they do, whether it is feast or famine.

To illustrate this point, look at Figure 6-5. This represents the stock performance of General Motors (GM) and TRW Inc. (TRW), starting with November 2000 and ending with November 2001. TRW designs, produces, and sells products and systems in several segments including occupant safety systems, chassis systems, automotive electronics, other automotive, space, and electronics systems, information technology, and aeronautical systems.

Clearly, the overall performance of General Motors and TRW are almost identical. The only time both stocks diverged was for a few months in the beginning. However, shortly after that and over the long run, they managed to pull toward each other and continued to experience a similar general trend. Therefore, we can equate TRW to the lions.

In terms of diversification, we can again argue the case that holding Ford, General Motors, and TRW will not provide the investor

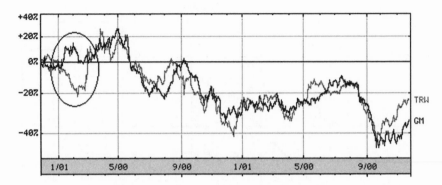

**Fig. 6-5.**   **Performance of General Motors and TRW over the same period.**

with true diversification. General trends such as interest rates and the economy affect many corporations, especially those that are involved in mature and established industries. When people talk about diversification, they generally attempt to describe various food chains. Buying different companies within the same industry or food chain inoculates an investor from poor management decisions or in some cases fraudulent behavior of corporate management, as in the recent case with Enron. However, it does not accurately represent the benefits of true diversification.

All of these examples, whether it's Dell-Intel-Applied Materials or General Motors-TRW, represent a mathematical concept the statisticians call *positive covariance*. In these examples we likened positive covariance to a food chain. Often, positive covariance is also compared to putting too many eggs in one basket, in this case a basket being a particular industry.

Since we thoroughly described and compared positive covariance as a food chain, our journey should lead us to a discussion of companies and animals that experience contrasting fortunes. This concept is referred to as *negative covariance*. Is there a food chain (or an industry) that benefits from a drought (or recession and high unemployment)? The answer to this question is yes.

In one of the best books ever written on the subject of investing and the benefits of diversification, *A Random Walk Down Wall Street* by Burton G. Malkiel, there is a wonderful story about a hypothetical island economy that describes the concept of negative covariance.

On this imaginary island, there are only two businesses. One is an umbrella manufacturer, and the other is a tourist resort with beautiful shorelines, sandy beaches, saunas, tennis, and good food. Each business in an average year produces an equal amount of revenue. For 6 months of the year, the sun shines and the resort generates $1 million in profits. Then, regrettably, it has to shut down because the weather changes drastically, and it rains for the next 6 months. In essence our little imaginary island becomes a rain forest. During this rainy period, the umbrella manufacturer starts cranking out the production of many umbrellas and generates $1 million of profits during these six months. This cycle repeats every year like clockwork.

At this point, if you were the owner of the resort, it would be safe to say that your annual expected profit would be $1 million per year. The same could be said for the owner of the umbrella factory. But suppose that one year the sun did not shine, and it rained throughout the entire year. Sorry to say the resort did not generate any income at all that year. This turn of events would obviously hurt you and your business. However, it would benefit the umbrella manufacturer immensely. During this rainy year, your earnings —assuming you have no expenses—were $0, but the umbrella factory earned $2 million.

Your horrible performance can be attributed to one thing and one thing only: You were not diversified. Now let's suppose that rather than owning the whole resort, you've decided to share it equally with the owner of the umbrella factory. In return, for your generosity, he promised to give you half of his share in the umbrella factory. Given that he is a bright businessman, he recognized that next year could be a sunny one instead of a rainy one, and his business might suffer just as much as yours did throughout the rainy year. After this transaction took place, both of you can sleep calmly at night without ever worrying about the weather. No matter what happens, rain or shine, you will make your $1 million per year going forward for the rest of your life.

This story illustrates negative covariance and the benefits of diversification. While one business thrives, the other deteriorates, and vice versa. When analyzing the performance of two or more stocks on the same chart over the long term, as in our previous examples of Intel and Dell, it becomes clear that these stocks have positive covariance. They frequently move up and down together. Figure 6-6 shows an example of negative covariance. It displays closing daily prices for Berkshire Class A (BRKA) and the NAS-DAQ. These two frequently diverge from one another on a regular basis, producing negative covariance.

Another example of companies that have negative covariance can be ultimately observed in the personnel recruiting business. Since the recruiting and hiring of new personnel in many companies largely depend on the state of the economy, the following two companies become very appropriate for our discussion. Companies that benefit directly from a slowing economy and rising unemployment happen to exist in the outplacement industry. For them the good times begin when almost all other companies suffer. They are like vultures in the jungle. Death and suffering are a time of plenty for these firms. Outplacement firms provide assistance and office space to people who are out of work. That means they benefit directly from rising unemployment.

Why does this trend occur? The simple response is that when corporations fire large numbers of employees, they engage outplacement firms to help some of those laid-off people find new jobs. For this service many corporations shell out up to $15,000 per laid-off worker. This creates a bonanza of earnings for outplacement firms.

Some will ask why large corporations spend so much money on employees they just let go. The answer is corporate image. In times

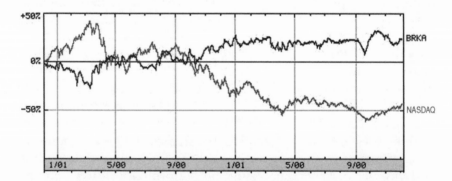

**Fig. 6-6.  Negative covariance between Berkshire Class A (BRKA) and the NASDAQ over the same period.**

of economic uncertainty, many employers reduce head count every day. This process creates a huge image burden for large corporations that hire thousands of people during good times, making promises and assurances to their new employees they often cannot keep. Stories of how wonderful they are and how much they care for their employees and their families end with economic sluggishness. Regrettably, when fortunes change and business slows down, all companies that are affected make 180-degree turns and begin laying people off by the truckload. A company like IBM that used to have an image of never firing its people, but needed to break away from this tradition to survive, had to generate a positive public relations campaign. IBM wanted to send a message to employees who were not dismissed that it was desperately trying to help its laid-off people find new jobs and/or change their careers.

In the most recent recession of 2000 and 2001, telecommunications, technology, media, financial, and other companies started laying off people in droves. This created an amazing opportunity for the countereconomic outplacement industry. It was a classic example of negative covariance.

Although some in this industry are private companies, one is a publicly traded firm and its name is Right Management Consultants Inc. (RMCI). The company's primary business is career transition services that offer individual and group outplacement. It is important to remember that as long as this company's main focus is outplacement services, the right time for this firm will be during economic slowdown and rising unemployment.

Administaff, Inc. (ASF), on the other hand, is in a totally opposite sphere from RMCI. This firm provides a number of comprehensive employee-management solutions, which encompass services such as benefits, payroll administration, employee recruiting, selection, performance management, training, and development. Indeed, Right Management Consultants stock and Administaff stock behave like two magnets with same polarity pushing away from one another. With their stock performance often mirroring each other, these two firms illustrate negative covariance (see Figure 6-7). The price chart (Figure 6-7) speaks volumes. It is quite similar to the story of the island economy discussed earlier.

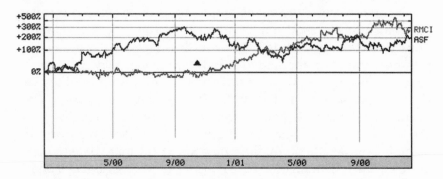

Fig. 6-7.   Negative covariance between price charts for Administaff
(ASF) and Right Management Consultants Inc. (RMCI).

Companies with such absolute negative covariance trends do not
exist in abundance. One of my finance professors years ago suggested that people who are serious about learning and understanding the beat of the markets must, among other things such as
investment errors and triumphs, compile a list of companies and
industries that share positive and negative covariance.

An additional scenario for serious investigators and investors
to write down in their little black book involves stocks in the secu-
rity-defense industry. War always benefits a certain segment of
capital market. As we know, the tragic events of September 11,
2001, were devastating to America's morale and at least in the short
term to her financial markets. Major stock indexes plunged rapidly when trading resumed on September 17, 2001. This slide
adversely affected almost all sectors and industries. However, companies manufacturing products that help government agencies
and/or other companies improve security measures saw their
stock prices advance to substantially higher altitudes just as quickly as the overall markets declined.

One of these firms was In Vision Technologies, Inc. (INVN). This
firm manufactures, markets, and supports explosive discovery systems for the public aviation security industry. In Vision's products
contain the first automated explosive detection systems to be certified by the Federal Aviation Administration. Whenever human-
made disasters strike, In Vision benefits automatically, at least in
the short term. However, given the unthinkable long-term impact

of the September 11 attacks, the benefits for this company could be much more lasting.

An alternative candidate that attracted additional investment interest due to the national tragedy was Magal Security Systems Ltd. (MAGS). This firm develops, manufactures, and markets computerized security systems that automatically detect, locate, and identify the nature of unauthorized intrusions. MAGS's clients include countries that need the capability to protect their national borders against illegal immigration, smuggling, and the infiltration of terrorists. MAGS's systems are also sold to airports, industrial sites, communication centers, military installations, nuclear facilities, and government agencies, to name a few. This firm's business improved after September 11. Figure 6-8 shows MAGS, In Vision and S&P 500 index before and after this tragic date.

It's interesting to note that neither firm received additional coverage from Wall Street analysts. In Vision Technologies has been rated a Hold by Prudential since 1999. As for Magal Systems, it did not receive any coverage at all. In the meantime In Vision Technologies managed to grow by 1500 percent in 2001 and Magal Systems was no slouch either. It performed extremely well and advanced 350 percent during the same time frame. Investors who rely solely on analysts and talking heads for their stock-picking advice would have missed giant opportunities to profit from these companies.

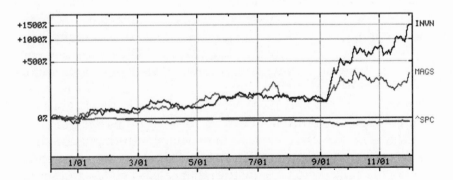

**Fig. 6-8. Performance of Magal Security Systems (MAGS) and In Vision (INV) stocks before and after September 11, 2001.**

Once investors realized that the American government was on war footing and that hostilities would be the inevitable outcome, the stocks in the defense industry received an enormous boost. Once again it was clear that companies such as L-3 Communications (LLL), which develops secure communication systems and specialized communication products, would clearly benefit. Lockheed Martin (LMT), a company that develops aircraft, spacecraft, launch vehicles, and missiles, would benefit as well. A few other candidates such as Raytheon (RTN) with its famous Tomahawk missiles and General Dynamics (GD), known for its shipbuilding, would profit from this conflict. There was no need to buy these shares on September 17, 2001, either. Sure it would have been nice, but in retrospect purchasing these stocks a week or two weeks later would still bring substantial returns.

Unfortunately, most analysts continued to exercise numbness. Very few upgrades were seen within this food chain when many of these firms were screaming Strong Buys. Thankfully, analysts did not issue too many downgrades either.

The situations we just described undeniably make sense, and there is a multitude of other similar examples. Negative and/or positive covariance is a powerful tool and should be utilized to investigate a potential investment. The fact of the matter is that because such examples are plentiful, it is impossible to remember them all. Therefore, just like the football coach has his playbook by his side at all times, investors would benefit from creating and keeping their little black book for the many different situations they will encounter in the future.

Before ending this discussion, it would be advantageous to discuss the impact of population and its effect on the economy. Baby boomers are an extremely visible and quantifiable force that continues to shape and influence our times as well as various sectors and industries. The baby boomer generation refers to Americans born between 1946 and 1964. After World War II, when American soldiers began to return home, many decided to start a family. The result was an explosive increase in new babies during those years. As this group of children was growing up and moving through the human life cycle, certain industries that catered goods and services to this generation benefited immensely in the process. According to the Baby Boomer Headquarters Web site, there are 76 million baby boomers. When this group of people shifts its focus and habits due to their age, the economy and our capital markets take notice.

As they continue to grow older, the following patterns among others will undoubtedly become more and more pronounced. The health-care industry in the next two decades will continue to experience increased demand for its products. Therefore, unless the legislature steps in and reshuffles existing laws, this sector will keep on and most likely accelerate its growth. An increased number of potential customers again parallels our rainy season and abundance of grass on Africa's Serengeti Plain. Companies that cater to the growing number of elderly Americans, such as health-care providers, will continue to benefit from an increased number of customers. Baby boomers will require all kinds of medical products and services. On a somber note, as this unstoppable trend continues and baby boomers' actual age draws nearer to projected life expectancy, companies that own and operate funeral homes will begin to see tremendous benefits as well.

# 7

# BROKER VERSUS MOUSE CLICK: THE EVOLUTION OF TRADING

*Alex Rabinovich*

## Trading in Europe

In the late Middle Ages, when the world had been progressing slowly and people had not known much change for centuries, a number of Italian city-states began issuing profitable government securities. This new method of raising money gave rise to the art of speculation. People began to engage in risky business transactions on the chance of quick or considerable profits. In Venice government securities were traded from the middle of the thirteenth century at the Rialto. At first speculators were frowned upon because of the fact that they were attempting to get rich quickly, regardless of how their earnings had been achieved. As early as 1351, a law was introduced forbidding gossip intended to lower the price of government funds. Such laws began the official enforcement of a market that would predict the prices of the future. All the evidence would point to these early laws and transactions as the cradle of the stock market located in the Mediterranean.

Although it wasn't a new creation, the early seventeenth century marked the beginning of a stock market in Amsterdam. Government stocks and the esteemed shares in the Dutch East India Company had introduced a modern approach to speculation and trade. Reaching a new scale of sophistication, the Amsterdam Stock Exchange had become an extraordinary trading center of Europe. Other than people buying and selling shares or speculating on their possible growth or decline, these new investors were now able to speculate without having any money or shares at all. By the early seventeenth century, the Dutch republic became the most advanced and flourishing economy in Europe, with Amsterdam as the financial capital of the world. All financial products and services were traded on the Amsterdam Exchange.

At this point speculators needed information on what was being traded as well as the current prices of these tradable securities. In 1692 John Houghton, an apothecary and coffee trader, began supplying regular lists of stock market prices twice weekly in his commercial periodical, "A Collection for the Improvement of Husbandry and Trade."

Although providing certificates as proof of a loan or of part ownership goes back to the late Middle Ages, by the late seventeenth century it had become widespread for individuals to invest in companies. Wealthy men were usually the shareholders, trading shares between one another, and they were the ones who had the time and resources to take an active interest in the dealings of the companies they traded.

Time went by as speculation became more attractive to people, and the practice of investing began to expand. As more of the public became investors, the original way of trading stock in a company had become increasingly impossible. No longer could investors be considered a small group of rich men who were able to handle their trades between one another. A necessity had developed for intermediaries: brokers who could handle the buying and selling of various companies' shares for their clients. It became common for brokers to meet in parks and coffeehouses to trade shares. This had become a major trend in cities such as London, Paris, and Amsterdam. In later times, with the emergence of the London Stock Exchange on a street called Exchange Alley, brokers transformed their old coffeehouse meeting places into private organizations that created and enforced rules to protect the business they had come to enjoy.

The colonization of America brought about a new and refreshed outlook on the future and its people. The colonial endeavor gave rise significantly to the speculative nature of the American public. People involved in the early days of American investments were full of dreams and high hopes that were being fulfilled in front of their eyes.

## Trading in Early America

The American stock market began on Manhattan's southern end after Independence had been achieved in the late eighteenth century. A speculative craze had developed dealing in government loans and bank stocks that imitated its predecessor in Exchange Alley a century earlier. The trade meetings were held on a narrow road called Wall Street, named after a wall that had been built there by Dutch authorities, governing their colony of New Amsterdam in the 1600s. What was once a small and insignificant street soon came to represent the country's financial markets. No other street in world history has represented such an embodiment of power and wealth.

In the spring of 1792, a group of twenty-four merchants and auctioneers got together and formed an association of Brokers for the Sale of Public Stock. The transactions of these brokers were to occur near a buttonwood tree, and therefore, the regulations that they established were called the Buttonwood Agreement. The original agreement of these brokers was to charge customers a minimum commission to stabilize their profits and prevent them from being driven lower. Regarding their dealings, they also agreed to give each other preferences.

The commodities market was the initial "hot" speculation of choice in the early 1800s. When the prices of cotton and silk rose, many outsiders were encouraged to enter the speculation field. At this point many other commodities followed in their tracks. The markets began to experience a rise in investors as well as in prices.

The New York Manufacturing Company, the first stock issued by a business other than a bank, canal, or insurance company, was published and quoted in 1815. Trading began at $105 a share, gradually dropped into the $60s, and eventually disappeared in 1817, proving yet again that IPOs have always been risky investments. As factories' needs for mechanical power rapidly increased, their need for large amounts of capital grew in parallel. This amount of capital was usually much greater than an individual could handle during those times. The solution to these problems gave birth to the modern corporation, or a *joint-stock company* as it was called in those days. This idea rapidly replaced partnerships and even sole proprietorships as a way of starting and running a large company. Joint-stock companies were able to raise large amounts of capital that they needed to sustain and improve their businesses with most of the help from the stock market.

As the banks began to supply margin loans to the stock market regularly, people saw more interest and advantages in investing. It enabled small-time speculators to make purchases that were larger than they normally could afford and stimulated a market turnover. The development of the "ticker" in 1867 spread the word about fluctuations in stock throughout the country and linked many small brokerages to Wall Street. It was estimated that nearly half of all the messages transmitted by telegraph involved speculative transactions by the end of the nineteenth century.

## Trading Enters the Twentieth Century

In 1917 a new middle class had entered the market of investing. This was largely due to the United States selling $27 billion in Liberty bonds and Victory bonds to fund the war against Germany. It was the single most effective cause of the boom in the market that followed in the next decade. What started out as a feeling of patriotic duty on behalf of the American people would later turn many beginners into serious and educated investors. More than 22 million people got involved in the securities market at the time, induced by these war bonds. In the previous years, railroads and a few industrial corporations sold securities to the public, and other American businesses took bank loans to fund their endeavors. Showing great success, the wartime bond market was the convincing stimulus for other corporations to expand shares of their company into the public and venture out for financial support. Dividends in the form of more shares became a common practice, saving cash for the company.

By 1929 there were approximately 1.5 to 2 million stockholders in American corporations, excluding people who owned multiple shares. At this time there were also 29 exchanges where securities were trading, and on the New York Stock Exchange alone, there were more than 1200 issues. Companies such as Goldman Sachs Trading Corporation and International Securities Corporation began issuing investment trusts with high expectations. They attracted interested customers with offers of professional supervision as well as diversified portfolios. The rapidly increasing paper economy brought forth new investment bankers, and their organizations made great profits from commissions and brokerage fees. Charging about $15 per 100 shares, securities brokers earned money when the transactions were buys or sells and when their client had made a profit or lost. With a bull market in full force, investors also took great advantage of margin trading, which is the buying of stock on credit from the broker. During this time, brokerage houses expanded rapidly, with nearly 600 branch offices opening in 1928 and 1929, an increase of over 80 percent.

Many watchful investors had difficulty attaining financial information that was helpful regarding the stocks they owned or wished to purchase. The New York Stock Exchange, enjoying its sudden increase of interest by the American public, did not hold their listed companies to a great measure of enforcement; hence, the disclosure of valuable information was minimal. The people involved in the financial dealings of these corporations, such as lawyers, accountants, and investment bankers, all shared the goal of selling stock rather than reporting the true balance of assets and liabilities.

As the bull market of 1929 sped up at a rapid rate, educated skeptics began to warn of a disaster that was waiting to strike. They pinpointed the causes of this inevitable danger to excessive securities floated by investment trusts, pool manipulations, inflated margin accounts, and questionable financial reports. A warning was issued by both Moody's Investment service and the Harvard Economic Society that the prices of many securities were at unreasonable levels and that corrections should be expected. Toward the end of October 1929, the crash of the stock market had begun. After many sell orders, including those from overseas, prices started to plummet to a level below the gains of the previous year. Since the stock market was regarded as the primary indicator of the

American economy, public confidence was devastated. More than $30 billion had disappeared from the American economy within a matter of half a month, and it took nearly 25 years for many stocks to recover.

The lessons of the great crash made a lasting impression on the American public, rich and poor, from common workers to government officials. The need for regulation had arrived. It was a bit too late to save the past but not too late to correct these mistakes from happening in the future. The Securities Act of 1933 was created to protect future investors from corruption in the representation of companies that were selling their stock. It required corporations and investment bankers who wished to sell stocks and bonds in the future to file thorough statements of disclosure with the Federal Trade Commission. There were now criminal and civil penalties enforced for those who failed to follow these rules and for those whose statements were false or misleading. In the same year, the Glass-Steagall Act was enacted to prohibit commercial banks from engaging in investment banking, a system that had encouraged speculation in the previous decade. Capital requirements of national banks were raised, and their officers were given 2 years to divest themselves of all personal loans given to them by their own institutions.

Congress established the Securities and Exchange Commission in 1934 to enforce these newly passed securities laws and, most important, to protect investors as well as to promote stability in the markets. Governing the securities industry derived from a clear and basic concept, which was that all investors, whether large institutions or private individuals, should have access to certain basic facts about their potential investments. To achieve these basic principles, the SEC required public companies to disclose meaningful financial and other information to the public. This information gave investors an upper edge on whether their goals would be met with the purchase of a particular security. Through the organized and steady flow of comprehensive and accurate information, investors could finally graduate from speculating to conducting actual research and making sound investment decisions. The SEC was also created to administer other partakers of the current and evolving securities market such as stock exchanges, broker-dealers, investment advisers, mutual funds, and public utility holding companies.

As the stock market cooled off and eventually regained its strength, investing into the future began to thrive as the business of all businesses. Thousands of smaller companies whose stock was not traded on any exchange began to appear. These stocks were bought and sold in what is termed the over-the-counter market (OTC). In 1961 Congress authorized the SEC to conduct a study into the OTC market. It was eventually proposed to use automation as a possible solution. The National Association of Securities Dealers Automated Quotations (NASDAQ) system was formed in 1971 to organize the trading system of OTC stocks. This innovation became the first fully automated market for securities. Brokers were now able to correspond over a computer network, all over the country, regarding their stock orders and no longer had to be located at a central exchange.

Full-commission brokers were the only way to go until the 1970s. Their services included recommending stocks to their clients, answering questions, and being available for consultations. Clients of these brokerages generally would have access to the firm's proprietary research. At the time there were *minimum fixed commission rates* that were set by the New York Stock Exchange. These prevented competition among the brokerage houses regarding their commissions. In 1975 the SEC decided that these minimum rates were a form of price fixing and ordered the New York Stock Exchange to abolish them. Discount brokers began to do business out of the belief that many investors did not need the advice as much as they needed the trading services. Since all legal information was attainable to the individual investor as well as the financial institution, these new types of brokerages had great success with less involvement in the trade decisions. Now regular investors would not have to worry about high fees and rates cutting into their modest gains. During this decade, a few U.S. investment banks, including Morgan Stanley, went public. This factor played a large part in the growth of the professional market trader.

*Portfolios,* the term for a particular individual's group of investments, were now being monitored and investigated more than ever. Since information was largely available, brokerages were widespread, and commissions had gone way down, the individual investor in some cases could do just as well as the institutions in percentage terms. Some years seemed to be bad ones for the securities in many portfolios, especially in the 1970s when there were several years of negative returns and only a few years of small positive returns. Showing a growth of only a few percent or even a loss would eventually be balanced out by exceptional times like those of the 1990s. Timing would be a crucial part of investing for years to come.

The regulatory structure in effect since the 1930s was relaxed as President Ronald Reagan came into office. The SEC budget was reduced, the Glass-Steagall separation of investment and commercial banking was not seriously enforced, and regulators were expected to be impressed with the atmosphere of the free market and deregulation. Although the market peaked in August 1987, it also went through one of the greatest crashes in history in percentage terms. The difference this time was that many investors did not back out as they did in the past, and the ones who held their positions since January were still able to record a modest profit in the aftermath of such a low point in the market. The interpretation by the advocates of market efficiency was that speculative booms and stock market panics were rarely, if ever, the cause of depressions. As opposed to the markets of 1929, this new market sent investors a completely different message. It now appeared that buying and holding stocks were the best strategy. Rather than a stock market crash representing a depression, it now could be treated as a chance to make bargain basement purchases considered "buying into the dip."

Faith in the stock market was revived when it was observed that stocks had provided higher investment returns over bonds since the 1950s. In 1996, on the 100th anniversary of the establishment of the Dow Jones Industrial Average, *The Wall Street Journal* reported that in 98 percent of all 20-year periods since 1925, stocks had outperformed bonds. *Trend following*, recently called *momentum investment*, has been a key feature of the financial markets since the 1990s.

## Mutual Funds

The concept of several individuals pooling their money for investment purposes arose in Europe in the 1800s. The faculty and staff of Harvard University were the first to create a pooled fund in the United States in 1893. The first official mutual fund, called the Massachusetts Investors Trust, was created in 1924. Such mutual funds were not widely used by investors until the birth of the individual retirement account (IRA) in 1981. From this point on, mutual funds would become popular in employer-sponsored defined-contribution plans 401(k), IRAs, and Roth IRAs.

People were being educated that a mutual fund was basically a financial liaison that allowed a group of investors to pool their money with a predefined investment goal. The financial institution handling the pooled money provided a fund manager who was responsible for investing this money into specific securities. A person who invested in a mutual fund bought shares of the fund and was considered a shareholder. Since mutual funds were cost-efficient and easy to invest in and because the investor did not have to figure out which stocks or bonds to buy, it was considered one of the best investments ever created. During a market correction in October 1997, a broker's poll found mutual fund investors expecting an average 34 percent annual return over the next 10 years. If this expectation were to occur, it would send the Dow Jones to 151,000 and the total U.S. stock market capitalization to 1500 percent of national income.

In recent years diversification has become the most important factor in surviving market dips as well as keeping a constant average return. The idea of spreading your money across many different types of investments should increase the chances of some investments being up while others are down. Risk is tremendously reduced as a portfolio's diversification increases. At the basic level of diversification, multiple stocks are purchased in hopes of keeping balance and stability. Mutual funds may contain hundreds or even thousands of stocks. Since it would take a lot of time buying and selling, as well as keeping track of so many investments, mutual funds have been an ideal solution. In addition to purchasing mutual funds more easily than many stocks separately, the funds are also diversified and often set up in predetermined categories of investments.

Traditionally, when investors wanted to buy or sell securities, they phone a broker and provide information about the desired transaction. This broker then transmitted the order to a trading desk at the broker's home office, and it followed through to the floor of an exchange or to the OTC market, linked by an electronic communication system, for execution. This system worked well for many years but prevented the common investor from taking immediate advantage of impulsive, sometimes small, price fluctuations. Even if the investor did have access to extremely current quotations, referred to as *real-time quotes,* it was still impossible to guarantee that a securities purchase would happen in the time required to take advantage of an attractive price.

The development of computers allowed brokers to create systems that gave them the ability to execute orders virtually instantaneously. Such computerized systems permitted brokers to place orders for traders, whether on exchanges or the OTC market, by computer connection and quickly send back receipts of each transaction. These computer order-execution systems let institutional investors take advantage of small price movements in publicly traded securities, allowing them to buy or sell closer to the price they anticipated. Proving to be very beneficial for the institutions and brokers, these systems also became appealing to regular investors. Individuals were highly interested in a system that they could use to ensure transactions that were as close as possible to the currently quoted price. Using computers was not unheard of for small investors, but they still only utilized them as a linkage to their brokerage firm for placing orders. As the Internet became a common phenomenon, new and old companies began to establish online trading capabilities, which could enact executions on their own rather than flowing through a chain of command. *Day-trading* has become a practice for many risk-taking investors, as they attempt to take advantage of small price movements and release their holdings by the end of each day. Although these risk takers do not buy for long-term investment purposes, many other investors still do, which maintains the typical price of most stocks.

The trend of online trading has been exceptional. In the beginning of 1998, SEC Chairman Arthur Levitt pointed out that online trading represented 25 percent of all retail stock trades. Recent examples of methods used by online firms to attract customers have been free trades or cash for opening a new account. Some companies have begun to guarantee speed on every trade and even waive the trade commission if it takes longer than promised. Online brokerages have also utilized the latest Internet technology and offer streaming quotes to their clients for up-to-the-minute prices. These online brokers are ideal for knowledgeable investors who plan to take advantage of the information available on the Internet.

As high-transaction sectors of investment services such as securities trading have made their way into the mainstream of online activity, the slower-moving and more conservative investment sectors like retirement plans and mutual funds are gradually following in their tracks. Investment management firms are anticipated to enhance their Web existence, offering more features and tools such as transactions, personalization, and real-time assessment. Most large firms already offer some of these services, as eventually customers will begin to expect and require these capabilities. Since mutual fund shareholders tend to be older than stock investors, it has taken that sector of investing longer to fully penetrate the Internet. As they become comfortable with the Internet and as it is becoming a standard for every firm to offer its services online, mutual funds among other original advancements will continue to evolve.

Online services range from financial news to bulletin boards of investors' opinions to full-service data research on any company listed in the stock market. Many online brokerages have had to provide these features along with their traditional trading applications. Some companies now sell the same research reports that the full-service brokerages provide to their clients. The expensive brokers or even discount brokers charging per amount of shares or amount of trade are slowly evolving into online research and real-time trading. More people have learned that the buys they made in the past were due to brokers being salespeople, trying to make money from commissions, rather than analysts helping their clients with honest first-rate analysis. Most recently, investment research companies such as Marketperform.com and Investars.com, among others, have appeared on the scene to help investors evaluate which brokers are preoccupied with generating commission through buying and selling and those who seek profits for their clients. Portfolio diversification is now more crucial than ever because investors feel discouraged by the recent drop of faith in the stock market. Investors are now becoming more involved in actively managing their own positions. The strategy of buying stocks for the long term and forgetting about them no longer seems valid.

In 1998 former U.S. SEC Commissioner Steven Wallman founded a company called FOLIO*fn*. In May 2000 FOLIO*fn* launched an investing revolution with the introduction of Folios: customized baskets of stocks that let virtually any individual investor combine the benefits of direct stock ownership with the simplicity and diversification of mutual funds. A Folio is a personalized basket of stocks that an investor owns. It combines the lower risk of broad diversification, the low cost of no trading commissions or asset-based fees, and the ability to control its taxes. Investors can change their basket anytime before or after purchasing it by adding stocks, removing stocks, or modifying the dollar amount. As offered by FOLIO*fn*, investors can make hundreds of changes each month commission-free in trades executed during two time periods each day called *windows.*

Other companies are slowly but surely following in the path of FOLIO*fn*. Investors can purchase "ready-to-go" or template baskets, which can be modified any way they wish, or they can assemble their own stock by stock. These baskets are sometimes called off-the-shelf baskets as well. An example of an off-the-shelf basket, now provided by E*TRADE, another company involved in basket trading, is the S&P20 Basket, which is a 20-stock sampling of the S&P 500 Index across all of Standard & Poor's defined sectors. This customized basket can be changed stock by stock if an investor wishes. In either case investors purchase the entire basket of stocks with the single click of a mouse. A basket can hold from 1 to 50 stocks, but the ready-to-go baskets generally have 20 to 30 stocks. Some focus on a particular sector or industry, whereas others are more broadly based. Rather than charging per trade, investors pay a low annual fee, and instead of buying stocks in shares, they are purchased in dollars. Shares in such a system are purchased on a fractional basis. Using investment research tools that are now widely available on the Internet, investors can figure out their strategy and choose their basket securities intelligently.

In theory, investors have always been able to buy diversified baskets of stocks. But in practice this type of investing has only been available to the wealthiest investors or those who had ample time or ability to analyze and research hundreds of stocks. Investors need 20, 30, or 40 stocks in their portfolios to maximize the benefits of diversification. Typically, investors also have to pay trading commissions for each stock and pay again each time they add to a portfolio or make any other change. Mutual funds seemed to have solved some of these problems, but investors would get hit with capital gains taxes at the end of the year, which are beyond their control, even if their fund had gone down in value. Investors didn't have the flexibility over their mutual funds to sell some losers to balance out the winners in their portfolio. Many mutual funds also tie in their shareholders to certain periods of time and require extra fees if one wishes to sell out earlier. Basket trading is the groundbreaking technology that has combined the gain potentials of the securities market, the diversification and ease of the mutual fund, and the user interactivity of the online experience.

## A New Breed Evolved

Some online ventures are also analyzing financial institutions, their analysts, and the advice they have given and continue to give to the investing population. This type of strategy can be used to see who has truly delivered results rather than who has just sold a large amount of stock. These advantages for investors have not been available in the past. Analysts would issue their recommendations, and investors would flock to their command. But history has shown that conflicts of interests have arisen between brokers and their firms. Investors have found—the hard way in many cases —much of the advice was not based on true and honest research. Problems such as this have spread the feeling of distrust within the investor community. Vague terms have been used as official stock ratings, and investors have acted upon them improperly. Analysts almost always have a Sell rating available, yet it's rarely used. Usually when a stock is no longer attractive, an analyst would simply drop coverage rather than issue a Sell rating. There have even been times when stocks with lower ratings have performed better than stocks with higher ratings.

Today, however, online companies that propose to analyze the returns of the past, based on analysts' opinions, are beginning to set the path straight once and for all. Investors can now combine the research of such companies with basket trading and truly create their own diversified and tax-controllable portfolios while saving greatly on trading fees. A committee of congress members, at a recent congressional hearing, criticized investment banks for not making research clear for ordinary individual investors. They also spoke about banks not sufficiently disclosing their business ties with the companies they covered. Financial institutions, in a reply to the recent drop in investor confidence, have begun to monitor their analysts more closely and have in many cases simplified their ratings systems. A number of firms are now promising to disclose, in their analyst reports, when they have had business relations with a company they cover.

A speech given by Frank Zarb, the chairman of the National Association of Securities Dealers (NASD), in 1999 predicted a future of investing where trading securities will be digital, global, and accessible 24 hours a day. People will be able to get quotes as well as execute trades instantly anytime of the day or night, anywhere in the world, with stock markets linked and almost all electronic. He also predicted certain aspects of the current market becoming obsolete in the up-and-coming technological era, such as the trading floor and even paper. Investors will commonly access their portfolios as well as do their research through various handheld devices and even use cellular phones to handle all their financial transactions. People will soon be able to receive customized reports on the performance of their portfolios to their car's onboard computer while driving to and from work—a dangerous proposition during a bear market.

The stock market has been evolving rapidly. As the investors of the world help improve technology, the stock market evolves its systems as well. Information is now widely available, with thousands of online investment-related companies ready to assist common, educated, and even aggressive investors. Many people, notwithstanding the market's occasional losses, continue to renew their interests in investing. Constant improvements and revisions to the existing system are the leading contributors to this phenomenon. Industry professionals have stated, "Past performance is no guarantee of future results," and they have used this disclaimer for many years. This may still hold true, but with recent advancements and vast amounts of data, powerful strategies can be created to improve one's chances for success.

# 8

# REPUTATION, TRUST, AND STATISTICAL VENGEANCE: TRUST BUT VERIFY

*At first you work for your reputation, and then your reputation works for you.*

Understanding this ancient saying attests that reputation and, consequently, the trust that follows are among the most precious things in life that money can't buy. When people trust someone, it's typically based on the honesty, integrity, and solid reputations these individuals or organizations possess. Most people think they know the meaning of trust based on their personal experiences; they also believe and look at trust as if it were a single entity.

But what is trust and how does it originate? According to Dr. Duane C. Tway, Jr., in his 1993 dissertation, *A Construct of Trust*, trust is "the state of readiness for unguarded interaction with someone or something." He developed a model of trust that consists of three components: the capacity to believe, the perception of competence, and the perception of intentions.

If we follow Tway's advice and subdivide trust into these three components, the word *trust* becomes easier to understand. The first element of trust is totally reliant on us and no one else. The capacity to trust is shaped from our own life experiences and our willingness to risk trusting others. The second element of trust is formed through our view that the people with whom we interact perform their function ably, given their established reputation in the field. The perception of someone's intentions, as defined by Tway, is our opinion that their actions, words, and motivating factors are set by mutually serving goals rather than self-serving goals.

After presenting this elaborate definition of trust, the following questions arise: Can investors—in view of recent Wall Street debacles—continue to have the capacity to trust analysts? Can investors perceive them to be competent? What are investors' perception of analysts' true intentions?

Analysts' intentions are indeed skewed somewhat, due to the conflict of interest inherent in their workplace. Therefore, their intentions are often questionable. Their competence level, however, although inconsistent, can be identified and sorted out. If investors could have access to tools that enabled them to sort analysts by their ability and then cross-reference their intentions to make sure they are mutual, the result would undoubtedly increase investors' capacity to trust the analysts and their recommendations.

The bottom line is that on many occasions analysts' own intentions will affect their overall performance. If their intention is to satisfy their investment banking houses or corporate management rather than investors, their recommendation performance will suffer. Therefore, the more their intentions diverge from investors' intentions or needs, the further their perceived competence will suffer. This trend in turn will damage the reputation of analysts and compel investors not to trust those analysts and their opinions.

The opposite is also true. If an analyst's intention is to satisfy the investor, then his or her performance should improve in the eyes of the investor. This leads to a positive perception of competence, improvement in his or her reputation, and a willingness for investors to listen to and lend credence to their recommendations. It's a vicious cycle (see Figure 8-1).

Nevertheless, just like people in every profession, analysts tend to reveal over time their shortcomings and lack of ability. No mat-

Perception of Competence

Perception of Intentions

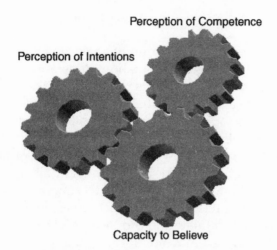

Capacity to Believe

**Fig. 8-1.   Construct of trust between investors and analysts.**

ter what their intentions might be, their performance may still be inadequate. The fact of the matter is that many are not very good at what they do.

Vilfredo Pareto (1848–1923) was an Italian economist who in 1906 observed that 20 percent of the Italian people possess 80 percent of their country's wealth, while the other 80 percent possess the remaining 20 percent. Since then, this finding has been applied to a variety of applications and has become known as Pareto's principle, or the 80–20 rule. This 80–20 blend reminds us that the relationship between input and output is not balanced. For example, Dr. Yuval Lirov, who was the head of the technology infrastructure support group at Lehman Brothers with 100 people in his organization, reminded me of this principle a long time ago. He said that in his organization, approximately 20 percent of the employees perform 80 percent of the workload, while the other 80 percent perform the remaining 20 percent. Could financial analysts conform to the same statistics? Is it possible that 20 percent of the analysts in any organization actually produce 80 percent of the good recommendations? It's certainly not out of the question.

In the end we are still faced with the question of whom we can trust and where we can turn to get reliable investment advice. Who deserves our undivided attention and hard-earned savings? The answers to these questions are easier to find than a lot of people might imagine.

The secret is to look for a group of analysts with good performance and, therefore, a good reputation. We want to identify those analysts whose recommendations produced market-beating results in the past. If we can identify that group of analysts, then the first barrier to finding outstanding research will be conquered. After overcoming that obstacle, the investor will have a list of great performers (analysts). The list will not contain the most popular ones like Henry Blodget, who made a substantial number of Buy recommendations that should have been Sell. Of course, no one is perfect, and investors must remember that fact. Investors need to identify analysts who can formulate and produce a greater number of good, as opposed to bad, recommendations.

Once this investigation is complete, the investor ends up with a list of reputable analysts. As chosen analysts on this list dispatch new recommendations, the investor needs to review and analyze each recommendation further to check for possible conflicts of interests or other discrepancies. The investor needs to become skilled at how to get a second opinion. Investors cannot only rely on analysts' recommendations alone. They must do some additional homework on their own. All this may sound like a lot of difficult and cumbersome work, but it is not. In most cases it's a clear-cut and straightforward process.

## Generating Potential Sources of Ideas

According to the SEC, there are more than 17,000 publicly traded companies. With so many firms out there, every investor knows that it's impossible to track them all. The universe for every investor must become smaller, and it often does. But smaller should not mean closed to expansion. Investors should keep it small but not make it an impregnable fortress for new ideas. Many individual investors make their stock universe so small that it interferes with rather than assists their quest to generate market-beating results. Even professional money managers take this small universe concept to the extreme. However, the individual investor does it more often. It is not unusual to observe people buying and selling the same stocks over and over again.

A question such as "What stocks do you own?" frequently generates an answer that is simply the most popular stocks such as America Online, Cisco, Microsoft, Intel, and the like. Individual investors often do not want to hear about exploring and investigating new investment ideas and strategies. The usual reply is, "I don't know this company." Regrettably, many investors are stubborn, and stubbornness often leads to ignorance, and ignorance always leads to defeat. On the other side of the spectrum, some investors rush out and purchase stocks without ever performing any due diligence. They buy a stock because their dentist recommended it, for instance.

In previous chapters we touched on the availability of numerous sources for investment advice. "Buy this stock" or "sell that stock" is heard all around us. Every financial TV show and every financial magazine has numerous advisers who generate new ideas for their viewers and readers, respectively. Wall Street spends hundreds of millions and perhaps billions of dollars per year to generate a ton of research daily. Upgrades, downgrades, resumed coverage, or initiated coverage is available for free and/or for a fee to individual investors. But how good is this research? It has become apparent that the only thing lacking with all this advice and research was an unbiased, third-party performance review. Or to put it differently, has anyone researched the research?

Academics for years have published studies on the performance and reliability of analysts' recommendations. Unfortunately, to my knowledge no one ever tried to sort this research by financial institution or individual analyst. The approach has been to take all Strong Buy and/or Buy recommendations, combine them across all brokerage houses, and produce overall performance results. This information was extremely interesting, but it did not produce conclusions that were of help to investors.

Then *The Wall Street Journal* came along and began to produce a section every summer entitled "All Star Analysts." The result of this work was about as helpful to the individual investor as the research from academics. The reason for this critical assessment is twofold. First, to become an all star analyst, the qualified participant needed only one outstanding stock recommendation. It was not based on the overall performance of all picks but just one. For instance, if I was a participant (analyst) and made ten Buy recommendations and nine of them tanked but one jumped 300 percent, I would become nominated and most likely join the all star analyst team. Yet another analyst who also made ten recommendations in the same industry that produced seven positive results and on average beat my overall performance handsomely would not be named an "all star analyst" because no single stock pick produced a 300 percent gainer. In the real world, it does not work that way. A Hail Mary pass rarely wins a football game.

The other problem confronting the individual investor's ability to interpret the results from the all star analyst report is the fact that small investors often do not hear or have access to analysts' names. Individual investors rarely hear that Bill Schmitt from CIBC World Markets just upgraded stock X from Hold to Buy or that Jason Ader of Bear Stearns downgraded stock Y from Buy to Neutral—and so on. If an individual investor tries to purchase recommendation data or earnings data that include the analyst's name from First Call, Multex, or Zacks, he or she will be turned down immediately. In the majority of cases, this information is off limits to a person who wants to manage his or her own money, even if he or she was willing to pay $5000 per month for it. There is a contractual obligation between certain financial institutions and data providers not to release this information to the general public. Only institutional clients are allowed to buy and access this information—period. So how can individual investors really benefit from *The Wall Street Journal's* all star analysts?

For an average individual investor, the only recommendation data available come in the format displayed in Figure 8-2. Many popular Web sites, including www.msn.com, www.yahoo.com, and others, display and update these data daily.

| Company | Symbol | Firm Issuing Recommendation | Previous Recommendation | New Recommendation |
|---|---|---|---|---|
| Scientific-Atlanta | SFA | Gerard Klauer Mattison | Neutral | **Buy** |
| ExtremeNetworks | EXTR | Needham & Co. | Underperform | **Hold** |
| Union Planters | UPC | Prudential | Sell | **Hold** |
| First Virginia Banks | FVB | Prudential | Sell | **Hold** |
| Compass Bancshares | CBSS | Prudential | Sell | **Hold** |

**Fig. 8-2. Typical list of stock recommendations as displayed on the Web.**

The information in this figure displays the following from left to right: companies that receive new or modified recommendations, their respective symbols, the financial institution that issued the recommendation, the previous recommendation, and the new adjusted recommendation. But where is the name of the analyst? It is quite hard to find analysts' names, unless you are a client of that specific financial institution or are willing to pay approximately $30 per average report that usually covers one stock with latest recommendation (see chapter 5). Therefore, analysts are not easy to find, and their past performances are elusive if you do find them.

Fortunately, at this juncture companies such as MarketPerform.com and Investars.com came along to analyze information that is easily accessible to the individual investor and is based on the performance of financial institutions rather than the analysts. Essentially, this concept underscores the philosophy that the buck stops with the organization, not with the analyst. Analysts, just like other employees, come and go. The franchise (i.e., brokerage house), on the other hand, endures. That is why investors must start holding financial institutions responsible for actions their employees undertake. If the investment banking side of the business is pressuring the research team to make ridiculous recommendations, isn't it time for research to fight back and tell those investment bankers, "Hey guys, we are being watched and analyzed. If we continue issuing positive recommendations solely to generate investment banking fees, pretty soon our recommendations will not be worth a dime."

On March 5, 2002, an article in *The Wall Street Journal* revealed the story of Chung Wu, an adviser who was fired from UBS Paine Webber for directing his clients to reduce their exposure to Enron stock in August 2001. Mr. Wu said, "I told the truth to my clients." The e-mail continued to say that the "financial situation is deteriorating." He was fired from UBS the same day the e-mail was sent. According to Mr. Wu, UBS Paine Webber renounced his Sell recommendation, saying the firm did not approve it. UBS countered that Mr. Wu was fired because he sent the aforementioned e-mail without authorization.

From this article we can deduce, even though we knew it all along, that all recommendations issued by financial analysts need an approval from the brokerage house's upper echelons. Thus, the following simple theory comes to mind. If investors want to create independent research departments within financial institutions, it's time to hold the firms and the analysts responsible for the overall recommendation performance. Currently, there is no accountability from financial institutions. Analysts are frequently treated as kindling. Wall Street investment banking and other departments use them for a certain period of time and then discard them. Henry Blodget, who recently took a package from Merrill Lynch, is a perfect example.

The performance results of many financial institutions and their respective rating systems (i.e., Buy, Hold, Sell) are now updated and offered on a daily basis (not just once a year) to anyone who cares to know. With that in mind, investors finally have the ability to research accessible data, and this enables them to find financial institutions whose research is possibly worth following. This leads us to our next subject: building and executing a recommendation-based trading strategy.

## Find, Build, and Execute a Strategy

Strategy consists of due diligence, planning, management, and execution. It's the groundwork that needs to take place before making a trade. If you are receptive toward the fundamental analysis side of research, it would be prudent to familiarize yourself with a company's business model and financial reports. For those who are inclined toward the technical analysis path, serious study (and a little bit of luck) is required. Once a strategy is selected, it's important to continue practicing common sense. And above all avoid using margin and buying IPOs. (For other fundamental elements, please refer to Chapter 2.)

Before you consider yourself a candidate to purchase stocks, it's paramount to make sure your financial house is in order: Get out of debt and establish through your employer a 401(k) or 403(b) plan and/or an IRA. Be sure you have enough money to take care of life's necessities. Only then consider investing in stocks. Remember that money allocated to stock investing—some funds should be invested into bonds—should be unnecessary for everyday living. You should not foresee the need to use it any time in the next 3, 5, 10, or more years.

After that, a champion-challengers strategy needs to be created, as discussed in Chapter 1. As a guiding principle, assign and invest 80 percent of these funds into the S&P 500 Index Fund and make that your champion-based strategy. It has been mentioned on more than a few occasions that this index fund beats eight of ten professional money managers. The other 20 percent of your funds should be assigned to individual stocks that adhere to your chosen rules and strategies. If one of your challenger strategies consistently—at least for 3 years—outperforms the champion strategy, consider switching the champion and replacing it with the winning challenger strategy. For a detailed explanation of this process, please refer to Chapter 1.

It must become clear to every investor who wants to start trading stocks and/or improve his or her stock-trading skills that it is wise to seek counsel and listen to advice. But at the end of the day, the buck stops with the investor and his or her own hard-earned savings. Don't allow someone else to press the trigger for you without knowing and understanding the consequences.

## The Formula

Up to this point, our story has spanned a variety of topics that individual investors can encounter in their quest to beat the market. We looked at the history and evolution of brokers and the various trading vehicles available. We also defined in Chapter 6 why it is of utmost importance to understand and appreciate the concept of food chains in capital markets. We provided an example of how Intel and Dell Computer Corporation businesses intertwine to provide evidence for this line of reasoning. In Chapter 4 we looked at analysts and the conflict of interests that can cloud their recommendations. In addition a clear and concise solution to interpreting financial statements was unwrapped and simplified in Chapter 5. The discussion of media and its effects on the psyche of the individual investor were analyzed as well. Furthermore, the significance of analyzing the results of your strategies and disciplines, if you have them, was furnished with the champion-challenger concept. The fundamental elements, with numerous examples of how they can hurt or benefit the investor, were discussed as well.

Ideally, all this information has prepared the reader for the chapters that follow.

The focus of the rest of this book will revolve around the process of building specific trading strategies that are based on recommendations and advice produced by sell-side analysts. The strategies and disciplines laid out in the pages ahead will demonstrate how to collect and decipher these recommendations systematically and then use them to beat the market. Initially, performance results will show what investors can expect if they follow these recommendations blindly—that is, without performing any additional investigation. Later we will apply certain strategies that will illustrate how accepting certain recommendations while rejecting others will produce better results and, therefore, aid them in becoming better investors. A patient reader will understand why he or she would not want to own Qualcomm Inc. (QCOM) at $500, Amazon (AMZN) at $400, Yahoo! (YHOO) at $250, or Enron (ENE) at $90.

The formula used to quantify results will be quite familiar to every investor. It will be portfolio-based and will operate on a what-if scenario. Since we will be dealing with and analyzing recommendations issued by major financial institutions, the following question will be applied: What if I bought an equal amount of stock ($1000) every time Lehman Brothers issued a Strong Buy recommendation? The starting, or purchase, price for every stock will be the closing price on the day the actual recommendation was issued and not the closing price of the day before. Financial institutions extensively use the closing price from the day before the recommendation was issued, which tends to inflate results somewhat. Our goal is to determine and use a purchase price at which an average investor can acquire the stock in substantial quantity.

Let's then keep this stock in this hypothetical Lehman Brothers' Strong Buy portfolio until Lehman Brothers changes its opinion and the recommendation to something other than a Strong Buy rating, perhaps a Buy or a Hold or, less likely, a Sell rating. Terminating coverage will also trigger a sell transaction. On the day this rating change occurs, the system will automatically sell that stock at the closing price on that same day. The profit or loss from this particular transaction will be recorded. This process will be repeated for all stocks that share Lehman Brothers' Strong Buy recommendation.

The system can perform the same process for every other recommendation that Lehman Brothers issues, such as Buy, Market Perform, and Underperform. It can also segment every recommendation into sector and industry. This will help the user identify which teams of analysts within a particular financial institution excel and which do not.

### Who Is Good and Who Is . . .

Bank of America (BAC) is one of the most active providers of recommendations to the investment community. All stocks that continue to receive coverage from Bank of America fall into one of four rating categories. It is important to know that financial institutions at times change the names and/or the number of rating categories they use. The top-rated category at Bank of America as of this writing is Strong Buy. Stocks in this rating category are judged by Bank of America's analysts to outperform the market during the following 12 months, typically by 10 or more percentage points. The second category is Buy. Stocks in this category are considered by the same analysts to outperform the market by 5 percent or more. The Market Perform category (which has nothing to do with the MarketPerform.com Web site) combines stocks that the same group of analysts believes will perform in line with the market, and the "Underperform" category represents stocks that will underperform the market, usually by 10 percent or more.

Now that the stage is set, let's start examining the goods. Our story of analyzing Bank of America and its analysts will begin on a cold February morning in 1999. The Dow Jones Industrial Average was trading in the 9300-point range, the NASDAQ was within the 2500 range, and the S&P 500 Index was hovering around 1250. As of this writing, the Dow Jones Industrial Average is at the 9800 mark, the NASDAQ is limping around the 1800-point range, and the S&P 500 Index, the most widely used benchmark, is at 1100.

Our hypothetical trading system included 3 years worth of data beginning in February 1999. During this time, a raging bull market of 1999 and two agonizingly bearish years contributed to the results. The group of stocks that shared a Strong Buy rating unfortunately managed to produce a loss of 10.57 percent. This result did not include trading fees or the impact of bid-ask price disparities.

To have a reference point, it's important to mention that during those 3 years the S&P 500 Index lost 10 percent. Thus, a hypothetical investor would perform in line with the market before expenses.

Looking at certain recommendations within this grouping, we naturally came across some great calls. For example, on August 10, 1999, Bank of America issued a Strong Buy recommendation on Integrated Device Technology Inc. (IDTI). The stock performed really well after that call, and although the analyst covering this stock did not downgrade IDTI all the way at the top, he did manage to downgrade it on October 27, 2000, allowing investors who followed this advice to pocket a 264 percent gain (see Figure 8-3).

Unfortunately, if investors continued to initiate trades during this 3-year period based solely on the news that Bank of America issued a Strong Buy recommendation, they would have ended up owning shares of Scientific-Atlanta, Inc. (SFA). This transaction would have taken place on April 20, 2001, at a purchase price of $63.05. By August 17, 2001, when Bank of America finally changed its opinion on Scientific-Atlanta and downgraded it to a Market Perform rating, the stock lost more than 66 percent of its value and closed at $21.24 per share (see Figure 8-4).

Regrettably, there were more Strong Buy recommendations that resembled Scientific-Atlanta than Integrated Device Technology.

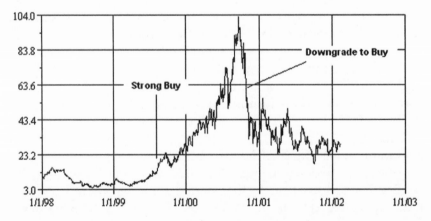

**Fig. 8-3.** Integrated Device Technology Inc. (IDTI) price chart.

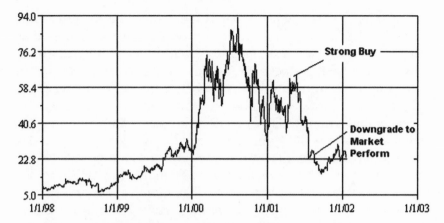

**Fig. 8-4.   Bank of America recommendations and price chart for Scientific-Atlanta, Inc. (SFA).**

But Bank of America's Buy rating produced better results. The overall return for stocks that shared this recommendation managed to squeeze out a tiny profit of 0.21 percent, thus beating the market, which lost 10 percent during this time and reaching the goals Bank of America's analysts set out to achieve for this rating. The Market Perform rating produced even better results, managing to deliver a 3.44 percent return. So much for the typical assessment that Strong Buy means Buy, Buy means Hold, and Hold—in this case Market Perform—means Sell. The group of stocks that shared the undesirable Underperform rating did indeed produce a poor showing by losing 17.1 percent.

One of the most frequently asked questions by our users revolves around the concern of being late in receiving upgrades/downgrades information. A typical question these people ask is: What happens if I execute a Buy transaction a day after a Strong Buy recommendation was issued? Wouldn't that wipe out most of the gains associated with this positive recommendation issued by a major financial institution? Another way to look at it is instead of buying stocks on the day a Strong Buy rating is issued, what would happen if you always bought the upgraded stock on the following day? Fortunately, the system allows you to test this hypothetical scenario with ease. Buying a stock 1 day after Bank of America issued a Strong Buy recommendation would produce a loss of

10.92 percent. This suggests that being a day late in purchasing stocks rated as a Strong Buy would increase your loss by less than half of 1 percent. From a statistical point of view, the difference between purchasing stocks on the day of the recommendation or waiting and executing the same transaction on the following day is insignificant, especially for long-term investors.

Interestingly, hundreds of people were interested in finding out how the overall results would be affected if they were to buy a day after the recommendation was issued, but no one posed the following question: What if I bought a stock on the day its Strong Buy recommendation was issued and sold it 6 months later or if the recommendation was changed, whichever occurred first? As an example let's trace the recent history of recommendations affecting a company called PC Connection, Inc. (PCCC). On January 26, 2000, Bank of America issued a Strong Buy recommendation on PCCC. Its closing price that day was $20.54 on a split-adjusted basis. However, instead of holding PCCC until the downgrade, which occurred on December 8, 2000, we sold it on July 26, 2000 (the 6-month "anniversary" of the recommendation) at $52.75 per share. This transaction produced a 157 percent gain. Waiting to sell this stock until Bank of America finally downgraded it on December 8, 2000, would have represented a 55 percent loss (selling price $9.81).

It is important to understand that this example underscores the point that holding on to a stock until a financial institution downgrades it is a futile strategy. Clearly, not all stocks receiving a Strong Buy recommendation will gain 150 percent within 6 months. However, this particular strategy (buying on the day a Strong Buy recommendation was issued and selling it 6 months later) would return an average 25.79 percent gain for the Strong Buy ratings at Bank of America. If you compare this result to a 10.57 percent loss when holding on to stocks until analysts issue the downgrade, the result becomes crystal clear. The difference in performance between these two strategies undoubtedly produces statistically significant results, even though the same Strong Buy recommendations from the same financial institution were used as the basis for trading.

In addition to the example from Bank of America, let's briefly analyze recommendation performance from Merrill Lynch. The rating model at Merrill Lynch is different from other financial institutions because each of their recommendations consists of two parts instead of one. The first part of every recommendation refers to near-term expectations—usually 12 months—and the second part refers to long-term expectations for the stock. For this example, we will analyze the near-term portion of the recommendation only.

Like many other financial institutions, Merrill Lynch has Strong Buy, Buy, Neutral, and recently combined Reduce/Sell ratings. And not unlike others, the performances of these recommendations have a very similar trend (see Figure 8-5).

Once more the dates for analyzing Merrill's recommendations span a 3-year time frame of February 1999 through February 2002. Strong Buy recommendations produced a disappointing 3.34 percent loss. If an investor decided to purchase these stocks 1 day after the recommendation was issued, the loss would increase to 3.96 percent. Once again the result is insignificant statistically. The Buy rating, as was the case with Bank of America's second-best rating, managed to outperform Merrill's best rating, delivering a positive 0.88 percent return. The Neutral rating also managed to outperform Strong Buy, losing only 1.01 percent of its value. Stocks that received a Reduce/Sell recommendation provided results consistent with the goals of this rating and lost 25.46 percent. This clearly illustrates that investors should not doubt Merrill's ability to identify stocks that will drop to a lower altitude.

But what would happen if we applied the same strategy to Merrill's Strong Buy rating that we did to Bank of America's Strong Buy? Suppose we purchase stocks that receive a Strong Buy recommendation from Merrill Lynch and hold them for 6 months rather than waiting for Merrill to downgrade them. The result is almost as convincing as the one achieved with Bank of America. Instead of a 3.34 percent loss, a gain of 16.26 percent would have been accomplished. Once again this produces a statistically meaningful variance.

| Merrill Lynch | Strong Buy | Buy | Neutral | Reduce/Sell |
|---|---|---|---|---|
| Purchase day 1 | −3.34% | 0.88% | −1.01% | −25.46% |
| Purchase day 2 | −3.96% | 0.74% | | −23.07% |
| Purchase day (1) and sell day (130), approximately 6 months | | | 16.26% | 1.53% |

**Fig. 8-5.    Merrill Lynch recommendations.**

At this juncture it would be appropriate to remind the reader that these results continue to group together all analysts within the selected financial institutions. However, what if 20 percent of the analysts within Bank of America and Merrill Lynch provided 80 percent of the good recommendations and 20 percent of the poor recommendations while the remaining 80 percent of the analysts provided 20 percent of the good recommendations and 80 percent of the poor recommendations? If that is the case, our next maneuver is to track down those teams of analysts who truly stand out and follow their advice for further investigation. But how can this be achieved? This is where the process of segmenting each recommendation into sectors and industries becomes so useful. Instead of looking at each analyst individually, we analyze teams of analysts who specialize in certain sectors and industries.[1]

The analyst recommendation data in this example revealed an interesting trait. Strong Buy recommendations tend to provide positive results for up to 6 months. After that point is reached, the performance of these recommendations runs out of steam and starts to head lower. This suggests among other things that analysts are too slow to downgrade stocks. Therefore, we must analyze results with a 6-month and/or 12-month cutoff option. Basically, every time a financial institution issues a Strong Buy recommendation, we will buy that stock and hold it for a period of 6 months. On the 6-month anniversary date, sometimes referred to as a 6-month artificial maturity date, we sell that stock. We analyze the results of this strategy on a sector level rather than across the whole firm to make our examples smaller and more manageable. After that we perform a second opinion check to accept or reject certain trades.

This process should improve our overall result. However, it is important to note that utilizing such strategies will occasionally lead to the rejection of stocks that would have a positive contribution. Nonetheless, many losers will be avoided, and the overall return will undoubtedly improve.

Here is a hypothetical stock-by-stock trade scenario if you were to follow Merrill Lynch's Strong Buy recommendation history blindly in the utilities sector. The only variables under your control

[1]Our system displays best performing recommendations by sector on home page. To view them, please log on to www.marketperform.com.

in this scenario are your purchase day and your sell (maturity) day. The purchase day is always the day the Strong Buy recommendation was issued, and the maturity day is always 130 business days (approximately 6 months) after that. Figure 8-6 shows the results. (The change box all the way to the right keeps track of why individual trades were accepted or rejected.) The exercise assumes $1000 per trade.

During the span of almost 3 years, the average return was 8.37 percent. On closer examination of these hypothetical trades, we find that one stock in particular has been a huge disappointment. That stock is Active Power Corp. (ACPW), which lost more than 63 percent in value. The question immediately arises whether the investor could have avoided this stock in the first place. And if the answer is yes, the next question is how. What element does ACPW contain, if any, that could have aroused the investor's suspicion? Let's investigate this stock a little more closely.

Merrill Lynch issued a Strong Buy recommendation for ACPW on February 5, 2001. The reason for issuing this upgrade was accompanied with the following note: "Shares have been weak ahead of today's lockup expiration." For an experienced investigator/investor, "lockup expiration" are dirty words. A lockup is a contractual obligation between the underwriters and insiders of the company that does not permit them to sell shares for a specified period of time. After lockups expire, insiders who were restricted to sell their shares are allowed to start selling, often resulting in a severe deterioration of stock price.

This note reveals another major tip. As you will recall from Chapter 2, fundamental rule 4 stated: Investing in IPOs is a trap. Fortunately, the investor does not need to examine these notes along with the ridiculous upgrade to know it's an IPO. All the investor had to do was examine the historical price chart of ACPW on the day this recommendation was issued. This would immediately reveal that ACPW has been trading for less than 1 year and thus qualified in our view to be labeled as an IPO. Clearly, an observation that "Shares have been weak ahead of today's lockup expiration" together with a Strong Buy recommendation does not make any sense whatsoever. How any investor, except the insiders who are about to start selling, can benefit from buying a stock on the day lockup expires is beyond any rational logic. Upgrading a

| Symbol | Name | Purchase-Date | Buy-price | #-of-shares | Sell-date | Sell-price | Gain Loss $ | Gain Loss % | Change |
|---|---|---|---|---|---|---|---|---|---|
| MDU | MDU Resources | 4/28/99 | 21.63 | 46.23 | 10/29/99 | 23.38 | 80.91 | 8.09 | |
| NFG | National Fuel Gas | 8/31/99 | 23.53 | 42.5 | 3/3/00 | 20.72 | -119.42 | -11.94 | |
| EXC | Exelon Corp | 12/6/99 | 33.5 | 29.85 | 6/7/00 | 41.81 | 248.06 | 24.81 | |
| AVA | Avista Corp | 1/12/00 | 18.38 | 54.41 | 6/21/00 | 19 | 33.73 | 3.37 | |
| KSE | KeySpan Corp | 3/17/00 | 24.69 | 40.5 | 9/19/00 | 36.19 | 465.67 | 46.57 | |
| NRG | NRG Energy | 6/6/00 | 17.19 | 58.18 | 12/7/00 | 23 | 338.18 | 33.82 | Spin-off |
| GAS | NICOR Inc | 7/20/00 | 34.06 | 29.36 | 1/24/01 | 38.44 | 128.44 | 12.84 | |
| CPN | Calpine Corp | 8/14/00 | 43.62 | 22.92 | 2/16/01 | 47.24 | 82.87 | 8.29 | |
| STR | Questar Corp | 8/17/00 | 21.25 | 47.06 | 2/22/01 | 27.58 | 297.88 | 29.79 | |
| ORN | Orion Power | 12/11/00 | 22.06 | 45.33 | 6/18/01 | 24.73 | 120.91 | 12.09 | IPO |
| ACPW | Active Power | 2/5/01 | 20.5 | 48.78 | 8/9/01 | 7.54 | -632.2 | -63.22 | IPO |
| VVC | Vectren Corp | 2/12/01 | 22.1 | 45.25 | 8/16/01 | 20.17 | -87.33 | -8.73 | |
| BGY | British Energy | 3/1/01 | 16.3 | 61.35 | 9/4/01 | 19.25 | 180.98 | 18.1 | ADR |
| TXU | TXU Corp | 11/5/01 | 48.65 | 20.55 | 2/11/02 | 50.25 | 32.89 | 3.29 | |

Fig. 8-6.  Merrill Lynch Strong Buy sector with utilities purchase day (1) and sell day (130).

stock such as ACPW on the day the lockup period expires clearly depicts a diverging motivating dynamic. If it wasn't for high-quality results from Merrill's analysts in the utilities sector in aggregate, a note such as this coupled with a Strong Buy recommendation can really affect our perception of their competence level. If such behavior is consistent, the investor should start looking for better advice.

Given what we have witnessed up to this point, it's reasonable to make the following logical observation. Avoiding IPOs in the utilities sector that Merrill Lynch rates as Strong Buy would result in rejection and elimination of the biggest loser in this portfolio. The other IPOs on this list included NRG Energy (NRG), Orion Power (ORN), and British Energy (BGY). Why should the investor consider purchasing NRG and BGY while rejecting ORN? The reason investor conceivably can break our rule has to do with how these companies became IPOs. NRG energy was a spinoff from a wholly owned subsidiary of Northern States Power Company. Spinoffs, unlike other IPOs, usually perform well. There are, of course, noted exceptions such as Palm Pilot (PALM); however, from a historical perspective, they generally tend to outperform the market. Big companies usually spin off subsidiaries to unlock value. Subsidiaries that start life as independent companies typically represent profitable, established, fast-growing organizations. British Energy, although not a spinoff, was a firm that traded on the London Stock Exchange for many years and continues to trade. It came to the North American markets as American depositary receipts (ADRs).

In summary, if the investor decided to bypass every IPO, whether it was a spinoff, a new ADR, or anything else, the result would have been a gain of 11.64 percent instead of 8.37 percent when trading on recommendation news only. However, if the investor decided that spinoffs and ADRs are acceptable to purchase, the overall gain would reach the 15 percent mark.

Morgan Stanley Dean Witter as well as Gerard Klauer Mattison & Company have also performed well in the utilities sector. Following is a hypothetical trading scenario based on recommendations received from Gerard Klauer Mattison in the utilities sector. This time there were no IPOs. Perhaps that is why we don't see a stock that managed to decline 60 percent or more in this figure.

Once more it would be beneficial to remind the reader that waiting to sell until analysts downgrade these stocks would result in a 2.72 percent gain. However, utilizing a 6-month artificial maturity option would earn a 22.05 percent return.

Figure 8-7 illustrates this scenario. The rightmost heading informs the investor whether the stock was under (U) the 50-day moving average or above (A) it. The second letter informs the investor about the 200-day moving average, and again U stands for under and A represents above. As you can see, the best performer of the group (Calpine Corporation) was trading above the 50- and 200-day moving averages on September 24, 1999. However, before the investor jumps to the conclusion to purchase stocks only if they trade above 50- and 200-day moving averages, I suggest a moment's reflection. Our tests of this option repeatedly revealed no conclusive results.

Learning from the earlier example and after further analysis, an investor might pose a question. Calpine Corp. (CPN), the biggest winner in this particular portfolio, was sold at $21.26 per share, yet it continued to go higher and reached the mid-$50s before dropping to approximately $8 per share in February 2002. Is there a way not to sell this stock so early and at the same time not to hold it until the bitter end when not only all your profits are wiped out but a nice portion of your principal—the money you invested in the first place—is wiped out as well? How can an investor hold on just a little bit longer and maximize the profit? The answer to this question is not easy. One thing that seemed to work was extending the maturity date from 6 months to 12 months. The overall results improved substantially. At 12 months Gerard Klauer Mattison returns jumped to a whopping 93.59 percent. (See the Appendix for step-by-step instructions on how to set up and execute this particular strategy.) Morgan Stanley Dean Witter managed a respectable 21.23 percent return, and Merrill Lynch—without ACPW and ORN —produced 18.86 percent.

There is a benefit to extending the maturity date a day or two past the 1-year anniversary of the purchase date that has to do with tax implications. Current tax laws treat stock sales after a 1-year holding period as capital gains. This means that a 20 percent federal tax rate would be applied to your gains, instead of your income bracket tax rate, which could be much higher. Therefore,

| Symbol | Name | Purchase-Date | Buy-price | #-of-shares | Sell-date | Sell-price | Gain Loss $ | Gain Loss % | MA 50/200 |
|---|---|---|---|---|---|---|---|---|---|
| EXC | Exelon Corp | 9/15/99 | 40.81 | 24.5 | 3/17/00 | 38.5 | $(56.75) | -5.68% | U/U |
| CPN | Calpine Corp | 9/24/99 | 10.24 | 97.7 | 3/28/00 | 21.26 | $1,077.10 | 107.71% | A/A |
| PNW | Pinnacle West | 9/27/99 | 35.69 | 28.02 | 3/29/00 | 27.5 | $(229.45) | -22.95% | U/U |
| DQE | DQE Inc | 9/28/99 | 37.63 | 26.57 | 3/30/00 | 46.38 | $232.32 | 23.23% | U/U |
| FPL | FPL Group Inc | 10/18/99 | 49.38 | 20.25 | 4/19/00 | 44.88 | $(91.18) | -9.12% | U/U |
| D | Dominion Resources | 4/10/00 | 40.25 | 24.84 | 10/11/00 | 55.94 | $389.55 | 38.95% | A/U |

Fig. 8-7. Gerard Klauer Mattison & Company recommendations in the utilities sector.

extending the maturity date appears to benefit the investor from two different angles.

But before accepting this solution of extending the holding period from 6 months to 12 months, there is a word of caution. The process does not improve performance results consistently. As in our previous example with PC Connection, when Bank of America issued a Strong Buy recommendation on January 26, 2000, waiting for the 1-year anniversary would have resulted in a substantial loss rather than a 157 percent gain. Extending the artificial maturity date to 12 months instead of 6 reduced overall results from a 25.79 percent gain to 10.7 percent.

We have found that setting maturity dates is valuable and needs to be practiced respectfully for successful results. Our examples from the utilities section illustrate this, and it is true in other sectors as well.

The technology sector has proven especially volatile over the past few years. Analysts' recommendations in the heat of the tech bubble often were Strong Buy or Buy, and there were very few Sell recommendations. Figure 8-8 helps illustrate the enormous power of setting artificial maturity dates. The numbers represent the computer and technology sector returns from Merrill Lynch, Morgan Stanley, and Goldman Sachs. Just as a reminder, the amount of every stock bought is always $1000. The table assumes purchasing

| Stocks in the Computer and Technology Sector Only | Morgan Stanley Strong Buy | Merrill Lynch Strong Buy | Goldman Sachs Recommended List |
|---|---|---|---|
| Purchase day of recommendation/ Sell on downgrade | −16.99% | −15.41% | −20.72% |
| Purchase day of recommendation/ Sell 130 business days later | 4.00% | 1.85% | 14.29% |
| Purchase day of recommendation/ Sell 255 business days later | 8.06% | 2.11% | 28.97% |

**Fig. 8-8.   Benefiting from recommendations.**

shares of the recommended company solely on financial institution's Strong Buy or comparable recommendation, without any fine-tuning for accepting or rejecting certain trades.

The results prove once again that waiting for downgrades to initiate sell transactions would bring huge disappointments (see results labeled Purchase Day of Recommendation/Sell on Downgrade). However, creating an artificial maturity date for these trades would reap enormous benefits. Figure 8-8 reveals that of the three financial institutions analyzed, stocks that Goldman Sachs's research team labeled Recommended List scored best with almost a 29 percent return. The only requirement for the investor was to make sure these stocks were sold 1 year after the purchase day. By applying the same 1-year artificial maturity strategy to Morgan Stanley's and Merrill Lynch's Strong Buy recommendations, the results managed to produce the same directional improvement. A 6-month and a 12-month artificial maturity strategy eliminated losses for all three firms in the technology sector and pulled their ratings out of deep waters and onto the shore.

The overall return from the three firms combined would have managed to provide the investor with 11.51 percent in the computer and technology sector. Even if we subtract approximately 5 percent from these results to cover commission costs and bid-ask spread, the results would still keep us in positive territory. And this is not a small feat given the fact that the NASDAQ (the index most closely aligned with the computer and technology sectors) managed to lose roughly 15 percent since those cold days in February 1999. The S&P 500 lost 10 percent since then as well. Once again the same trend is clearly observed. Whether it's in the utilities sector, the technology sector, or across all sectors combined, selling on artificially created maturity dates increases return. Waiting for the analysts to give investors a sign that it's time to sell poses major problems.

Consequently, we can say with a high degree of confidence that analysts do have the insight to tell the investor what stocks to buy. The problem they continue to demonstrate time and again primarily has to do with the fact that analysts are too late to downgrade the stocks they cover. We have seen it in the utilities sector and have now observed the same weakness in the computer and technology sectors. As a result the dirty job of downgrading stocks is left to the investor. There is a famous saying that applies here like almost nowhere else: It's a tough job, but someone has got to do it.

Before moving on to the next leg of our journey, it is important to stress again the importance of avoiding IPOs. Without a doubt there were winners among these highly recommended stocks. A few of these winning IPOs would include firms such as Inktomi Corp. (INKT), Allegiance Telecom Inc. (ALGX), and Broadcom Corp. (BRCM). But they were winners only if you sold them in time. However, losers solidly outweigh the winners. For instance, stocks such as Lending Tree Inc. (TREE), Digex Inc. (DIGX), Allscripts Healthcare Solutions (MDRX), and many more fall into that category. If the investor would practice rejecting IPOs across the board—including spin-offs and ADRs—from recommendations supplied by the firms we just analyzed, regardless of who was the lead underwriter, the overall return would jump from 11.51 to 16.71 percent. This approach would result in increased returns by over 5 percent, which by the way will pay for your commissions and bid-ask spread.

In concluding this chapter, which started with a description of trust and reputation followed by examples of how an investor can benefit from executing recommendation-based strategies, I would like to recall a great Russian saying used by President Ronald Reagan late in the 1980s. Ice from the Cold War era had just begun to thaw, and relationships between the Soviet Union and the United States started to become friendly. President Reagan said, *"Doveryai no proveryai,"* which means, "Trust but verify." From an investor's point of view, analyst recommendations have become suspect in many respects, yet not all calls are off the mark. The secret is to adhere to a system of analyzing the analysts and investing accordingly.

# 9

# WHEN "SELL" REALLY MEANS "BUY"

*Katherine Dovlatov and Eric Shkolnik*

## The Story of the Ugly Duckling

We begin this chapter by reminding everyone of a famous Hans Christian Andersen fairy tale. A swan's egg is somehow mixed up with Mother Duck's eggs and hatches in the nest along with three ducklings. Mother Duck is shocked that one of her babies looks nothing like the others or anyone else in the barnyard. The biggest fear is that this ugly baby is a turkey chick and cannot swim. These fears are, however, quickly dismissed as the unusual duckling jumps in the pond, swimming beautifully. The mother is full of pride, but the other ducks in the barnyard are not easily impressed. They taunt and torment the little outsider, making his life unbearable. In spite of Mother Duck's efforts to protect her unfortunate offspring, to reassure him that it is all right to be different, the Ugly Duckling, as he is teased by the others, is inconsolable and one day, when his "cup runneth over," leaves his home.

On his journey the Ugly Duckling meets many fascinating characters and faces numerous tricky situations. By hook or by crook, our little hero manages to keep up his good spirits and overcomes life's obstacles. Finally, the following spring a miracle occurs, and the Ugly Duckling is transformed from an awkward, ugly baby

169

bird into a magnificent Swan, the envy of all his former enemies. This ageless classic is a wonderful old story that still holds many truths for us all as well as a great lesson for investors.

For all companies that are going strong, there are always some that are ailing. These companies often find themselves in rather unpleasant and unpopular situations and are habitually shunned and discarded by inexperienced and experienced investors alike. Many of them do not share in the fate of the hero of Andersen's fable and prove to be turkey chicks indeed, unable to swim. Hampered by poor strategic vision and heavily encumbered by debt, they will find themselves gasping for air and, ultimately, drowning. Fortunately, the ones that will never become glorious swans or anything else are in the minority. They undoubtedly epitomize every investor's greatest fear. However, numerous other companies will not be denied in this way. They will be forced to shed their liabilities, replace their lackluster management, and as a result of some effort, grow into money-making businesses, our beautiful swans.

The theory we are about to introduce revolves around and is contingent on the research produced by sell-side analysts. From a statistical point of view, Sell recommendations are extremely rare, and fewer recommendations provide fewer data points to offer statistically meaningful results. This very fact should make us wary and compel us to investigate stocks, as well as their respective performance, that bear recommendation, names such as Hold, Neutral, Market Perform, and the like. All of these recommendations are typically one category above the rarely issued Sell rating. (Some brokerage houses have a policy of not issuing any Sell recommendations, and Hold or its equivalent is their lowest rating.) The media and other organizations such as the SEC frequently remind investors that these recommendations are euphemisms for Sell. This wordplay is a way for research analysts to soften the blow they are about to inflict on an ailing company. It placates that company's management, satisfies everyone's interests, and avoids burning bridges in the process, as discussed in earlier chapters. The sheer volume of companies tagged by Wall Street research teams with these so-called Hold recommendations is staggering. Thus, drawing our analogy with Andersen's fairy tale, it is safe to say that "ugly ducklings" abound in the Wall Street barn.

The reasons analysts downgrade stocks to a Hold (or worse) differ. At times, however rare, a stock has been overvalued and needs adjustment. As illustrated in the previous chapter, this occurs very infrequently. Analysts seem reluctant to downgrade a stock and usually do so much later than they should, leaving inexperienced and unsophisticated investors feeling a bit foolish and a few dollars poorer (and usually none the wiser). At other times downgrades to Hold are in direct response to the supply and demand dynamics of the market, which affect a specific industry sector. This is reminiscent of our food chain theory introduced in Chapter 6, where we observed that when Dell suffered, so did Intel, being another link in the technology sector chain, followed by Micron Technology, and so on. This domino effect is characteristic of any sector once chips start to fall.

The last but not least reason Wall Street sometimes issues Hold recommendations is based solely on a financial analyst's opinion as a result of his or her investigation. In some situations research may reveal that a company is not living up to its potential and its management is acting inefficiently and making inopportune or ill-advised judgment calls. Management is getting the company heavily into debt, pursues too many mergers and acquisitions, which strains the company's resources, or is taking on too much risk. Sometimes it is the analyst's belief that a long-awaited product line will flop due to improbable market demand or the quality of the product. This cataloguing of the company's or management's shortcomings can go on, but the fact remains that it is the analyst's call and he or she may, upon discovery of such failings, issue a Hold rating.

It is impossible to list all reasons analysts may use in proclaiming a certain company an ugly duckling. Most companies with such a pessimistic prognosis tend to go through a negative adjustment period. During this time, the company's management and its shareholders perpetuate a further downward slide due to the negative general mood lingering over a company with such an ominous diagnosis. The stock will most likely face selling pressure from having been downgraded and will see its price plummeting.

The database of recommendations we have examined lead us to make the following conclusion: In general, stocks that have been downgraded to a Hold were probably under selling pressure for some time before the downgrade. We can make this conjecture on the basis of our earlier assertion that stocks, once downgraded, even if it is from a Strong Buy to a Buy and especially if it is to a Hold, will continue sliding down on inertia. However, just like in Sir Isaac Newton's law of motion, an object in motion wants to stay in motion, but friction forces that object to stop. Hence, this downward slide will not continue forever. Unlike Newton's law, however, this process does often reverse itself, and the sun does begin to shine on these companies rated Hold. We will focus our attention on these companies and search for hidden treasure among them.

By using existing data readily available on numerous financial Web sites, we will test our "contrary" theory by analyzing two sets of results based on a hypothetical investor. This investor first buys stocks immediately after a Hold recommendation has been issued on a stock and then buys stocks on an artificially created maturity purchase date for every such Hold recommendation. We hope our experiment will provide ample evidence in support of our purchase theory for stocks rated with a Hold. We will prove that our "contrary" theory can be an extremely rewarding and profitable strategy.

## Sink or Swim Simulated Portfolio

To corroborate this proposition, we evaluated the performance of research teams from three of the most influential financial institutions on Wall Street: Salomon Smith Barney, Lehman Brothers, and Goldman Sachs. Cumulatively, these financial bulwarks spend millions of dollars on research and employ many financial analysts who are considered by *Institutional Investor* and All Star Analysts (an annual supplement to *The Wall Street Journal*) to be the brightest in their field.

Salomon Smith Barney's equity research team, ranked number 1 by *The Wall Street Journal*,[1] delivered quite a large number of Neutral ratings, the equivalent to a Hold, with regard to companies they were researching Neutral stock recommendations from Smith Barney's financial analysts are generally expected to perform in

---

[1]*"Best of the Street,"* a supplement to *The Wall Street Journal*, June 26, 2001.

line with the market at their best. They are expected to underperform the market by a fairly significant margin at their worst.

As the starting date for our first performance evaluation, we chose February 2000 with the end date falling in February 2002. During February 2000, the S&P 500 Index was trading around the 1350-point range. The NASDAQ, in what seems like the glorious past in retrospect, was trading around the 4050-point range at the beginning of that February, reaching a 4600-point mark by the end of the month. A little more than 2 years later, in March 2002 the S&P 500 had slumped to around 1150, and the NASDAQ, weighed down by technology stock, dropped to around 1850.

Let us see how our hypothetical investor fared after purchasing "unlikely" stocks in February 2000, subsequent to the issue of a Neutral rating by Smith Barney, and holding on to them for 2 years. In this case our investor would have lost 1 percent. With the calculation of commission costs associated with each buy and sell transaction and the bid-ask spread, an additional 5 percent can be added onto the losses. Therefore, the total losses have increased to roughly 6 percent. However, when comparing the total loss against the overall market drop, we can unequivocally state that although the results are disappointing, they still support our proposition. Our hypothetical investor has managed to beat the market—the S&P 500 Index declined by approximately 15 percent and the NASDAQ fell by roughly 60 percent—by following the Neutral recommendation strategy of buying stock with a Hold rating immediately after the recommendation was issued.

Lehman Brothers is a company with a 150-year history that used to be associated primarily with the fixed-income (bonds) securities business. It made great strides during the exuberant 1990s and managed to build a successful equities trading operation that attracted many top-ranking financial analysts. Let us imagine that our hypothetical investor bought a Lehman Brothers' Market Perform–rated stock, which is similar to Smith Barney's Neutral rating, both in context and substance. Once again we will use a 2-year time frame, from February 2000 to February 2002, for our simulation. The overall results for companies that received a Lehman's Market Perform rating were disappointing, as was to be expected. The price of company shares belonging to this rating group dropped by 2.75 percent. Factoring in an additional 5 percent, a rough estimation of trading costs, the results for buying on a Market Perform or Hold recommendation immediately after its pronouncement produced a loss of approximately 8 percent. However, even with such negative results, our investor still was ahead of the market, with the S&P 500 Index and the NASDAQ trudging through huge losses.

As our third point of reference, we chose Goldman Sachs, the banking world "royalty" and "blue blood" of Wall Street. Goldman Sachs uses a Market Performer rating as the equivalent of a Hold recommendation. Of the three banks examined, Goldman's stocks rated Market Performer yielded the most positive results—a gain of 8.02 percent by March 2002. Thus, our investor, if following the strategy of buying stocks rated Market Performer by Goldman Sachs immediately after the call is made, would have ended up gaining approximately 3 percent if we added all related trading costs to the gains. This is not a bad track record, given the overall market and economic conditions in 2000 and 2001.

It should be easy to summarize what we have seen up until now. The three Hold recommendations from three different financial institutions have managed to outperform the market, after including the estimated cost of trading, by anywhere from 6 to 18 percent. Our findings should not be surprising at all when we consider what we established in the previous chapter. That is, Wall Street researchers have a tendency to be reluctant when it comes to downgrading stocks. The downgrade is usually issued later than data would indicate, after considerable losses have been incurred on stocks still rated a Strong Buy and not a Hold, as one would expect. In the previous chapter, we demonstrated that it is possible to transform losing stocks rated with a Strong Buy into winners. All we had to do was establish a 6- or 12-month maturity date. By applying our fundamental rules, we were able to extend our winnings even further. Could this theory hold true for stocks rated with a Hold? Can we reverse a Hold stock's fortune if we created an artificial purchase maturity date? The answer is an unequivocal and undeniable yes. But we are not asking you to take our word for this; we are going to prove it.

Our theory will hold true if certain rules are observed. In the earlier examples of Hold stock purchases, our investor effected the transaction on the day the terminal Hold recommendation was issued. But what would happen if the investor waited, say, another year? We have illustrated by looking at back data wich suggests that by buying Hold recommendations our investor has beaten the market. However, even in the best performance (i.e., Goldman Sachs), the investor ended up making a measly 3 percent. Could this contrary investor actually improve these market-beating results by going against the grain. Let's see.

We often hear the old adage that "patience is a virtue." But, as with all clichés, it has lost all meaning due to its repetition. However, it would not be a cliché if it were not true. And this old truism is integral to our theory on buying stocks rated Hold. We conducted our experiment on the assumption that a stock would have reached its bottom or been close to its bottom within 1 year after receiving a Hold rating. Therefore, we chose 1 year for our artificial purchase-maturity date. By waiting the investor can keep a close watch over the targeted stock and become better informed for making an educated decision on whether the ugly duckling is indeed a turkey or potentially a gracious swan. Not unlike the historical process, when it is impossible to focus on any single incident to explain a major event, a company fails for multiple reasons. It usually takes a multitude of details, which over a period of time perpetuates a certain event. Therefore, without an isolated incident, it becomes impossible to isolate the date of said incident. Without this date it is nearly impossible to recognize when conditions actually begin to change, either from good to bad or vice versa. The point we are making, that it is unfeasible to prognosticate the exact moment of reversal of fortune, finds ample support on Wall Street. The turning point for stocks in the Strong Buy valuation group, when their performance first began to slide from good to poorer, was identified only after serious dips in prices had been recorded. Is it possible then that the turning point in the other direction, from bad to better, for stocks rated Hold is also undetectable right away? Is there a possible pocket of time, a potential gold mine, that has been completely overlooked? This is certainly worth further investigation.

The following simulated scenarios all involve the purchase of Hold rated stocks 1 year after the issuance of this recommendation. It is possible that a 2-year period will yield better results. It is important to bear in mind that we are only interested in Hold (or its equivalent) stocks that have maintained their Hold rating with the institution that issued it for 12 months. If the same institution upgrades or downgrades the Hold stock within a period of 1 year from its original valuation date, this stock will be disqualified from participation in our simulated portfolio. We have referred to this period of 12 months as an artificial purchase-maturity date. Let us simply call it a maturity date, and instead of executing a sell transaction on this date, let us treat it as a time to buy.

As in our previous simulation, we will begin our analysis with February 2000. And let's not forget that the Hold stocks our hypothetical investor is purchasing have maintained this rating for at least 1 year, which means they were downgraded in February 1999. (In some instances Hold recommendations may have been issued even earlier due to reiterations, which will be treated as new recommendations if earlier records cannot be found in our database.) The results we are about to witness are amazing as well as astonishingly consistent. Although the illustration we provide is based on recommendations issued by three financial institutions only—Salomon Smith Barney, Lehman Brothers, and Goldman Sachs—the fact remains that this particular trading strategy of buying stocks 1 year after they have been downgraded to a Hold reveals a consistent positive performance pattern as witnessed for every financial institution. We found this strategy to be the most rewarding. Anyone practicing it automatically avoids all IPOs as well as a majority of other factors that lead to conflict of interests.

Let us first look at stocks rated Neutral by Salomon Smith Barney, which our investor purchased 12 months after their downgrade. By March 2002, our date of reconciliation, these stocks yielded a positive 13.83 percent. If you recall, Neutral recommendations purchased immediately, without the date adjustment, resulted in a 1 percent loss and Buy recommendations were a negative 14.44 percent. What these numbers show is that had our investor waited a year to buy these stocks, the portfolio would have improved its performance by almost 15 percent.

Results from Lehman Brothers' recommendations showed a mind-blowing 36.33 percent increase. (See the Appendix for step-by-step instructions on how to set up this simulation and notification strategy.) Thus, instead of losing 2.75 percent when purchased on the date a Hold was issued, our investor gained more than 36 percent by doing nothing more than waiting 1 year before executing the transaction. This equates to a 39.08 percent increase in performance. Even after we calculate the transaction costs at the standard 5 percent rate, an investor who followed Lehman's recommendations with patience, having utilized that time pocket of 1 year, has managed to make quite a bit of money in these unfavorable market conditions. The investor beat 99.9 percent of professionals!

Goldman Sachs's Market Performer recommendations have similarly managed to produce a phenomenal rate of return and delivered a dazzling 33.12 percent profit before expenses. Compare this to the 8 percent return before our investor learned patience and waited 12 months before buying. Once again subtract 5 percent for trading costs, and we still have a substantial improvement of 25.10 percent. Let us see how these numbers fared against the market. On Salomon Smith Barney's Neutral recommendation, our investor stood at 29 percent gain against S&P 500 Index. On Lehman Brothers' and Goldman Sachs's Market Perform and Market Performer recommendations, our investor beat the market by a whopping 51 percent and 48 percent, respectively.

These results indicate that financial analysts are not better equipped at determining when market conditions are about to turn, whether it is from good to worse or bad to better. These results also show with certainty that a number of companies labeled as ugly ducklings are fostering a potential swan. What every investor needs is a bit of patience. If in addition to this virtue an investor shows the ability and desire to investigate, to perform additional due diligence, these extraordinary and systematic results can be further improved (see Figure 9-1).

Another point to remember that is of paramount importance to the overall success of our strategy is that you should never, under any circumstances, "put all your eggs in one basket." The key element in our approach is diversification. And that does not mean two or three stocks either. Our system estimates that if we follow Hold recommendations from one of these three financial institutions, having previously investigated their performance history, we would be facing approximately 160 buy and sell transactions per year. This translates into approximately three transactions per week. This is not exactly a buy and hold strategy, but it is far from a chaotic day-trading system.

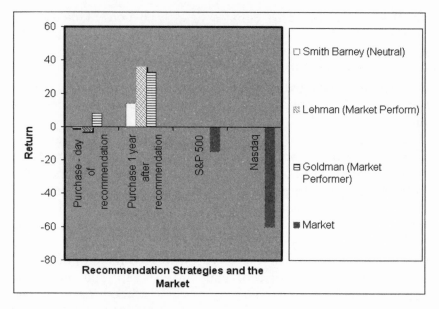

**Fig. 9-1. Hold ratings performance.**

In the past, when individual investors were trading through full service or discount brokers only, trading strategies such as the one we are proposing were cost prohibitive and thus impossible to execute. However, with the advent of companies that provide basket-trading technology, such as www.foliofn.com, or others that charge $5 per trade, such as www.brownco.com, executing this strategy has become easy and inexpensive. Even full-service brokerages are now offering accounts where fees are based on assets rather than on transactions. If an investor has that type of trading account, our proposed strategies are feasible to execute even with a full-service broker.

Now that we've established that this strategy is feasible and realistic, we can examine the benefits of the approach. First, there are the advantages of diversification. According to the Risk Metrics Group, an independent company spun out of J. P. Morgan, "adding stocks to a portfolio generally lowers risk" (K. Brown, "Analysts' Top Stock Picks Get Failing Grade on Risk Meter," *The Wall Street Journal*, August 17, 2001). Second, it keeps the investor disciplined. As in any systematic approach to a task, it demands that a certain schedule and regimen are observed. And third, the risk associated with Hold-rated stocks is on the average far less than Strong Buy and Buy picks, again, according to the discovery made by the Risk Metrics Group. However, our strategy lowers the risk factors even more than the discoveries just mentioned. The reason for this additional risk buffer is the 1-year wait before purchasing a Hold-rated stock.

As discussed, the number of stocks involved when following this strategy is rather considerable. Therefore, for illustration purposes only, we have decided to minimize this universe by selecting a single industry and a single financial institution.

## Turkeys or Swans? The Goldman Sachs Nest

For our demonstration we have chosen Goldman Sachs and its table of stocks rated Market Performer. Each stock was bought on its artificial maturity date, or its 12-month anniversary. Please be reminded that only stocks that have maintained their Market Performer status for an entire year are pertinent to our study and all those whose rating fluctuated have been disqualified. The information in Figure 9-2 was calculated on February 15, 2002. The closing price for that day is shown next to securities that are still rated as Market Performer. Stocks that have been upgraded or downgraded while under our ownership have again, for the purposes of this illustration, been sold on the day such a rating change was issued. The expediency of these sell dates is not being examined here because it was addressed in detail in the previous chapter. In this simulation we are only interested in approximating the overlooked time pocket between the date of issuance of a Hold recommendation on a particular stock and its subsequent reversal of fortune.

Let's examine Figure 9-2. All stocks listed have been rated Market Performer by Goldman Sachs, and their artificial maturity purchase date happened to fall anywhere between February 1, 2000, and February 15, 2002. These 18 fortuitous stocks rated by Goldman Sachs are the 18 mysterious eggs that may or may not hatch to become turkeys that cannot swim or our beautiful swans. To continue with the fairy tale analogy, we will break down our simulation portfolio into turkeys, ducks, and swans. The division criteria will be as follows: Stocks that appreciated by more than 10

| Symbol | Company Name | Day Bought | Buy Price | # of Stocks | Closing Day Sell Day | Closing Price | Gain/Loss Amount | Gain/Loss Percent | Type Bird Type |
|--------|--------------|------------|-----------|-------------|----------------------|---------------|------------------|-------------------|----------------|
| KM | Kmart Corp. | 02/01/00 | $8.69 | 115.07 | 1/24/2002 | 0.93 | $(−892.98) | -(89.30) | Turkey |
| PSS | Payless Shoe Source, Inc. | 02/22/00 | $40.81 | 24.50 | 2/15/2002 | 56.94 | $395.25 | 39.53 | Swan |
| SMRT | Stein Mart, Inc. | 03/01/00 | $4.50 | 222.22 | 2/15/2002 | 9.07 | $1015.56 | 101.56 | Swan |
| WAG | Walgreen Co. | 03/01/00 | $25.63 | 39.02 | 2/15/2002 | 37.61 | $467.42 | 46.74 | Swan |
| GYMB | The Gymboree Corp. | 04/13/00 | $4.00 | 250.00 | 2/15/2002 | 13.54 | $2385.00 | 238.50 | Swan |
| DYS | Distribucion y Servicio D&S S.A. | 05/01/00 | $17.00 | 58.82 | 2/15/2002 | 12.65 | $(−255.88) | (−25.59) | Turkey |
| RSTO | Restoration Hardware, Inc. | 05/05/00 | $5.63 | 177.62 | 2/15/2002 | 11.05 | $962.70 | 96.27 | Swan |
| JWN | Nordstrom, Inc | 05/12/00 | $25.31 | 39.51 | 2/15/2002 | 24.91 | $(−15.80) | (−1.58) | Duck |
| SKS | Saks, Inc. | 08/16/00 | $9.50 | 105.26 | 2/15/2002 | 9.89 | $41.05 | 4.11 | Duck |
| DDS | Dillard's Inc. | 08/18/00 | $13.88 | 72.05 | 2/15/2002 | 17.4 | $253.60 | 25.40 | Swan |
| WIN | Winn-Dixie Stores, Inc. | 10/05/00 | $14.69 | 68.07 | 2/15/2002 | 14.4 | $(−19.74) | (−1.96) | Duck |
| PBY | Pep Boys | 11/13/00 | $4.38 | 228.57 | 2/15/2002 | 14.46 | $2305.12 | 230.51 | Swan |
| WSM | Williams-Sonoma, Inc. | 03/08/01 | $28.98 | 34.51 | 2/15/2002 | 45 | $552.80 | 55.28 | Swan |
| LE | Lands' End, Inc. | 03/13/01 | $27.32 | 36.60 | 11/7/2001 | 42.15 | $542.83 | 54.28 | Swan |
| NMG.A | The Neiman-Marcus Group, Inc | 05/15/01 | $36.50 | 27.40 | 1/28/2002 | 35.07 | $(−39.18) | (−3.92) | Duck |
| COST | Costco Wholesale Corp. | 05/30/01 | $37.29 | 26.82 | 2/15/2002 | 45.89 | $230.62 | 23.06 | Swan |
| OATS | Wild Oats Markets, Inc. | 06/25/01 | $10.00 | 100.00 | 2/15/2002 | 8.8 | $(−120.00) | (−12.00) | Turkey |
| CC | Circuit City Stores | 08/22/01 | $15.88 | 62.97 | 1/7/2002 | 29.75 | $873.43 | 87.34 | Swan |

**Fig. 9-2.  Market performers in the retail industry.**

percent in value are swans, stocks that lost more than 10 percent are turkeys, and the stocks ranging between negative and positive 10 percent are ducks.

To test this strategy, we again employed the services of our hypothetical investor who purchased $18,000 worth of stock within the retail industry sector. For our purposes we will assume that the 18 stocks were purchased in equal dollar amounts of $1000 each. Looking at the figure, as of February 15, 2002, there are three turkeys, four ducks, and eleven swans. These results dramatically favor the swans, or companies whose stock has climbed by more than 10 percent in value. Mathematically, these results are on the side of the investor. By February 15, 2002, this simulation portfolio would have increased by $8680 from the initial investment of $18,000, raising its overall value to $26,680—a 48 percent rate of return.

The system is certainly not foolproof (no system is). Kmart, the first stock our hypothetical investor would have purchased, was a turkey that lost almost 90 percent of its value. However, take a look at the number of beautiful swans we now have in our nest. The Gymboree Corporation (GMBY) is up 238 percent, Pep Boys (PBY) is up 230 percent, among a score of others. The advantages and rewards of this theory are incontrovertible, but we are not through yet.

You don't need to have a Ph.D. in finance to realize that the majority of stocks rated with a Hold or its equivalent will eventually go up or down in rating. Most of these, whenever this happens, will be upgraded (our swans). For the purpose of the simulation, we made our hypothetical investor sell stock the minute its rating changed from a Hold, whether it was an upgrade or a downgrade. However, there is no reason to sell stock on the day of an upgrade; instead it has proved expedient to hold on to it for a while longer. It is worth mentioning that an average retail stock that receives an upgrade from Goldman Sachs shows a tendency to appreciate another 10 percent within the next 3 months (see Figure 9-3).

## Are All Ugly Ducklings Created Equal?

In Chapter 7, through the evaluation of Strong Buy recommendations, we hope to have proven that regardless of the underwriter, it

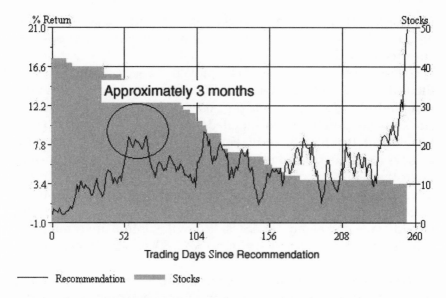

**Fig. 9-3. Stock performance trend in the retail industry after an upgrade by Goldman Sachs.**

is a good strategy to avoid IPOs (initial public offerings). Similarly, all our information points to the fact that avoiding Hold-rated penny stocks will improve our results even further. By weeding out our simulated portfolio comprising Hold recommendations from all three financial institutions, our results have shown an additional improvement of approximately 2 percent across the board. The reason is that many companies whose stock prices fell below $1 a year after they were rated a Hold did not survive the hardships that lay ahead and eventually faded into obscurity. Other companies whose shares continued trading as penny stocks and managed to keep their head above water have done so just barely. Their performance as a group did not inspire any confidence. For your reference two such companies are the TenFold Corporation (TENF) and Engage, Inc. (ENGA). There are many others.

Having said this, the longer these companies manage to stay afloat, to continue trading below $1 per share, the better is their diagnosis for the future. This reminds us of the famous lottery slogan: You have to be in it to win it.

We would like to remind you once again of the story of the ugly duckling. Many companies tagged by Wall Street researchers with Hold recommendations will have to go through a very difficult period and struggle to survive. Chastised and neglected by financial analysts and, consequently, by the majority of investors, they will face a long and harsh period of adjustment. However, for a large number of publicly traded companies, this period will be replete with many of life's lessons, just like the long and harsh winter in the life of our neglected little hero, the Ugly Duckling. This painful period of growing pains will without a doubt benefit the companies that are not afraid to face their fears and will aid them in their transformation into beautiful swans. We hope that this chapter has convinced you that being a part of this transformation process is a rewarding and profitable experience.

# 10

# STATISTICS, PROBABILITY, CHANCE, AND UNCERTAINTY

*I have learned to predict the movement of celestial bodies but not the movement of man in markets.*
*Sir Isaac Newton*

There is an ongoing debate in academia and common practice about what is "uncertainty" and what is "risk." For our purposes risk and uncertainty are treated as equals.

In the preceding chapters, a various number of recommendation-based strategies were explored and illustrated. Some of them had weak performance, whereas others produced exceptionally encouraging results. Nonetheless, questions arise: Can patterns of what has happened clearly define the road that lies ahead? Is it prudent to draw on past experiences to define actions that are yet to come? Can we intelligently decipher our past? These are some of the questions economists, mathematicians, and philosophers to this day are trying to answer.

Probability describes the likelihood that a condition, a situation, or an event will come about. The nature of probability dictates a methodical and rational approach to problem solving and decision making. It is an area within mathematics that can motivate people's awareness and encourage their rational assessment. Investors who conduct probability experiments using financial data are challenged to make sense of circumstances in which they cannot be entirely sure of the outcome. This exercise improves their ability to think critically but does not always guarantee that critical thinking will lead them to a profitable decision. Opening a new business is always based on the belief by the entrepreneur that the business will become profitable. Yet approximately 90 percent of new businesses fail during their first year. Therefore, what people believe should happen and what actually happens do not necessarily coincide.

## Objective Probability

Examining probability in its simplest form such as tossing a die describes and identifies something mathematicians call *objective probability*. A die—unless it was rigged—has no "emotions" or "beliefs" that can affect its final outcome. After it has been tossed, it will always have an equally weighted and, therefore, objective number of possible answers. The die does not have a favorite side. It can't fall in love or feel sorry for any particular side. Thus, a die —unlike a human being—is totally objective. From a statistical point of view, studying and understanding objective probability involve a fairly straightforward process. When a die is tossed twice, does the outcome of the first toss affect the outcome of the second? The answer is no. The die on its second roll still has six equally weighted sides; thus, the chances are still 1 in 6 for any side to end up on top.

Academics and a large number of investors who are proponents of the random walk theory use this hypothesis as their trump card. They argue, and not without merit, that prices for any security on any given day can rise, decline, or stay unchanged. Therefore, each security traded on a public market has the same three choices. When the next trading day begins, nothing has changed. The price can increase, decrease, or stay the same. Burton G. Malkiel, the author of *A Random Walk Down Wall Street*, concludes that technical analysis, which tries to predict future trends that are based on past prices, volumes, and so on, makes astrology look like concrete science. Technical analysts, however, strongly dislike and disagree with this statement for obvious reasons.

The same theory can be applied to a coin toss. Each coin toss is independent of the other. However, if you toss a coin 10,000 times, you will reach a number that is close to 5000 heads and 5000 tails. Experiments such as this were the foundation and proof for the law of large numbers. It stated that although it's impossible to be certain what side would come up on your next coin toss, it will almost certainly reach an equilibrium after a substantial number of tosses have been performed.

The law of large numbers is responsible for spawning many business models throughout history that thrive and flourish in modern times as well. Casinos are one of them. After establishing rules for the games of chance, the gambling house fosters its prosperity by creating odds and, hence, probability within these rules that are stacked in its favor. No matter how good a player is, whether the game is blackjack, craps, or roulette, the casino will win in the long run. Gamblers inevitably are all victims of objective probability. Yet they continue to play.

Insurance companies use a similar technique. The information they compile, update, and maintain about events such as car accidents, deaths, burglaries, and other unwanted occurrences allows them to develop a reliable and profitable business model that can estimate with a substantial degree of certainty the number of car accidents that can occur within a certain geographical area segmented by age group, for instance. Insurance premiums for people who own BMWs in Brooklyn are higher than for people who own the same model BMW in Westchester. The same logic applies to insurance premiums that are based on age groups. Again because of probability, we see substantially higher insurance premiums for a 19-year-old male driver as opposed to a 40-year-old female driver. The reason for these disparities revolves around historical data showing that more BMWs were stolen in Brooklyn than in Westchester and more 19-year-old male drivers were involved in car accidents than 40-year-old females. This type of information allows insurance companies to create a fee structure tailored for each client that will cover the anticipated losses due to car thefts and car accidents. It will also cover operational costs and leave the rest for profit. They can't inflate their fees too much to increase profit due to competition and at times due to government regulations.

Yet in this brief insurance business model illustration, we already can sense a potential for uncertainty that insurance companies may face. A disaster of the magnitude of the terrorist acts that occurred on September 11, 2001, clearly threw many insurance companies off balance. The number of claims and the amounts of payouts were unforeseen even by the smartest mathematicians. Although mathematicians are able to estimate the number of deaths that can occur under so-called "normal" circumstances, they regrettably cannot foresee three planes filled with jet fuel and frightened passengers deliberately smashing into the World Trade Towers and the Pentagon.

Pierre Simon Laplace, a mathematician who contributed enormously to the subject of probability and was considered to be one of the greatest scientists of his time, and perhaps of all times, muttered these words on his deathbed: "What we know is not much. What we *do not* know is immense."

## The Trap: Subjective Probability Mistaken for Objective Probability and the 1929 Crash

During the Roaring Twenties, people became fascinated with the stock market. The reason for this fascination and ultimately participation for many clearly had to do with the fact that the stock market was headed higher. Back then the market traded 6 days a week, including Saturday. Thus, perhaps we can compare it to our objective die toss for parallelism in that a die also has six sides. In the end the number of days the markets are open or number of sides a die has is beside the point and is used in our example strictly for illustrative purposes.

For instance, what if someone offered you to play a game of die where you could bet $1 or more before each toss. The rules for the game would be as follows: You win if the die shows a 1, 2, 3, or 4 and you lose if the die shows 5 or 6. The amount won or lost depends on the amount you wagered before the toss. Wouldn't you accept this challenge? Clearly, this type of rule would be in your favor. The fact that you can't win on every toss is irrelevant in view of the fact that playing this game over a long time would allow you to amass a fortune due to odds that are in your favor. After a certain period, you would tell your friends, coworkers, and others about this great game that made you rich, and they would undoubtedly start playing it as well. After experiencing success, they would tell their friends, coworkers, and so on.

This is exactly how ordinary people without much knowledge of the financial markets flock in droves when markets are experiencing a bull run. They mistake financial markets with an objective game such as tossing a die, even though markets are anything but equally weighted or objective. Just because during the past year, 2 years, or 10 years the stock market returned positive results on 4 of 6 days does not mean it will continue to do so. The rules under which bull markets operate can change radically and unexpectedly. Without warning, you begin to lose when sides of 1, 2, 3, and 4 come up and win only when sides 5 and 6 come up. Alas, for many investors the realization that probabilities were reversed and are now stacked against them comes too late. One of the reasons has to do with the fact that after a prolonged winning streak a player would start borrowing funds (i.e., margin) to increase his or her ante to the limit. Get-rich-quick stories that were bountiful before this change in probabilities occurred are suddenly replaced with stories of financial grief and vanished dreams.

In 1929, when the Dow Jones Industrial Average reached a historic high of 381.17, most investors felt they were playing an objective game in which probability was on their side and, frankly, not without reason. Figure 10-1 illustrates how the years 1924 through October 1929 produced consistently positive returns.

However, when the crash struck in October 1929, the rules of the game changed, throwing what was widely thought to be an objective game on its side. While the actual crash took a number of days to unfold, the first fracture appeared on Thursday, October 24, but on that day there was an afternoon recovery that reduced morning losses. This was followed by a small rally on Friday, October 25. On Saturday the index was shaky and then came the famous one-two punch that so often knocks out even the best boxers in the ring. On Monday, October 28, the Dow fell 12.8 percent. The next day, remembered as Black Tuesday, it lost an additional 11.7 percent. There were some rallies in days to come, but even so, from that point on and for the 34 months that followed, the direction was downward. As in our previous example, the rules changed in October 1929 and so did what were wrongly perceived as objective

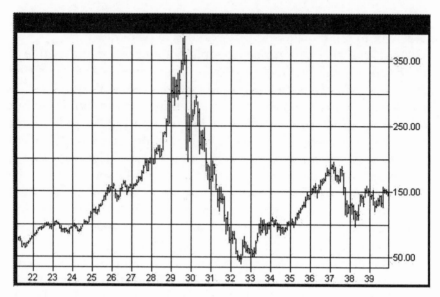

**Fig. 10-1.  Dow Jones Industrial Average, 1922–1940.**

probabilities. As a result, when the market hit bottom on July 8, 1932, the Dow closed at 41.22, down 89 percent from its 1929 peak.

## The 1987 Crash

On August 26, 1987, the day after the market peaked and the Dow Jones Industrial Average reached a record high of 2722.40, *The Wall Street Journal* had a message portraying the overall mood that was prevalent at the time. In a market like this, all stories are positive. Every bit of news is good news. It's pretty much decided at this point that markets are headed higher. From this communiqué along with its reflection, it can be sensed how people once again began to mistakenly perceive subjective probability for objective probability. Once again people started to believe—because of most recent history—that the chances to win were stacked in their favor and would continue to be so evermore. However, as we know today, the stock market collapsed on October 19, 1987, and the Dow Jones Industrial Average fell 508 points and closed at 1738.70. This was the biggest 1-day drop in history.

Many financial commentators and so-called probability gurus following the crash of 1987 predicted a depression. These forecasts were amplified by the media reports, which forever favor the spectacular to the mundane. The gurus' views were supported by data from the first crash of 1929. They pointed out that investors who tried to take advantage of the oversold market after the crash of 1929 were wiped out. Back then they pointed out that the market continued an unstoppable slide and lost an additional 80 percent before recovery had begun. Therefore, many of them concluded that the crash of 1987 would provide similar results. They advised their listeners, clients, readers, and others to sell all equity holdings immediately. Yet this time we avoided both a depression and an additional 80 percent decline in the markets.

There were major differences in monetary policy between 1987 and 1929 as well as other variables that made the two crashes different. But at the time of the 1987 crash, these variables were not as clearly visible as they are today in hindsight. On charts both crashes looked almost identical in nature. Keynes at one time concluded that the purpose of statistics and probability theory is frequently hopeless: "There is a relation between the evidence and the event considered, but it is not necessarily measurable."

Making market predictions based on historical data and probabilities that are derived from them is a very inexact science. To accurately predict what people will do tomorrow based on the information of what they did yesterday is easier said than done. Anyone who tells you differently must be a convincing salesperson. In the end stock markets symbolize and demonstrate people's emotions on any given day and little else. Markets are an emotional melting pot, and emotions are impossible to quantify.

## Extent of Mistakes

Sayings such as "History repeats itself" and "Those who do not learn from past mistakes are doomed to repeat them" abound. Yet how do we know that the lessons learned are interpreted correctly? Don't we face the peril that our theories can be flawed, our reasons invalid, and our proof unreliable? If there is one thing certain about the future besides death and taxes, so famously noted by the great Benjamin Franklin, it must also include uncertainty. The future is inherently uncertain: At best it is unevenly foreseeable, and frequently, it is completely unpredictable. Accordingly, the estimations that we make today about the future outcome are at best faulty and at worst completely wide of the mark. The extent of mistakes we make about the future today, whether small or large, is therefore inevitable and completely unavoidable.

The applications of these ideas are fitting for all types of decision makers, including investors. When two investors are exchanging one asset (e.g., stock) for another asset (e.g., cash), they both have expectations that this transaction will deliver them a financial gain over time. This transaction can only take place when both investors sense that the value of an asset obtained surpasses the value of an asset abandoned. Obviously, this prudence for one or both of the investors in this transaction may be incorrect. The methods and reasons for arriving at these conclusions may differ. For instance, an investor who practices fundamental analysis typically will come to the conclusion that an asset will appreciate in price based on information contained in financial statements. An investor who practices technical analysis could come to a similar or different assessment based on a moving average or some other technical variable. Even two investors who generally see eye to eye in their approach on how to value stocks may come up with a different verdict during an evaluation of a particular company. Therefore, investment decision making and markets that essentially are composites of billions of decisions every day are extremely subjective in nature. Uncertainty in the end will manifestly escort every decision maker, including the invaluable investor.

Figure 10-2 displays the price for Boeing (BA) stock from January 1998 through March 2002. It also displays upgrades represented by the letter U inside a circle and downgrades represented by the letter D inside a square that were issued by the equity research department at Prudential Securities. Reading the graph from left to right demonstrates a troubling trend of mistakes by Prudential's research team. The first upgrade for the stock is followed by a sharp decline in price. After that fiasco, a downgrade was issued that led to the second fiasco because the stock price, instead of declining this time, climbed higher. All the way at the top, an upgrade was issued for the second time, yet again the result is intolerably similar. The stock price proceeded to decline after that call. Regrettably,

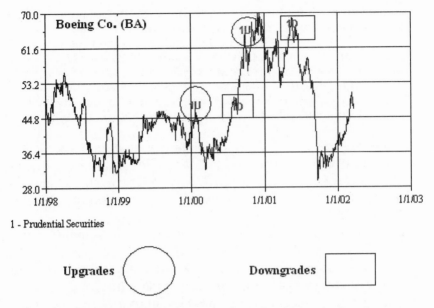

1 - Prudential Securities

**Fig. 10-2.   Stock prices for Boeing with indications of when it was recommended for an upgrade or downgrade by Prudential Securities.**

from Prudential's point of view, their recommendations for Boeing produced reverse results three times in a row. Anyone examining this chart before the last downgrade could have drawn the following conclusion: When Prudential upgrades Boeing, sell the stock, and when Prudential downgrades Boeing, buy the stock. However, the last downgrade was finally right on the money. This time the downgrade was followed by a sharp price decline. This particular example should make it obvious that just because someone was incorrect in making predictions three times in a row does not mean he or she will continue to do so in the future.

## Decision Making Under Uncertainty

Some of the greatest minds in economics during the twentieth century had very little tolerance for those who made their choices based on the frequencies of past occurrences. John Maynard Keynes in "General Theory of Employment" said:

[Under uncertainty] there is no scientific basis on which to form any calculable probability whatever. We simply do not know. Nevertheless, the necessity for action and for decision compels us as practical men to do our best to overlook this awkward fact and to behave exactly as we should if we had behind us a good Benthamite calculation of a series of prospective advantages and disadvantages, each multiplied by its appropriate probability waiting to be summed. (*Quarterly Journal of Economics*, 1937)

Another remarkable and profound thinker in modern economics, Nicholas Georgescu-Roegen, said: "Many idle controversies involving the nature of expectation could be avoided by recognizing at the outset that man's conscious actions are the reflection of his beliefs and of nothing else."

Since the future is continually vague and the anticipated consequences of our actions hold the possibility of the unanticipated, how can we endure? Too many people rationalize things differently, and so many things are unforeseen. At any instant our knowledge is partial. A change in any variable can change our viewpoint and prompt us to alter our opinion. If there is one word that can describe markets, it's *chaos*. And chaos leads us to *subjectivism*, which is associated with the notion that we cannot know everything or even know anything for sure.

Technology investors were amused with Warren Buffett during the late 1990s. They snickered when Buffett admitted that because he did not understand the technology sector, he had avoided investing in it. According to tech investors, he failed to grasp the greatest bull market in history. This talk, however, ended abruptly in 2001. Instantly, with the tech wreck, Buffett became a hero once again. What goes around comes around, but not exactly in the same old fashion. Some things inevitably will be different. The extent of the difference is always unknown.

Peter Bernstein, in his book *Against the Gods*, describes a situation when during a professional investment conference a friend passed him a note that had the following message:

The information you have is not the information you want.
The information you want is not the information you need.

The information you need is not the information you can obtain.

The information you can obtain costs more than you want to pay.

I would take this a step further and add the following:

The information you obtained, paying more than you were willing to pay, in most cases will lead you to:

The information you have is not the information you want and so on.

Every financial prospectus displays this message: "Past returns are no guarantee of future returns." This describes financial risk and uncertainty in their entirety. A prospectus is used by the sponsor to attract the potential investor with successful past results, but at the same time, the language in it protects the same sponsor from the fact that the future is unpredictable and therefore cannot be guaranteed.

Subjective probabilities are an extension of human perceptions of odds and ends, such as world affairs, the economy, or a specific company. The list can go on forever. Markets are extremely confused and often act like a person with bipolar disorder, and for that reason they are chaotic. When chaos reigns, it's impossible to find everything you are looking for. Our understanding is incomplete and forever will be so. And yet we need to go on. Life does not stop. The greatest and the brightest economists and mathematicians that the world has ever produced could not deny the possibility that knowing and understanding a tiny amount more than others could be enough to prevail in the end.

The fundamental rules that were described earlier in the book can certainly facilitate and improve investors' understanding about how the market works. Hence, practicing them will force investors to reduce, not eliminate, their exposure to stocks that inevitably will experience downtrends. Not buying IPOs, not using margin, and not buying companies that extensively continue to purchase other companies will always reduce potential losers.

With a genuine interest in knowing and understanding more, investors will find that success is within their reach. Applying hard work and intellect will accomplish a great deal.

Here is an illustration that perhaps is easier to identify with. For example, if you were to purchase 5 prize tickets of 200 in the drawing, your chance of winning would be 2.5 percent. On the other hand, instead of purchasing 5 tickets in a drawing of 200 possible outcomes, what if you were able to purchase the same number of tickets for the same price but in a drawing that had 100 tickets with an equal winning prize. This would increase your potential of winning to 5 percent. That is all an investor can do. The one who knows how to reduce uncertainty will prevail.

## Looking for Winners and Avoiding Losers

We have described a number of strategies and examples of how investors can use recommendations issued by Wall Street analysts to increase their return on investments. In essence the approach operated around a theme that tried to reduce uncertainty.

Our examination illustrated that, among companies rated Hold, there were many potential winners and losers. Initially, our research was based on trying to find winners. Performing this task met insurmountable resistance. Technical analysis was highly erratic and did not provide us with results that were worth our time and effort. Fundamental analysis coupled with the directional progress report that was detailed in Chapter 5 was much more consistent than technical analysis. Unfortunately, the directional progress report did not produce better results than the strategy described in Chapter 9. Nevertheless, it is highly recommended that investors use it, especially for companies that are rated Strong Buy.

At that point we decided that instead of looking for winners, what would happen if we tried to avoid losers? We made great efforts to find ways to reduce the number of losers in that pot of companies rated Hold. By means of delaying the purchase transaction for approximately 1 year, we were able to reduce the overall pool of potential losers dramatically. Surely, some winners left the station too. But this was irrelevant. Our odds of buying winners as opposed to losers grew, and, thus, uncertainty was reduced.

The same can be said about stocks rated Strong Buy. The longer a stock was rated Strong Buy, the more chances it had to decline in price sharply. In Chapter 8 we illustrated a number of steps that reduced the number of losers among stocks rated Strong Buy. Getting out in time and selling stocks on artificially created maturity dates improved our system substantially. Avoiding IPOs reduced the number of losers even further. There will be a number investors who will point out certain stocks that were highly rated for years, perhaps even decades, and managed to produce phenomenal returns. Microsoft (MSFT), General Electric (GE), and America Online (AOL), until it merged with Time Warner and broke one of our fundamental rules, certainly come to mind. Yet overall, stocks that are rated Strong Buy for too long represent a large number of potential losers. And these losers undoubtedly overwhelm the potential winners among them. In aggregate holding on to stocks rated Strong Buy for too long increased investors' odds to lose. Additional reasons for this phenomenon will be addressed in the next chapter.

Can the recommendation-based trading strategies we described work in the future? The answer is yes. (Well, at least until millions of people start using them.) Of course, one must remember that our system is so rich and so extensive in choices that its power is timeless. Perhaps it can even work endlessly. Only time will tell.

In the end it's important to remember that the economy and the financial markets are dynamic forces. Every economic cycle is different and forever will be so. Just like all people are different and unique, so are the economy and financial markets. The only time they will become identical to what they were in the past is when scientists learn how to perform "time cloning." Until then, we need to look to the past for conceptual rationale only and not for a concrete verdict.

Keynes once said, "In the long run we are all dead." But at the same time, he also pointed out and agreed that even though uncertainty will always be our companion, "the necessity for action and for decision compels us as practical men to do our best to overlook this awkward fact."

# 11

# TAKING ADVANTAGE OF REGRESSION TO THE MEAN

On June 22, 1941, at 4 A.M., the undefeated armies of the Third Reich plunged into the frontiers of Soviet Russia. No conflict in history can compare with the clash that began that fateful day. The sheer number of men, military hardware, and the size of the front were, en masse, the most colossal that human history has ever seen. The exhilaration of the German armies on that horrible summer morning and in the weeks and months that preceded it was at an unprecedented high. They were better trained, better equipped, and better led than their Russian opponents. After a number of easy victories that involved powerful foes, one of them being France, the confidence and self-assurance of the German army climbed even higher. They felt invincible.

The armies of the Soviet Union, although quantitatively massive in terms of soldiers and equipment, were completely and undeniably inferior to the German enemy. They were poorly trained, poorly equipped, and poorly led. After the clash began, no one thought they could last more than 6 months against such a vastly superior rival. Within 3 months of cruel and vicious fighting the situation appeared, as predicted, even gloomier for the Russian defenders. However, as this unrelenting struggle continued,

Russian armies slowly gained incalculable knowledge, experience, and confidence. German armies, on the other hand, which had started this fight confidently assured of their superiority and the final outcome, began to harbor a growing sense of uneasiness, skepticism, and doubt about what was unexpectedly turning into a difficult engagement. The easy conquest promised by the German leadership was slowly slipping away.

German armies approached the doorsteps of Moscow in December 1941. Despite their growing doubts, they must have still felt that victory was assured. Fortunately, it wasn't so. Within four long and difficult years the German war machine, which was unquestionably the best in the world at that time, was obliterated and defeated. The armies of the Soviet Union, which were below average in June 1941, were at their strongest and thus above average at the end of this conflict in May 1945.

History provides many examples of how empires rise to astonishing levels of wealth and power only to fall behind and become insignificant in economic and/or military terms. Some disappear entirely, including the Roman Empire, the Ottoman Empire, and the Soviet Union, to name just a few.

Regression to the mean—the notion that what goes up must come down, and vice versa—regulates nature, empires, and people alike. The seasons come and go like clockwork, but people's perceptions and decisions do not recur as regularly. For example, some empires lasted for as long as 11 centuries, as was the case with the Roman Empire, but others such as the Third Reich carried on for only 12 years. Therefore, human by-products such as nations and financial markets, among other things, are extremely uneven.

Francis Galton, a British anthropologist who was the cousin of Charles Darwin, was instrumental in developing the concept "statistical regression." Analyzing the tallness of men, Galton established that the tallest men frequently produce shorter sons, whereas the shortest men frequently produce taller sons. Given that numerous tall men come from families of average height, they are likely to have offspring shorter than they are, and vice versa. In both cases the height of the children was less excessive than the height of their fathers.

The examination of this observable fact gave rise to the term *regression*, which has since been recognized in a number of fields.

Regression to the mean offers a number of decision-making techniques. Few things in life, if any, grow infinitely large. It is also true that few things in life become infinitely small. If these simultaneous, counterbalanced changes in course were not continually at work, the world would consist of tiny and giant inhabitants like the Morlocks and Eloi of H.G. Wells. Life on Earth would be a bizarre and eerie place. But fortunately, trees never reach the sky. Regression to the mean sooner or later conquers and defeats many of its opponents.

Regression to the mean theory has a large number of practical applications on Wall Street and for good reason. All investors early during their indoctrination into the subculture get exposed to adages such as "buy low and sell high" or "markets fluctuate." In a perfectly rational state of mind, every investor understands that shares cannot rise forever. Eventually, a glass ceiling is reached, and prices will start to decline. Bubbles always have and always will eventually burst.

Yet for many new investors, these lessons of the past are not convincing enough. Unfortunately, many need to learn these lessons the hard way—through their own pocketbooks. When markets are up, it gives people a false impression that they will go up forever. When markets encounter a downward spiral, it makes them feel as if the rug is being pulled out from under them. The urge to jump off immediately is instinctive and hard to resist. Again we can recognize the herding mentality at work. Once the masses start marching in the same direction, they seem to be an unstoppable force, until this force collides painfully with a brick wall.

## Beating the Dow

The dogs of the Dow strategy gained investors' attention in the early 1990s. A book entitled *Beating the Dow* by Michael B. O'Higgins advocated this strategy and was published in 1991. The strategy hinged on the premise that buying 10 stocks (which are part of the Dow Jones Industrial Average) that were paying the highest dividends, and thus were most undervalued, would provide the investor with market-beating results. The author revealed that starting in 1973 onward through 1990, the strategy outperformed the Dow Jones Industrial Average by more than 6 percentage points. As more and more investors started to follow this strategy, its performance became self-defeating. As a result people started to abandon the strategy toward the end of the 1990s, especially after its performance started to lag substantially compared to the exuberant returns offered by dot-com companies. In 1997 the dogs of the Dow strategy lost roughly 3 percent. In 1998 the loss increased to roughly 12 percent, and in 1999 it dropped by an additional 23 percent.

However, in 2000, when dot-com companies themselves started dropping like flies, the dogs of the Dow strategy had a remarkable comeback. It gained 11 percent that year and in 2001 gained an additional 2 percent, outperforming the overall market for the second year in a row. Regression to the mean eventually obliterated the high-flying dot-com investors and uplifted the dogs of the Dow strategy from its doldrums.

The evidence collected from decades of historical data reveals that behavior which is rewarded tends to be reinforced and is chronically practiced until it fails. For example, in the computer industry, when a computer programmer gets paid twice as much to write code using Java and C++ as opposed to writing programs using COBOL, you'll find many COBOL programmers switching to learn and develop programs using Java. This trend continues until Java programmers get paid just as much as their COBOL counterparts.

The wealth of academic research confirms that regression to the mean is the most powerful strategy available to investors. Legendary investors practicing this approach include Warren Buffett, Benjamin Graham, Bernard Baruch, Bill Miller, and countless others.

Since the 1960s, the University of Chicago Graduate School of Business Finance Professor Eugene Fama has promoted the efficient market hypothesis, an idea that soon will have its 40th anniversary. The hypothesis states that stock prices reflect the entire spectrum of available information. Index funds that were created have received their support from this theory. They have been shown to persistently outperform the majority of, but not all, active investors who are tenaciously trying to find ways to beat them. If the markets are efficient, the verdict for investors is plain and simple: You can't consistently surpass the returns of an index fund.

Nonetheless, over the last few years, a new school of investing called *behavioral finance* has developed and become popular with professional and amateur investors alike. Behavioral finance and its creators have confronted the fundamentals of efficient market theory. Chicago researcher Richard Thaler, a behavioral finance theorist, asserts that investors can outperform the market consistently. By thoroughly examining investor behavior, active money managers can isolate profitable traces vis-à-vis what stocks to purchase and when. Supported by convincing information from cognitive psychology, the new school believes that a substantially large number of investors frequently formulate predictable, systematic blunders when examining information about the stock market. Because of common human shortcomings such as overconfidence, greed, or fear, people make mistakes in reasoning, and these mistakes, consecutively, can be observed and exploited by other investors who are cleverer and don't follow the crowd.

## Behavioral Finance

One of the earliest documents to initiate the behavioral finance field became available in 1985. Werner DeBondt of the University of Wisconsin and Richard Thaler wrote an evaluation of the long-standing performance of stock prices dating back to 1933. They categorized stocks into winners and losers by their past 3- to 5-year returns. Stocks that underperformed the market during the past 3- to 5-year time frame ended up labeled losers, and stocks that outperformed the market during the past 3- to 5-year time frame were labeled winners.

The results were amazing. Stocks labeled winners during the past 5 years performed very poorly on average over the next few years. Yet stocks that were labeled losers in the past performed very well over the next few years. According to this finding, they concluded that it is a superior investment strategy to purchase stock that underperformed in the past. They argued that past underperformance was responsible for creating undervalued securities.

Thaler and DeBondt attribute these performance turnarounds to investors' overreaction. The notion that investors overreact to new information regarding companies frequently carries stock prices to excessively high or low price levels. Conversely, during the ensuing years, investors begin to recognize the overreaction on their part, and stock prices begin to march in the opposite direction. If behavioral finance theorists are right, it seems that investors can outperform the market by taking advantage of other investors' erroneous beliefs and emotions. Clearly, this study is based on the concept of regression to the mean. Greed and fear often seize people's sentiments and drive stock prices to ridiculous levels, both high and low. Emotions triumph over logic and reason, but not without end. Eventually, reason prevails, only to lose again, and so on. This game of cat-and-mouse is never ending.

### The Best on Wall Street Practice Regression to the Mean

One mutual fund manager in particular has managed to outperform the Standard & Poor's 500 Index every year since 1990: Bill Miller at Legg Mason Value Trust (LMVTX). Miller is undeniably one of the best stock pickers of our time. Some of his holdings at the time of this writing include retail food and drug chain Albertson's, Inc. (ABS), financial services company Washington Mutual Inc. (WM), provider of waste management services Waste Management, Inc. (WMI), and retailer Amazon.com (AMZN).

Miller's strategy and approach often look like mistakes early on, only to transform into long-term success. The focal point of his approach is to discover securities he deems to be undervalued. Such pricing anomalies are frequently forced by cyclical declines or company-specific forms of distress that could take a certain period of time to run their course. In 2001, for example, Miller bought a number of telecom-equipment companies such as Corning (GLW), Lucent Technologies (LU), and Tellabs (TLAB). As has been mentioned, it seems he is keenly aware of and applies regression-to-the-mean strategy before taking a position. After tremendous declines during 2000 and 2001, the shares in the telecom sector are beginning to look attractive again. He could be early with his purchase, but it seems logical and likely that the telecommunications industry will not disappear and thus eventually will experience a rebound.

We would like to point out that an investor who followed our proposed strategy of purchasing stocks that were rated Hold for at least 12 months would have ended up possessing some of the stocks that are part of Mr. Miller's legendary value fund. For example, an investor who decided to follow Morgan Stanley's Neutral rating with a 12-month delay would end up buying Waste Management on July 8, 2000, for approximately $19 per share. Today it's trading around $27 per share, representing a 40 percent increase.

Another investor who chose to follow Lehman Brothers' Market Perform rating instead of Morgan Stanley's Neutral rating would end up having, among others, two stocks owned by Bill Miller. Amazon would have been purchased on or around July 26, 2001, for approximately $12.33 and Albertson's would have been purchased on September 17, 2000, for approximately $19.24. By March 8, 2002, Amazon would have risen by 33 percent and Albertson's would bring in a 62 percent return.

Why does our strategy of buying stocks rated Hold with a 12-month delay continue to offer market beating results? The answer leads us to our old friend, regression to the mean. It seems to be the underlying reason our strategy continues to succeed. Our approach helps to discover a large number of securities that appear to be undervalued. Such pricing can be created by various factors, one of which appears to suggest that a Hold rating eventually contributes to downward price pressure and thus the development of pricing anomalies. And it is for this reason that an investor practicing our strategy can triumph.

## Value Creation and Value Destruction

Perhaps for some it will appear an oversimplification, but the fact of the matter is that because of bad news and subsequent overreaction, a quickly declining stock price in many cases forms intrinsic value for the underlying security. The notion that a particular company is not living up to its perceived expectations often results in trouncing the company and its stock beyond sanity. As we have proven, this does not mean that investors need to flock and buy the stock immediately. Perceptions are an important element in valuing any stock. Bad news is frequently followed by more bad news. And due to our human nature and herding mindset, it becomes even more magnified in our mind because of the media that sensationalize all bad news. As unappealing news accumulates, the stock price declines and suffers. However, if the companies suffering this downturn have solid business models, the turnaround will come through sooner or later. We frequently observe this trend in cyclical businesses.

Declines and subsequent rises for securities in the tobacco industry during the last few years offer a perfect example. During President Clinton's administration, tobacco lawsuits by the government and individuals proliferated. Phillip Morris (MO), RJR Tobacco Holdings (RJR), and others faced enormous pressures on many fronts. It seemed as if the tobacco industry would fold and disappear. At one point RJR stock price declined to such unrealistically low levels that anyone who purchased it would have been collecting a 17 percent dividend. Phillip Morris was paying more than a 10 percent dividend. And these dividends did not appear in jeopardy of being phased out. Both firms continued to stay profitable. Any penalties imposed on them by the courts would be easily transferred to their loyally addicted client base. As stock prices for the tobacco industry persistently languished in the cellars and bad news endlessly filtered through, their stock prices relentlessly slipped lower and lower.

Perception was the key here as it always is. Investor insight continued to suggest that there was no reason to buy these stocks. What for? They are the enemy. Their products are awful to health, their liabilities due to lawsuits are awful to investors, and the companies are awful, period.

Technology, on the other hand, was a friend. Technology was the growth engine. Technology was the underlying reason for increased productivity. Technology was the place to be! Semiconductors, telecommunications, software, hardware, and all the others subindustries of the technology sector were experiencing continued growth, expansion, and exuberance. While all this was going on, not too many people noticed the creation of value through stock price declines in the tobacco industry. Not too many people noticed how the value was destroyed through stock price appreciation in the technology sector.

Company-specific fundamentals habitually lag investors' perceptions. After all, when stock price declines much more rapidly than fundamentals, value is created, unless value is destroyed to the point that the company perishes. The reverse is also true. When stock price appreciates much faster than fundamentals, the intrinsic value these shares represent has deteriorated much more quickly as well.

## We Need a New Enemy to Recognize Value

To have an enemy is an important factor for nations and investors alike. Prices for stocks within a certain industry may appear low, and yet they do not rebound until there is motive to focus investors' anger and attention somewhere else. Tobacco stocks represented a good value long before their price hit bottom. Yet few investors were able to focus and recognize the value that was right before their eyes. Tobacco was the enemy, and until a new enemy emerged, nothing seemed to help. The industry had no reprieve from investors' wrath. Nonetheless, as soon as the technology sector was identified as overpriced and extremely overvalued, it formed the new enemy. Love and hate are only one step apart is an old axiom. The old enemy in the form of the tobacco industry was not only forgotten, but it also became a new friend. Markets now had a new enemy: the technology sector. As investors' fury was now directed at technology, the old enemy in the form of the tobacco companies finally had a chance to catch their breath and recover. Their stocks quickly rebounded. Today, as these words are put on paper, the technology sector continues to remain investors' number one enemy. Overcapacity, poor demand, and pricing pressures linger on. The telecommunications industry is probably getting beaten up more than any other segment of the technology sector. Cellular operators such as Sprint PCS and ATT Wireless, in concert with their suppliers such as Lucent (LU) and Nortel (NT), are barely breathing. Yet some of them in one form or the other undoubtedly will survive. Telecommunications will not disappear, and their stock price will eventually rebound. The question is when? The answer is when a new enemy is found.

## Fortune Cookie: Many Receive Advice, but Only the Wise Profit from It

Our goal has been to identify financial institutions whose recommendations were superior. We wanted to know if Goldman Sachs was better than Merrill Lynch, or vice versa. We wanted to know if Morgan Stanley was better than Salomon Smith Barney. We wanted to know if Hold recommendations outperformed Strong Buy recommendations. In a broad spectrum, we wanted to rate every financial institution and every recommendation and provide these data to any investor who wanted to build trading strategies based on our findings. Our goal was to create a system that would continuously compile and segment recommendation data and perhaps in turn would help us locate undervalued stocks. It did!

Regression to the mean convincingly outmaneuvered all other strategies. Paying attention to who was best in the past and building trading strategies around their advice did not surpass Francis Galton, the ancestor of our ideas. Yes, some financial institutions did excel in the health-care sector, whereas others produced better results in the technology sector, and so on. However, this does not mean they will accomplish the same feat repeatedly. They too are subjects of regression to the mean. Analysts' ability to predict the future fluctuates. Yesterday they were hot, but today they are cold. Don't be surprised if they become hot again tomorrow.

Financial institutions hire and maintain analysts for a reason. They help Wall Street raise money for newly created businesses. They support mergers, acquisitions, and spinoffs. Last but not least, they stimulate trading activity and thus liquidity. The fact that Wall Street analysts have an enormous amount of clout and drive stock prices up and down remains one of the pillars of Wall Street. Some even say that it's the only game in town. That seems like an exaggeration. Yet we can't deny that analysts move stock prices through their upgrades and downgrades. Most investors think that these moves have a very short life span. It will probably not be an overstatement to say that investors perceive analysts' recommendations as being valid only during the actual day a recommendation was issued. However, it is not so. Looks can surely be deceiving.

Figure 11-1 conveys the essence of our story. It is a new spin on the old theme called regression to the mean. In it the reader can recognize two patterns. The top line reveals a general trend for stocks that receive Strong Buy recommendations. Many of them are considered growth stocks. Their P/E multiples tend to be higher. Their management tends to be more aggressive. They tend to be

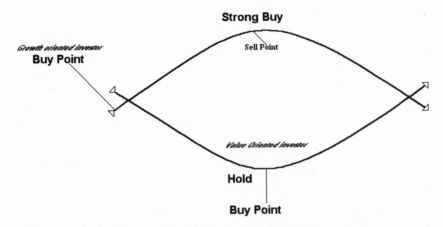

**Fig. 11-1. Growth-oriented investment versus value-oriented investment: A schematic comparison.**

more leveraged and, thus, more risky. Professional and amateur investors alike have expectations for these firms that are at times labeled "castles in the sky." Investors believe that their stock price can rise forever. During the late 1990s, there were many stocks that appeared to be just that. They were phenomenal performers. Financial analysts seemed to be on target with many of their positive predictions. This was a great time. Raising money was not a problem. Money was cheap. There was plenty of it around.

However, as our research has shown, these stocks need to be treated with caution. On average they tend to appreciate in price for only a certain period of time. After that they experience sharp sell-offs and see considerable declines in their stock prices. A certain number of these firms will realize that their business models are flawed. They will either try to adjust quickly or disappear. Others will face downward pressures from the fact that expectations for their growth were set too high. In either case investors who hold on to these stocks for too long will suffer defeat. Performing fundamental analysis is always recommended. This recommendation is especially important for stocks rated Strong Buy. You really don't need to be an accountant to get a basic picture. Before turning to the value stock line in Figure 11-1, we will briefly discuss the Enron catastrophe.

**The Enron Catastrophe**

Congress recently began hearings on why Enron failed. Wall Street analysts were called to testify and explain why they continued to rate Enron as Strong Buy almost until the bitter end. All kinds of reasons were given. We didn't know, we didn't see, we were lied to, and so on. Frankly, the lying part perhaps may turn out to be true. But the parts about we didn't know and we didn't see are questionable.

For investors who practiced our system of selling stocks rated Strong Buy with a 12-month artificial maturity date, Enron would have been sold a long time ago regardless of the financial institution he or she has chosen to follow. For example, an investor who was following a top recommendation from Merrill Lynch would have purchased Enron on January 21, 2000, for $71.63 and sold it on January 22, 2001, for $75.06. Another investor who followed a J.P. Morgan Chase top recommendation would have bought Enron on June 9, 1999, for $39.16 and sold it on or around June 10, 2000, for $73.25. And finally, a third investor who followed a Dain Rauscher Wessels—currently called RBC Capital Markets—top recommendation would have purchased Enron on April 5, 2000, for $66.56 and sold it at a loss on April 6, 2001, for $55.50. No, the sale wouldn't capture the top price. Each investor would have seen different results, yet for two of three, it would be a profitable transaction. Our third investor who experienced a loss would feel pretty good in the end, knowing what happened to Enron afterward.

Those who continued to insist on holding Enron stock for the long haul and did not sell it on time should take a quick look at Figure 11-2. You will see a top portion of Enron's income statement for the year 2000. This document was available to investors approximately early in April 2001 and without a doubt should have served as a warning sign.

Although sales increased from $40 billion to $100 billion, representing 250 percent top line growth (indisputably a phenomenal performance), the gross profit managed to grow from $5.351 billion to only $6.272 billion. This means that Gross Profit Margin plummeted from over 13 percent in 1999 to slightly above 6 percent in 2000. Net income from continued operations declined from $1024 in 1999 to $979 in 2000. Need we say more? It seems that Enron grew,

| ii | 12/31/2000 | 12/31/1999 |
|---|---|---|
| Sales | 100,789.00 | 40,112.00 |
| Cost of Goods | 94,517.00 | 34,761.00 |
| **Gross Profit** | **6,272.00** | **5,351.00** |
| **Gross Profit Margin** | **6.22%** | **13.34%** |
| Selling & Administrative & Depr. & Amort. Expenses | 4,319.00 | 4,108.00 |
| Nonoperating Income | 529 | 752 |
| Interest Expense | 838 | 656 |
| **Pretax Income** | **1,644.00** | **1,339.00** |
| Income Taxes | 434 | 104 |
| Minority Interest | 231 | 211 |
| Investment Gains/Losses (+) | 0 | 0 |
| Other Income/Charges | 0 | 0 |
| **Income from Cont. Operations** | **979** | **1,024.00** |

Note: The fiscal year end for Enron falls in December.

**Fig. 11-2.  Annual income statement for Enron (in millions except EPS data).**

but unfortunately mostly in the wrong places. Later, of course, it was revealed that this growth in all the wrong places was bogus too.

It is important to remember that growth companies are not meant to grow forever. Eventually, in the best case scenario, they revert to normal growth. Their stock during that time will suffer. For investors the lessons described in this book are along these lines: Getting out in time is essential to stay ahead of the crowd and succeed. Sooner or later, regression to the mean will catch up with all growth stocks, and when it does, watch out. It will not spare or have mercy on any of them.

The bottom line on Figure 11-1 essentially represents our story in Chapter 9. This line denotes the average performance of stocks rated Hold. Wall Street expectations for this group of stocks are subdued and cool. They are the ugly ducklings in the barn of lower Manhattan. Not many analysts or investors seem interested in their fate. Many of them include the growth companies of the past. Their adjustment from being Wall Street beauties to Wall Street beasts is undeniably cruel and spiteful. But financial markets don't care. After all, this is Wall Street!

One broker told me that he couldn't call his clients and suggest they buy shares of a company that financial analysts rate Hold. *Forbes* magazine concluded that no one cares about stocks rated Hold. Their final verdict was that it's useless to write about their performance because people will not consider buying them anyway. No wonder experienced traders always say, "When pessimism and negative outlook abound, it often marks the bottom." Again, we recognize an old friend, regression to the mean, tirelessly at work.

If there is one point investors need to remember it is that few things in life become infinitely small. By utilizing an investment methodology that spreads investment dollars across a good number of firms that have been rated Hold for a while and constantly replenishing them produces great returns. And that is our final verdict.

## The Endless Possibilities

The system we laid out embraces extremely diverse capabilities; this is not the dogs of the Dow system. That has the same 10 stocks every year. The options and possibilities of our system are almost limitless. One group of investors might choose to buy stocks rated Recommended List by Goldman Sachs on the day of the recommendation and sell them 1 year later. Another group might choose to purchase stocks rated Market Perform by Lehman Brothers and hold them until they are upgraded or downgraded. Still others might embark on building even more sophisticated recommendation-based stock strategies. Another possibility is mixing up and investing 30 percent of allocated equity funds in companies rated Strong Buy by Morgan Stanley and selling them 6 months later while investing the other 70 percent in stocks rated Hold for at least 12 months by Prudential Securities. With the trading tools currently available to investors, they can compose and engineer stock portfolios based on recommendations with the underlying notion of regression to the mean.

For many investors the problems they face are frequently self-created. Even if some investors try to execute trading strategies based on historical probabilities or regression to the mean or some other system, they often fail to see them through. Emotions and instincts within most of us are more primitive and frequently override rational calculations that are secondary in nature. Remember, in the financial world, your gut feel is often wrong. Once a strategy is chosen, stick with it; however, it must adhere to certain rules. Diversification is number one because it reduces risk. Not using margin account is number two because slow and steady wins the race. Regression to the mean is number three because it works.

Aron Nimzovich, one of the greatest chess philosophers and players of all time, wrote an immensely popular book, *My System*, in 1925. It contained the following interesting observation about chess players. He said that a professional chess player is satisfied with a slightly better position on the board. He or she is ecstatic with an advantage of a weakly pawn, for instance. On the other hand, a beginner always looks for a killer combination of either announcing a quick checkmate or, for some reason even more satisfactory, the feeling of snatching the opponent's queen. Investors' exhibit very similar tendencies. Professional investors are exuberant after beating the S&P 500 Index. Amateur investors are frequently looking to retire on one or two stock picks.

Humility is an important virtue. Markets represent a powerful and unrelenting foe. Underestimating them is a huge mistake. We mentioned at the beginning of this chapter what happened when the Third Reich miscalculated the power and resilience of its opponents. Far too many individual investors, unlike professional investors, have little regard for the market. Many are too sensitive, too unseasoned, too impetuous, and perhaps even too temperamental. They must change their behavior quickly, or they unavoidably will lose.

Before ending our story about regression to the mean and our book, a portion of a popular Pink Floyd song called "Time" comes to mind:

> And you run and you run to catch up with the sun, but it's sinking
> And racing around to come up behind you again.

Interpreting these words from a stock market point of view might go as follows: Don't chase stocks that have made their run and are ahead of you. They inevitably will sink just like the sun. Rather, become a patient investor who is willing to wait because inevitably many of these same stocks will come up behind you again. In fact a few more are waiting to appear tomorrow.

# Appendix
# The
# Marketperform.com
# System

This section will allow the user to keep in touch with the latest recommendations within the financial institutions and act upon the criteria that have been researched to bring in the best results.

1. This application sends you e-mails based on criteria you set. There are ten slots of criteria available, meaning you can set up ten various alerts that you customize.
   a. You can select a financial institution from the drop-down list and click "ADD." This will create a notification alert for any recommendation that this institution issues.
   b. In order to see a recommendation list belonging to a specific financial institution, select the institution from the drop-down list and click on "See Recommendations." By clicking on "ADD," you will set up a notification for that specific recommendation.
   c. You can also add criteria such as a symbol, a sector, or an industry to further narrow down your notification. This can also be added as criteria without choosing a recommendation so that your alert will trigger when a specific institution makes any recommendation within that sector or industry, or

for that symbol. If you do not want to use criteria, you can leave the default of "Any." To choose any of these criteria, you must select the radio button to its left.

d. There is a way to be reminded a specified number of days after the recommendation is made and then again a specified number of days thereafter, when you feel that these criteria have matured with regard to buying and selling at the proper times. This is done by making a selection from the "Day to Buy" and "Day to Sell (Mature)" drop-down lists. This can be determined by looking at the graphs in the financial institutions section. Setting a "Day to Buy" number equal to your "Day to Sell (Mature)" number results in one notification being sent.

2. The following list represents the up-to-10 slots available for an individual investor to set up notifications.

a. The "ADD" button adds new notification criteria to an available slot in your list.

b. The "REPLACE" button swaps a chosen notification slot with the new criteria set above in the form. You must select a slot to replace by clicking on its corresponding radio button to the right.

c. The "DELETE" button gets rid of a chosen notification if it is no longer proving to be effective. You must select a slot to delete by clicking on its corresponding radio button to the right.

d. The "RESET FORM" button, below the list, clears your choices and selections in your form so that you may rearrange your selections. (Note: This will not delete your slots.)


## Portfolio Simulation

Purpose: This section will allow the user to create slots as in the notification section, but the user will be able to use specific dates as if the investment had been made then. This allows the user to run a simulation of what would have happened if the user had acted upon the criteria for each stock within the timeframe specified.

1. There are 10 slots of criteria available, meaning you can set up 10 varied portfolios that you customize yourself.

a. In order to see a simulation of what would have taken place, you must set a date where that slot of particular investments would have started. The years in the drop-down list begin at 1999 and extend to the most recent year.

b. In order to see a recommendation list belonging to a specific financial institution, select an institution from the drop-down list and click on "See Recommendations." By clicking on "ADD," you will set up a simulation for that specific recommendation. (Note: In the portfolio simulation, you must choose a recommendation to add it to your slots.)

c. You can also add criteria such as a symbol, a sector, or an industry to further narrow down your simulation. If you do not want to use criteria, you can leave the default of "Any." To choose any of these criteria, you must select the radio button to its left.

d. You can also simulate your criteria based on buying after a certain number of days after the recommendation was made and then selling after a certain number of days. This is done by choosing from the "Day to Buy" and "Day to Sell (Mature)" drop-down lists. This can be determined by looking at the graphs in the financial institutions section.

2. The following list represents the up-to-10 slots available for an individual investor to set up and run a simulation.

a. The "ADD" button adds new simulation criteria to an available slot in your list.

b. The "REPLACE" button swaps a chosen slot with the new criteria set above in the form. You must select a slot to replace by clicking on its corresponding radio button to the right.

c. The "DELETE" button gets rid of a chosen slot if it is not proving to be effective to your portfolio. You must select a slot to delete by clicking on its corresponding radio button to the right.

d. The "RESET FORM" button, below the list, clears your choices and selections in your form so that you may rearrange your selections. (Note: This will not delete your slots.)

3. Once you have created a suitable portfolio to simulate, click on the "RUN SIMULATION" button at the bottom of your list.

a. The resulting screen will display the following information on your simulation:

   i. Trades executed within the portfolio.

   ii. Total amount invested.

    iii. Total value after divesting, equity earned, and cash needed to make the initial investment.

    iv. Total gain or loss.

    v. Realized gain or loss.

    vi. Unrealized gain or loss.

    vii. Dow gain or loss (since the date you entered in your criteria) to compare your portfolio to.

    viii. NASDAQ gain or loss (since the date you entered in your criteria) to compare your portfolio to.

    ix. S&P gain or loss (since the date you entered in your criteria) to compare your portfolio to.

## Examples

The following are three examples that you can follow and learn how to use the Marketperform.com system. (These examples have been discussed in the book.)

## Example 1.

| Financial Institution | Recommendation | Criteria | Day to Buy | Day to Sell (Matures) |
|---|---|---|---|---|
| Lehman Brothers | Market Perform | any | 255 | 255 |

## Notification

1. In the Notification section, locate "Lehman Brothers" in the first drop-down list within the form.
2. Click on the "See Recommendations" button directly below the drop-down list. This will display the recommendations that are issued by Lehman Brothers. Select "Market Perform" from this list.
3. Select "255" from the "Day to Buy" as well as "255" from the "Day to Sell (matures)" drop-down lists. (This will tell the system to notify you 255 business days after the recommendation has been issued and when the recommendation changed.)
4. To finally add this to your Notification slots, click on the "ADD" button directly below the form.
5. The result will be an e-mail notification 255 days after the next time that Lehman Brothers issues a recommendation of Market Perform on any stock, within any sector, and within any industry.

## Portfolio Simulation

1. In the Portfolio Simulation section, locate "Lehman Brothers" in the first drop-down list within the form.
2. Click on the "See Recommendations" button directly below the drop-down list. This will display the recommendations that are issued by Lehman Brothers. Select "Market Perform" from this list.
3. Select "255" from the "Day to Buy" as well as "255" from the "Day to Sell (Matures)" drop-down lists.
4. To finally add this to your Portfolio Simulation slots, click the "ADD" button directly below the form.
5. You may leave the date as 1/1/1999 to see how Lehman Brothers has done since that date in this recommendation. (After trying this example, you may also change the date to run various other scenarios.)
6. Clicking on "RUN SIMULATION" on March 19, 2002, resulted in the following data. (Note your results will differ due to stock price and recommendation updates.)

### Simulation Results

| | | | |
|---|---|---|---|
| Trades executed: | 320 | | |
| Total amount invested: | $162,452.60 | | |
| Total value/Equity/Cash: | $221,465.26 | $221,465.26 | $0.00 |
| Total gain (loss): | $59,012.66 | 36.33% | |
| Realized gain (loss): | $29,547.40 | | |
| Unrealized gain (loss): | $29,465.26 | | |
| Dow (INDU) gain (loss): | 1453.82 | 15.83% | |
| NASDAQ (COMPX) gain (loss): | (311.82) | −14.22% | |
| S&P (SPAL) gain (loss): | (58.94) | −4.79% | |

### Example 2.

| Financial Institution | Recommendation | Criteria | Day to Buy | Day to Sell (Matures) |
|---|---|---|---|---|
| Gerald Klouer Mattison & Company | Buy | Utilities sector | 1 | 255 |

## Notification

1. In the Notification section, locate "Gerald Klouer Mattison & Company" in the first drop-down list within the form.

2. Click on the "See Recommendations" button directly below the drop-down list. This will display the recommendations that are issued by Gerald Klouer Mattison & Company. Select "Buy" from this list.
3. Select "1" from the "Day to Buy" and "255" from the "Day to Sell (Matures)" drop-down lists.
4. Select the "Sector" radio button and choose the "Utilities" sector from the drop-down list.
5. To finally add this to your Notification slots, click the "ADD" button directly below the form.
6. The result will be an e-mail notification 1 day as well as 255 days after the next time that Gerald Klouer Mattison & Company issues a recommendation of "Buy" on any stock, within the Utilities sector, and within any industry.

**Portfolio Simulation**
1. In the Portfolio Simulation section, locate "Gerald Klouer Mattison & Company" in the first drop-down list within the form.
2. Click on the "See Recommendations" button directly below the drop-down list. This will display the recommendations that are issued by the Gerald Klouer Mattison & Company. Select "Buy" from this list.
3. Select "1" from the "Day to Buy" and "255" from the "Day to Sell (Matures)" drop-down lists.
4. Select the "Sector" radio button and choose the "Utilities" sector from the drop-down list.
5. To finally add this to your Portfolio Simulation slots, click on the "ADD" button directly below the form.
6. You may leave the date as 1/1/1999 to see how Gerald Klouer Mattison & Company has done since that date in this recommendation. (After trying this example, you may also change the date to run various other scenarios.)
7. Clicking on "RUN SIMULATION" will result in the following data.

## Simulation Results

| | | | |
|---|---|---|---|
| Trades executed: | 13 | | |
| Total amount invested: | $6,000.00 | | |
| Total value/Equity/Cash: | $11,615.26 | $1090.91 | $10,524.35 |
| Total gain (loss): | $5615.26 | 93.59% | |
| Realized gain (loss): | $5524.35 | | |
| Unrealized gain (loss): | $90.91 | | |
| Dow (INDU) gain (loss): | 1453.82 | 15.83% | |
| NASDAQ (COMPX) gain (loss): | (311.82) | −14.22% | |
| S&P (SPAL) gain (loss): | (58.94) | −4.79% | |

## Example 3.

| Financial Institution | Recommendation | Criteria | Day to Buy | Day to Sell (Matures) |
|---|---|---|---|---|
| Merrill Lynch | Strong Buy | Utilities sector | 1 | 130 |

## Notification

1. In the Notification section, locate "Merrill Lynch" in the first drop-down list within the form.
2. Click on the "See Recommendations" button directly below the drop-down list. This will display the recommendations that are issued by the Merrill Lynch. Select "Strong Buy" from this list.
3. Select "1" from the "Day to Buy" and "130" from the "Day to Sell (Matures)" drop-down lists.
4. Select the "Sector" radio button and choose the "Utilities" sector from the drop-down list.
5. To finally add this to your Notification slots, click on the "ADD" button directly below the form.
6. The result will be an e-mail notification 1 day as well as 130 days after the next time that Merrill Lynch issues a recommendation of Strong Buy on any stock, within the Utilities sector, and within any industry.

**Portfolio Simulation**

1. In the Portfolio Simulation section, locate "Merrill Lynch" in the first drop-down list within the form.
2. Click the "See Recommendations" button directly below the drop-down list. This will display the recommendations that are issued by Merrill Lynch. Select "Strong Buy" from this list.
3. Select "1" from the "Day to Buy" and "130" from the "Day to Sell (Matures)" drop-down lists.
4. Select the "Sector" radio button and choose the "Utilities" sector from the drop-down list.
5. To finally add this to your Portfolio Simulation slots, click on the "ADD" button directly below the form.
6. You may leave the date as 1/1/1999 to see how Merrill Lynch has done since that date in this recommendation. (After trying this example, you may also change the date to run various other scenarios.)
7. Clicking on "RUN SIMULATION" will result in the following data.

**Simulation Results**

| | | | |
|---|---|---|---|
| Trades executed: | 29 | | |
| Total amount invested: | $4887.76 | | |
| Total value/Equity/Cash: | $5871.73 | $1097.23 | $4774.50 |
| Total gain (loss): | $983.97 | 20.13% | |
| Realized gain (loss): | $886.74 | | |
| Unrealized gain (loss): | $97.23 | | |
| Dow (INDU) gain (loss): | 1453.82 | 15.83% | |
| Nasdaq (COMPX) gain (loss): | (311.82) | −14.22% | |
| S&P (SPAL) gain (loss): | (58.94) | −4.79% | |

# Index

# ABOUT THE AUTHOR

**Eric Shkolnik** is president, CEO, and founder of market-perform.com, the first research/strategy tool that measures the performance of stock recommendations made by financial institutions. He also is president of Integrated Data Consulting Services, Inc., a privately held information technology services company recognized as an industry leader by the likes of Chase Manhattan, Bear Stearns, Morgan Stanley Dean Witter, Lehman Brothers, and others. Formerly a credit risk management professional at Chase Manhattan Bank, Shkolnik and market-perform.com have been featured in a variety of media, including *BusinessWeek, Bloomberg, Hedge World*, and CNNfn.com.